Lecture Notes in Computer Science   **10071**

Commenced Publication in 1973
Founding and Former Series Editors:
Gerhard Goos, Juris Hartmanis, and Jan van Leeuwen

More information about this series at http://www.springer.com/series/7407

Carlos Martín-Vide · Takaaki Mizuki
Miguel A. Vega-Rodríguez (Eds.)

Theory and Practice of Natural Computing

5th International Conference, TPNC 2016
Sendai, Japan, December 12–13, 2016
Proceedings

 Springer

Editors
Carlos Martín-Vide
Rovira i Virgili University
Tarragona
Spain

Miguel A. Vega-Rodríguez
University of Extremadura
Cáceres
Spain

Takaaki Mizuki
Tohoku University
Sendai
Japan

ISSN 0302-9743   ISSN 1611-3349   (electronic)
Lecture Notes in Computer Science
ISBN 978-3-319-49000-7   ISBN 978-3-319-49001-4   (eBook)
DOI 10.1007/978-3-319-49001-4

Library of Congress Control Number: 2016955997

LNCS Sublibrary: SL1 – Theoretical Computer Science and General Issues

This Springer imprint is published by Springer Nature
The registered company is Springer International Publishing AG
The registered company address is: Gewerbestrasse 11, 6330 Cham, Switzerland

Preface

These proceedings contain the papers that were presented at the 5th International Conference on the Theory and Practice of Natural Computing (TPNC 2016), held in Sendai, Japan, during December 12–13, 2016.

The scope of TPNC is rather broad, including:

- Theoretical contributions to: amorphous computing, ant colonies, artificial chemistry, artificial immune systems, artificial life, bacterial foraging, cellular automata, chaos computing, collision-based computing, complex adaptive systems, computing with DNA, computing with words and perceptions, developmental systems, evolutionary computing, fractal geometry, fuzzy logic, gene assembly in ciliates, granular computing, intelligent systems, in vivo computing, membrane computing, nanocomputing, neural computing, optical computing, physarum machines, quantum computing, quantum information, reaction-diffusion systems, rough sets, self-organizing systems, swarm intelligence, synthetic biology.
- Applications of natural computing to: algorithmics, bioinformatics, control, cryptography, design, economics, graphics, hardware, human–computer interaction, knowledge discovery, learning, logistics, medicine, natural language processing, optimization, pattern recognition, planning and scheduling, programming, robotics, telecommunications, web intelligence.

TPNC 2016 received 33 submissions. Papers were reviewed by three Programme Committee members. There were also a few external reviewers consulted. After a thorough and vivid discussion phase, the committee decided to accept 16 papers (which represents an acceptance rate of about 48 %). The conference program included three invited talks and some poster presentations of work in progress.

The excellent facilities provided by the EasyChair conference management system allowed us to deal with the submissions successfully and handle the preparation of these proceedings in time.

We would like to thank all invited speakers and authors for their contributions, the Program Committee and the external reviewers for their cooperation, and Springer for its very professional publishing work.

September 2016

Carlos Martín-Vide
Takaaki Mizuki
Miguel A. Vega-Rodríguez

Organization

TPNC 2016 was organized by the Cyberscience Center, Tohoku University, Japan, and the Research Group on Mathematical Linguistics - GRLMC, from Rovira i Virgili University, Tarragona, Spain.

Program Committee

Andrew Adamatzky	University of the West of England, UK
Zixing Cai	Central South University, China
Óscar Castillo	Tijuana Institute of Technology, Mexico
Óscar Cordón	University of Granada, Spain
Gianni Di Caro	Dalle Molle Institute for Artificial Intelligence Research, Switzerland
Marco Dorigo	Free University of Brussels - ULB, Belgium
Austin G. Fowler	Google, USA
Michel Gendreau	Montreal Polytechnic, Canada
Debasish Ghose	Indian Institute of Science, Bangalore, India
Jin-Kao Hao	University of Angers, France
Inman Harvey	University of Sussex, UK
Wei-Chiang Hong	Nanjing Tech University, China
Amir Hussain	University of Stirling, UK
Robert John	University of Nottingham, UK
Joshua Knowles	University of Birmingham, UK
Kwong-Sak Leung	Chinese University of Hong Kong, SAR China
Seth Lloyd	Massachusetts Institute of Technology, USA
José A. Lozano	University of the Basque Country, Spain
Vittorio Maniezzo	University of Bologna, Italy
Carlos Martín-Vide	Rovira i Virgili University, Spain (Chair)
Philip K. McKinley	Michigan State University, USA
Jerry M. Mendel	University of Southern California, USA
Marjan Mernik	University of Maribor, Slovenia
Radko Mesiar	Slovak University of Technology in Bratislava, Slovakia
Chrystopher Nehaniv	University of Hertfordshire, UK
Vilém Novák	University of Ostrava, Czech Republic
Linqiang Pan	Huazhong University of Science and Technology, China
Frederick E. Petry	Naval Research Laboratory, USA
Dan Ralescu	University of Cincinnati, USA
Francisco C. Santos	University of Lisbon, Portugal
Friedrich Simmel	Technical University of Munich, Germany
Andrzej Skowron	University of Warsaw, Poland

John A. Smolin	IBM Thomas J. Watson Research Center, USA
Ying Tan	Peking University, China
Guy Theraulaz	Paul Sabatier University, France
Tommaso Toffoli	Boston University, USA
Vicenç Torra	University of Skövde, Sweden
Edward Tsang	University of Essex, UK
Sergi Valverde	Pompeu Fabra University, Spain
José Luis Verdegay	University of Granada, Spain
Fernando J. Von Zuben	University of Campinas, Brazil
K. Birgitta Whaley	University of California, Berkeley, USA
Darrell Whitley	Colorado State University, USA
Xin-She Yang	Middlesex University, UK
Hao Ying	Wayne State University, USA
Mengjie Zhang	Victoria University of Wellington, New Zealand
Zhi-Hua Zhou	Nanjing University, China

Organizing Committee

Masayuki Fukumitsu	Ebetsu
Carlos Martín-Vide	Tarragona (Co-chair)
Takaaki Mizuki	Sendai (Co-chair)
Hideaki Sone	Sendai
Miguel A. Vega-Rodríguez	Cáceres
Florentina Lilica Voicu	Tarragona

Additional Reviewers

Weiwei Hu
Junzhi Li
Chao Qian

Invited Talks

Managing Natural Noise
in Recommender Systems

Luis Martínez[1]([⊠]), Jorge Castro[2,3], and Raciel Yera[4]

[1] Department of Computer Science, University of Jaén, Jaén, Spain
martin@ujaen.es
[2] Department of Computer Science and A.I.,
University of Granada, Granada, Spain
[3] Centre for Quantum Computing and Intelligent Systems,
University of Technology Sydney, Ultimo, Australia
[4] University of Ciego de Ávila, Ciego de Ávila, Cuba

Abstract. E-commerce customers demand quick and easy access to suitable products in large purchase spaces. To support and facilitate this purchasing process to users, recommender systems (RSs) help them to find out the information that best fits their preferences and needs in an overloaded search space. These systems require the elicitation of customers' preferences. However, this elicitation process is not always precise either correct because of external factors such as human errors, uncertainty, human beings inherent inconsistency and so on. Such a problem in RSs is known as *natural noise* (NN) and can negatively bias recommendations, which leads to poor user's experience. Different proposals have been presented to deal with natural noise in RSs. Several of them require additional interaction with customers. Others just remove noisy information. Recently, new NN approaches dealing with the ratings stored in the user/item rating matrix have raised to deal with NN in a better and simpler way. This contribution is devoted to provide a brief review of the latter approaches revising crisp and fuzzy approaches for dealing with NN in RSs. Eventually it points out as a future research the management of NN in other recommendation scenarios as group RSs.

Multiobjective Evolutionary Computation, Decomposition and Regularity

Qingfu Zhang

Department of Computer Science, City University of Hong Kong,
Kowloon Tong, Hong Kong
qingfu.zhang@cityu.edu.hk

Abstract. Many real world optimization problems have multiple conflicting objectives by nature. Unlike a single optimization problem, a multiobjective optimization problem has a set of Pareto optimal solutions (Pareto front) which could be required by a decision maker to make her final decision. Evolutionary algorithms are able to generate an approximation to the Pareto front in a single run, and many traditional optimization methods have been also developed for dealing with multiple objectives. Although there is not much work that has been done, combination of evolutionary algorithms and traditional optimization methods should be a next generation multiobjective optimization solver. Decomposition techniques have been well used and studied in traditional multiobjective optimization. It is well known that the Pareto optimal solution set of a continuous multiobjective problem often exhibits some regularity. In this talk, I will describe two multiobjective evolutionary algorithms: MOEA/D and RM-MEDA. Both of them borrow ideas from traditional optimization. MOEA/D decomposes a multiobjective problem into a number of single objective subproblems or simple multiobjective subproblems, and then solves these subproblems in a collaborative manner. RM-MEDA makes use of the regularity property to model the distribution of Pareto optimal solutions in the search space, and then generates new solutions from the model thus built. I will also outline some possible research issues in multiobjective evolutionary computation.

Contents

Formal Models

Machine Learning

Invited Talk

Managing Natural Noise in Recommender Systems

Luis Martínez[1]([✉]), Jorge Castro[2,3], and Raciel Yera[4]

[1] Department of Computer Science, University of Jaén, Jaén, Spain
martin@ujaen.es
[2] Department of Computer Science and A.I., University of Granada, Granada, Spain
[3] Centre for Quantum Computing and Intelligent Systems,
University of Technology Sydney, Ultimo, Australia
[4] University of Ciego de Ávila, Ciego de Ávila, Cuba

Abstract. E-commerce customers demand quick and easy access to suitable products in large purchase spaces. To support and facilitate this purchasing process to users, recommender systems (RSs) help them to find out the information that best fits their preferences and needs in an overloaded search space. These systems require the elicitation of customers' preferences. However, this elicitation process is not always precise either correct because of external factors such as human errors, uncertainty, human beings inherent inconsistency and so on. Such a problem in RSs is known as *natural noise* (NN) and can negatively bias recommendations, which leads to poor user's experience. Different proposals have been presented to deal with natural noise in RSs. Several of them require additional interaction with customers. Others just remove noisy information. Recently, new NN approaches dealing with the ratings stored in the user/item rating matrix have raised to deal with NN in a better and simpler way. This contribution is devoted to provide a brief review of the latter approaches revising crisp and fuzzy approaches for dealing with NN in RSs. Eventually it points out as a future research the management of NN in other recommendation scenarios as group RSs.

Keywords: Recommender systems · Natural noise · Fuzzy logic · Computing with words · Group recommender systems

1 Introduction

The development of the e-commerce has made available huge information amounts of interest for customers in their purchasing processes. With large amount of options, customers usually cannot filter them effectively, hence frustration and early purchasing leaving can happen. Therefore, the support to finding out quick and easily items that fits customers' preferences and needs become an important challenge nowadays. Recommender systems (RSs) are the most successful tool for supporting personalized recommendations [1,13]. RSs have been

C. Martín-Vide et al. (Eds.): TPNC 2016, LNCS 10071, pp. 3–17, 2016.
DOI: 10.1007/978-3-319-49001-4_1

broadly used in different scenarios like e-commerce [28], e-learning [29], tourism [19], and so on.

Different approaches have been used in RSs, being the content-based (CBRS) [6,21] and the collaborative filtering (CFRS) [1] the most widespread. CBRS methods are based on items' descriptions to generate the users' recommendations, meanwhile CFRS have performed this task just using users ratings about items. The latter approach is the most popular one in real world RSs because of their good performance even when items descriptions are not available. But, the necessity of customers preferences in CFRSs has produced some problems that limit their performance, such as *cold start* and *sparsity* [1,25], and more recently new related problems regarding the quality of the rating data have raised up [14,22,30]. Specifically, Ekstrand et al. [9] pointed out that the rating elicitation process is not error-free, hence the ratings can contain noise. They mentioned that such a noise, previously coined *natural noise* (NN) in [20], could be caused by human error, mixing of factors in the rating process, uncertainty and other factors. They stated that its detection and correction should provide more accurate recommendations.

The main research stream in RSs has been and still is the development of algorithms that increase the accuracy of the recommendations. Due to the fact that NN biases the recommendations and affect negatively to the RSs performance, it is worthy to research its management for improving the recommendations. For this reason, different proposals in the literature have introduced processes for managing the errors of rating elicitation in recommendation scenarios. The management of NN depends on the data available and some approaches require additional user interactions [22] and others just remove noisy data either ratings or users [2]. Recently, however, new proposals manage the NN by using the current rating values in the user/item rating matrix while keeping as much information as possible and without any new user's interaction [30,31].

This contribution aims at providing a brief review about the latter approaches for managing NN, which only need current ratings in the RS, by revising both crisp and fuzzy approaches. Additionally, it points out future research challenges.

This contribution is structured as follows. Section 2 provides a brief background for understanding RSs and NN. Section 3 provides a view about the basic model to manage NN with the information stored in the user/item rating matrix. Section 4 focuses on a fuzzy extension of the previous approach for dealing with natural noise in CFRS. Eventually, Sect. 5 points out the application of NN management in group recommendation scenarios.

2   Preliminaries

This section provides the required background for the current research, including basics about CFRS and a short review of natural noise processing in CFRS.

2.1 Basics in Collaborative Filtering

A Recommender System (RS) has been defined as *"any system that produces individualized recommendations as output or has the effect of guiding the user in a personalized way to interesting or useful objects in a large space of possible options"* [5]. Therefore, the main tasks of a RS are: (i) to gather information about the users' needs and interests, and (ii) to present the items that might satisfy such needs and interests. The recommendation problem can be formally defined as finding the most suitable item, or set of items, that maximizes the rating prediction for a target user:

$$Recommendation(I, u_j) = arg \max_{i_k \in I}[Prediction(u_j, i_k)] \qquad (1)$$

being $I = \{i_1, \ldots, i_n\}$ the set of all the items and $Prediction(u_j, i_k)$ is a function to predict how satisfied would be the user u_j with the item i_k, regarding the data available about u_j and i_k.

Different approaches have been proposed in the literature to recommend, such as content-based [17], knowledge-based [16], or demographic-based [27]. However, collaborative filtering (CFRS) is the most widespread approach in RSs [9,13], because of its ability to provide effective recommendations only requiring minimal information [23]. This information is usually composed by explicit or implicit feedback from the users. This work is focused on CFRS with explicit feedback preferences, r_{u_j,i_k} (see Table 1), which are given by user's preference values over a subset of items.

Table 1. Users' preferences over items, the rating matrix

	i_1	$\cdots$	i_k	$\cdots$	i_n
u_1	r_{u_1,i_1}	$\cdots$	r_{u_1,i_k}	$\cdots$	r_{u_1,i_n}
$\vdots$	$\vdots$		$\vdots$		$\vdots$
u_j	r_{u_j,i_1}	$\cdots$	r_{u_j,i_k}	$\cdots$	r_{u_j,i_n}
$\vdots$	$\vdots$		$\vdots$		$\vdots$
u_m	r_{u_m,i_1}	$\cdots$	r_{u_m,i_k}	$\cdots$	r_{u_m,i_n}

Among the approaches for CFRS, two pioneer and yet effective methods are the user-based and item-based collaborative filtering approaches [8]. Both methods rely on the nearest neighbours algorithm. Due to the fact that both represent key methods in the CFRS research, both of them will be used as the base for the evaluation of the natural noise approaches revised across this contribution.

2.2 Natural Noise in Recommender Systems

Several authors have pointed out that the user preferences in RS could be inconsistent due to several reasons [20]. These inconsistencies have been classified in two main groups: (i) *malicious noise*, when the inconsistencies are intentionally inserted to bias the recommendation [7], or (ii) *natural noise*, when the inconsistencies appear without malicious intentions [4]. While the malicious noise received much attention since the beginning of the use of RS [12,18], natural noise has attracted less attention from researchers.

The concept of natural noise was introduced by O'Mahony et al. [20], in which the authors focus on discovering noisy ratings, both malicious and natural noise. Amatriain et al. [4] performed a user study to obtain a better understanding about how natural noise tends to appear. Afterwards, in [3] they propose strategies to correct the inconsistent preferences. More recently, Pham and Jung [22] proposed the use of item attributes, such as genre, actors, or director, in the case of movies, to detect and correct natural noisy ratings. They focus on finding a preference model based on this information for each user, and then identify as anomalous those positive ratings that do not match the model. The inconsistent ratings are then corrected using the information associated to other users identified as experts.

While the previous methods focus on the detection of noisy ratings, Li et al. [14] propose the discovery of *noisy but non-malicious users* by detecting user's *self/contradictions*, following the principle that highly-correlated items should be similarly rated. This study focuses on noise detection at user level, which could not be detailed enough in some scenarios.

All previous methods manage natural noise in CFRS in different ways, for instance O'Mahony et al. [20] and Li et al. [14] remove noisy information from the dataset. Others use additional information beyond the rating matrix, such as Pham and Jung [22] and Amatriain et al. [3]. Table 2 characterizes these proposals for dealing with NN according to the management of noise and the necessity of additional information beyond current ratings. Table 2 shows a shadowed cell that represents the lack of research centered on noisy ratings correction without additional information that should be filled and it is the aim of this contribution.

Table 2. Related works in Natural Noise

		Information required beyond ratings	
		Additional information	No additional information
Management of noise	Remove noise		O'Mahony et al. [20] Li et al. [14]
	Correct noise	Amatriain et al. [3] Pham et al. [22]	

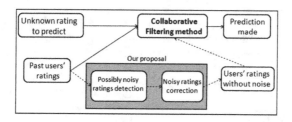

Fig. 1. General scheme of the natural noise approach

3   Managing Natural Noise Relying Just on Ratings: A Basic Approach

Yera, Caballero and Martínez [30] proposed a method for correcting noisy preferences that only relies on the ratings and it processes them at a rating level in order to fill the gray cell in Table 2. This approach takes into account just rating values, in which it was not necessary to use any additional information about users either items.

In such an approach, apart from preferences variation over time, it was considered that erroneous ratings can appear in recommender systems dataset due to several reasons:

– Users can unintentionally express information that does not correspond with their preferences and profiles. This is the classical scenario for natural noise.
– They could also insert anomalous-but-correct information intentionally added, that is not actually aligned with their global profiles and could be considered as noisy.

In all cases, erroneous ratings or ratings that do not represent real user's preferences can cause accuracy decay in collaborative filtering. Incorrect ratings could alter user's profile, and the biased user could fall in a different neighborhood compared with an unbiased one. This could affect current user's predictions, and also predictions for users in the neighborhood.

In order to manage natural noisy ratings, a framework is proposed, which includes two steps (see Fig. 1):

1. *Noisy ratings detection*: it classifies user and item profiles into four different classes considering their ratings. Each rating can also be classified into three different classes. A rating is marked as possible noise if there are contradictions between the rating class and the classes associated to its user and item.
2. *Noise correction*: it uses a basic collaborative filtering method to predict a new rating for each possible noisy one. If the difference between both ratings is greater than a predefined threshold, then the old rating is definitively considered as noisy and its value is replaced with the new one.

A further detailed description of previous phases is introduced below:

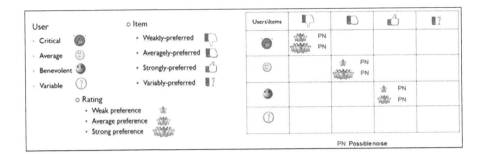

Fig. 2. User, item, rating classification and possible noisy ratings

3.1   Noisy Rating Detection

This approach follows the principle that users and items have their *own tendency* giving or receiving ratings respectively. Once the tendencies have been identified, the ratings that contradict such tendencies can be classified as possibly noisy. Therefore, to detect natural noisy ratings, a classification for ratings, users, and items is initially performed.

The approach assumes that each user has his/her own tendency when rating items (see Fig. 2): (i) A group of users tends to positively evaluate all items, (ii) another group provides average values, (iii) a third one usually gives low ratings, and also, (iv) there is a fourth group of users whose behavior varies among any of the former categories, and do not fall into a specific one.

This classification is also extended for items: (i) There is a group that is highly preferred by all users, (ii) a group whose items are averagely preferred, (iii) a group of items that are not preferred by the majority of users, and like in users, and (iv) a group that contains items with divided opinions about their preferences degree.

Eventually, each rating $r(u, i)$ (for a user u and an item i) is classified into three different classes according its value:

1. Weak preference: A rating $r(u, i)$ is a *weak preference* if r(u,i) < κ.
2. Average preference: A rating $r(u, i)$ is an *average preference* if $\kappa \leq$ r(u,i) < ν.
3. Strong preference: A rating $r(u, i)$ is a *strong preference* if r(u,i) $\geq \nu$.

This classification depends on a weak-average threshold κ and an average-strong threshold ν that are prior defined, satisfying $\kappa < \nu$ (See Remark 1).

Considering U and I as whole sets of users and items, preferences for each user u can be grouped in sets W_u, A_u and S_u, :

1. $W_u = \{r(u, i), \forall i \in I \ where \ r(u, i) \ is \ a \ weak \ preference\}$
2. $A_u = \{r(u, i), \forall i \in I \ where \ r(u, i) \ is \ an \ average \ preference\}$
3. $S_u = \{r(u, i), \forall i \in I \ where \ r(u, i) \ is \ a \ strong \ preference\}$

And for each item i in sets W_i, A_i and S_i:

1. $W_i = \{r(u,i), \ \forall u \in U \ where \ r(u,i) \ is \ a \ weak \ preference\}$
2. $A_i = \{r(u,i), \ \forall u \in U \ where \ r(u,i) \ is \ an \ average \ preference\}$
3. $S_i = \{r(u,i), \ \forall u \in U \ where \ r(u,i) \ is \ a \ strong \ preference\}$

Considering rating classes and user and item sets, user profiles can be formally classified into four different categories: *benevolent, average, critical, and variable*. On the other hand, items can be classified in four categories: strongly-preferred, averagely-preferred, weakly-preferred and variably-preferred (see Table 3).

Table 3. User and item classes proposed

User classes	
Critical user	Verifies $card(W_u) \geq card(A_u) + card(S_u)$
Average user	Verifies $card(A_u) \geq card(W_u) + card(S_u)$
Benevolent user	Verifies $card(S_u) \geq card(W_u) + card(A_u)$
Variable user	Does not satisfy the others user conditions
Item classes	
Weakly-preferred item	Verifies $card(W_i) \geq card(A_i) + card(S_i)$
Averagely-preferred item	Verifies $card(A_i) \geq card(W_i) + card(S_i)$
Strongly-preferred item	Verifies $card(S_i) \geq card(W_i) + card(A_i)$
Variably-preferred item	Does not satisfy the others item conditions

Table 3 summarizes user and item classification, being, $card(A)$, the cardinality of the set A. Users and items are classified in one of the first three categories in each case if the amount of ratings belonging to the corresponding class rating (following rating classes) exceeds the amount of the other two. Specifically, for each user and item, it is counted the amount of ratings belonging to each preference class.

Once each rating, user and item has been classified, the detection process looks for contradictions among them. In general, it is assumed that if a rating belongs to similar classes regarding its user and item, then it must belong to the similar rating class. Otherwise, the rating could be erroneous. Specifically, the following procedure is presented to determine if a rating could be noisy (see Fig. 2):

1. Classify the rating, and classify its corresponding user and item.
2. Mark the rating as possible noise if:
   (a) User class is critical, item class is weakly-preferred, and rating class is an average or a strong preference.
   (b) User class is average, item class is averagely-preferred, and rating class is a weak or a strong preference.
   (c) User class is benevolent, item class is strongly-preferred, and rating class is an average or a weak preference.

Remark 1. The proposal depends on three parameters: κ, ν and δ. These parameters are highly domain-dependant in [30] can be found a further detailed analysis about them.

3.2 Noise Correction Process

Some authors propose to discard noisy ratings, while others consider that these ratings must be corrected. Yera, Caballero and Martínez [30] proposal adopted the latter view. Before correction, another reason that classifies ratings as noise is verified. For each value marked as possible noise (PN), another value is predicted using traditional memory-based user-user collaborative filtering with Pearson's similarity and k = 60. The predicted value is compared with the current value. If the difference between them exceeds a predefined threshold δ then the new value is set as rating. Otherwise, the initial one is kept.

Summarizing, the whole correction process is:

1. Classify each user and item according definitions.
2. For each rating
   (a) Classify it according to definition.
   (b) Following the procedure presented in the previous section, mark it if represents a possible noise.
3. For each rating marked as possible noise
   (a) Predict its value using traditional collaborative filtering
   (b) Calculate the difference between predicted and original value.
      i. If the difference exceeds a threshold, then substitute the original with the predicted value.
      ii. Otherwise, remain the value as the original one.

3.3 Case Study

Following the experimental protocol suggested by Gunawardana and Shani in [11] a case study is carried out to evaluate the effects of the previous proposal over Movielens, which is a well-known dataset containing 100,000 movie ratings on 943 users and 1,682 items where each rating is discrete and is given in the range $[1,5]$.

For the mentioned dataset, it is evaluated the MAE of the CFRS methods *user-user* and *item-item* with and without rating correction. To prepare data for experiments, 900 users were randomly selected conforming the training and test set as aforementioned. This task is then performed five times, selecting each time a different set with the same amount of users. The approach parameters were set as $\kappa = 2$, $\nu = 4$ and $\delta = 1$. The Table 4 shows the results obtained.

The case study illustrates that the proposed approach obtained positive results for the datasets used in experiments. It proves that the correction approach decreases MAE value disregarding the algorithm used. It is remarkable that the correction process improves MAE value in a similar degree comparing with the other two traditional recommendation methods (Pearson's user-user and item-item). For a further detailed analysis see [30].

Table 4. MAE values with and without rating correction

	User-User CF	UUCF + NN management	Item-Item CF	IICF + NN management
k = 10	0.7741	**0.7713**	0.7771	**0.7723**
k = 20	0.7658	**0.7644**	0.7713	**0.7680**
k = 30	0.7646	**0.7632**	0.7705	**0.7673**
k = 40	0.7644	**0.7630**	0.7704	**0.7672**
k = 50	0.7644	**0.7631**	0.7704	**0.7673**
k = 60	0.7647	**0.7632**	0.7705	**0.7674**

4   A Fuzzy Approach to Detect Noisy Ratings

In previous section it has been shown that the use of *NN* management approaches in RSs generally improves the accuracy of recommendations. However, existing approaches do not properly manage the inherent uncertainty associated to ratings because they represent and manage the ratings and its noise in a precise way. This precise management lacks of flexibility and robustness, hence a way to properly mitigate this drawback is to use fuzzy tools based on fuzzy logic and fuzzy linguistic approach for modelling the uncertainty and vagueness associated to user's preferences.

Therefore, Yera, Castro and Martínez [31] focused on overcoming the lack of flexibility and robustness by proposing a novel fuzzy *NN* method to deal with the inherent uncertainty of *NN*, improving in such a way the noise management and consequently the recommendation accuracy. This approach extends the one revised in Sect. 3 because it focuses on the *NN* management just using ratings. This fuzzy approach for managing *NN* extends the proposal in Fig. 1 and it is composed by the following phases (see Fig. 3): (i) fuzzy profiling, (ii) noise detection, and (iii) noise correction.

These phases are further detailed in the coming sections.

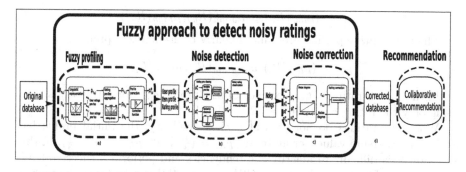

Fig. 3. General scheme of the fuzzy approach to eliminate noise in ratings database

4.1   Fuzzy Profiling

The fuzzy profiling consists of transforming ratings values into a fuzzy linguistic representation. This representation allows to obtain users', items' and ratings' fuzzy profiles. These initial profiles are then transformed by using Computing with Words (CW) [15,26] into modified profiles to boost their tendencies in a flexible way. Initially, the membership functions that characterize the ratings over its universe of discourse are defined. These functions are respectively associated to the fuzzy linguistic labels [10], $S = \{low, medium, high\}$, whose fuzzy semantics are shown in Fig. 4.

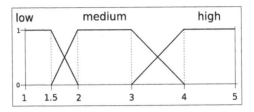

Fig. 4. Fuzzy definition of the ratings domain for the one to five stars domain

Once the ratings are represented using fuzzy linguistic terms, they are used to build the users', items', and ratings' profiles. Specifically, a user's profile p_{R_u} is built using the fuzzy representation of the user's ratings denoted by R_u (see Eqs. 2 and 3).

$$\mu_{low}(R_u) = \frac{\sum_{r_{ui} \in R_u} \mu_{low}(r_{ui})}{|R_u|} \qquad \mu_{medium}(R_u) = \frac{\sum_{r_{ui} \in R_u} \mu_{medium}(r_{ui})}{|R_u|} \tag{2}$$

$$\mu_{high}(R_u) = \frac{\sum_{r_{ui} \in R_u} \mu_{high}(r_{ui})}{|R_u|}$$

$$p_{R_u} = (\mu_{low}(R_u), \mu_{medium}(R_u), \mu_{high}(R_u)) \tag{3}$$

The items' fuzzy profiles are built similarly to users' fuzzy profiles:

$$p_{R_i} = (\mu_{low}(R_i), \mu_{medium}(R_i), \mu_{high}(R_i)) \tag{4}$$

In the case of rating's fuzzy profile, a fuzzy profile $p_{R_{ui}}$ for rating r_{ui} is built using only the rating r_{ui} itself, i.e., $R_{ui} = \{r_{ui}\}$.

When the ratings do not present a clear tendency, the initial profile has similar membership values for all terms, $p_{R_u} = (\frac{1}{3}, \frac{1}{3}, \frac{1}{3})$, $p_{R_i} = (\frac{1}{3}, \frac{1}{3}, \frac{1}{3})$. In this situation it is difficult to identify the tendencies and perform a successful NN management. The proposal applies a CW process [24] that transforms the profiles by maintaining high membership values and discarding low ones. The function f_1 (Fig. 5) is used with this purpose, depending on the parameter k whose value must be greater than $\frac{1}{3}$ to allow certain flexibility, for instance $k = 0.35$.

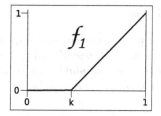

Fig. 5. The fuzzy transformation function to boost the fuzzy profile detected tendency

The transformed profiles are defined as:

$$p^*_{R_x} = (p^*_{R_x,low}, p^*_{R_x,medium}, p^*_{R_x,high}) = (f_1(\mu_{low}(R_x)), f_1(\mu_{medium}(R_x)), f_1(\mu_{high}(R_x)))$$

4.2   Noise Detection Phase

It classifies each rating of the dataset as noisy or not noisy. To do so, it checks if a given rating r_{ui} is noisy by analysing the rating tendency of its user u and item i, therefore the transformed fuzzy profiles are used to identify whether the rating matches the user's and item's tendencies or it lies out of the detected tendencies. The noise detection phase consists of two main steps:

(i) Rating pre-filtering: Each rating is analysed to determine whether it is eligible for the noise classification step. The corresponding user and item fuzzy profiles are compared to determine their closeness. Ratings whose corresponding user or item profiles have zero membership for all terms are discarded. For the remaining ones, their corresponding user and item profiles are compared by using the Manhattan distance, d, and a threshold d_1:

$$d(p^*_{R_u}; p^*_{R_i}) < d_1$$

If a given rating r_{ui} satisfies this inequality, then r_{ui} is eligible for noise classification. The best value for d_1 has been determined empirically [31], concluding that for $d_1 = 1$ the proposal obtains an optimal performance.

(ii) Noisy rating classification: For the chosen ratings in the pre-filtering step, its user, item and rating fuzzy profiles are compared to determine if the rating follows the user and item tendency. Thereby, for a rating r_{ui}, the distances among the profiles are computed and a threshold d_2 is used:

$$min(d(p^*_{R_u}; p^*_{R_{ui}}), d(p^*_{R_i}; p^*_{R_{ui}})) \geq d_2$$

If the rating verifies this inequality then r_{ui} is noisy. Several experiments [31] were performed to determine the most suitable value for the threshold, d_2, determining that $d_2 = 1$ is the best value.

4.3 Noise Correction Phase

Once the noisy ratings have been detected, this approach not only fixes noisy ratings but also it provides a *noise degree* of each rating that makes the rating correction much *more flexible* and *adaptable*. To define the noise degree of a noisy rating, the normalised Manhattan dissimilarity between profiles is used:

$$dissimilarity(p^*_{R_x}, p^*_{R_y}) = (d(p^*_{R_x}, p^*_{R_y}) - d_{min})/(d_{max} - d_{min}),$$

where $p^*_{R_x}$ and $p^*_{R_y}$ are the two profiles being compared, and d_{min} and d_{max} the minimum and maximum distance value between two profiles.

The noise degree of a noisy rating is defined as:

$$NoiseDegree_{r_{ui}} = T(\ dissimilarity(p^*_{R_u}, p^*_{R_{ui}}),\ dissimilarity(p^*_{R_i}, p^*_{R_{ui}})\ ),$$

being T a t-norm. In our context, the minimum is used as t-norm. After this, a new rating value n_{ui} for the same user and item is predicted, using a CF method (in this case the UserKNNPearson prediction approach [9]) using only the not noisy ratings. Afterwards, noisy ratings are corrected using the $NoiseDegree_{r_{ui}}$, original value and prediction:

$$r^*_{ui} = r_{ui} * (1 - NoiseDegree_{r_{ui}}) + n_{ui} * NoiseDegree_{r_{ui}}$$

4.4 Case Study

The proposal is evaluated in MovieLens dataset (ml-100k), which is prepared according to the procedure proposed by Gunawardana and Shani [11] to build training and test sets. The method performance is then evaluated through the following steps:

1. Apply a noise correction method over the training set, obtaining the modified training set.
2. Recommend with a given recommendation method using the modified training set.
2. Evaluate the recommendation results using the MAE.

This protocol is used to compare the current proposal (NN-Fuzzy) with related previous works. Specifically, the approaches presented by O'Mahony et al. [20] (DiffBased in Table 5), Li et al. [14] (NNMU) and Yera et al. [30] (NN-Crisp), and a baseline that does not use any noise correction approach (Base) are compared.

The results shown in Table 5 demonstrate that NN-Fuzzy obtains the best results for all cases. This evidence proves that it overcomes the performance of all previous works.

Table 5. MAE results on the MovieLens dataset

Predictor	Base	DiffBased	NNMU	NN-Crisp	NN-Fuzzy
UKNN	0.7647	0.7662	0.7644	0.7632	**0.7608**
IKNN	0.7705	0.7749	0.7699	0.7674	**0.7656**

5 Natural Noise in Group Recommendation Scenarios

Group recommender systems (GRSs) filter relevant items to groups of users regarding their preferences. These preferences can be explicitly given by the members, hence natural noise can also affect these scenarios. However, the natural noise problem has not been addressed on GRSs yet.

It seems worthy to research the NN management (NNM) in this scenario but taking into account that the complexity is much higher than in individual scenarios and at least in the group recommendation scenario two levels of data should be considered: (i) *local level*: preferences belonging to the group members, and (ii) *global level*: preferences of all the users in the entire dataset. The level considered most suitable to perform the NNM should be then studied. Four alternatives for NNM in GRSs should be then analyzed in both levels of data:

- First, two approaches that focus the NNM on the local level before the recommendations. The approaches are local NNM based on local information, NNM-LL, and local NNM based on global information.
- Second, an approach that focuses the NNM on the global level before the recommendation, disregarding the group to which each user might belong.
- Eventually, a cascade hybridization of the previous approaches that performs a global NNM approach, and then a local NNM that corrects the group ratings by using the information already corrected.

Acknowledgments. This research work was partially supported by the Research Project TIN2015-66524-P, and the Spanish Ministry of Education, Culture and Sport FPU fellowship (FPU13/01151).

References

1. Adomavicius, G., Tuzhilin, A.T.: Toward the next generation of recommender systems: a survey of the state-of-the-art and possible extensions. IEEE Trans. Knowl. Data Eng. **17**(6), 734–749 (2005)
2. Amatriain, X., Jaimes, A., Oliver, N., Pujol, J.M.: Data mining methods for recommender systems. In: Ricci, F., Rokach, L., Shapira, B., Kantor, P.B. (eds.) Recommender Systems Handbook, pp. 39–71. Springer, New York (2011)
3. Amatriain, X., Lathia, N., Pujol, J.M., Kwak, H., Oliver, N.: The wisdom of the few: a collaborative filtering approach based on expert opinions from the web. In: Proceedings of the 32nd International ACM SIGIR Conference, pp. 532–539. ACM, New York (2009)

4. Amatriain, X., Pujol, J.M., Oliver, N.: I Like It.. I Like It Not: evaluating user ratings noise in recommender systems. In: Houben, G.-J., McCalla, G., Pianesi, F., Zancanaro, M. (eds.) UMAP 2009. LNCS, vol. 5535, pp. 247–258. Springer, Heidelberg (2009). doi:10.1007/978-3-642-02247-0_24

5. Burke, R.: Hybrid recommender systems: survey and experiments. Adapted Interaction 12(4), 331–370 (2002)

6. Castro, J., Rodríguez, R.M., Barranco, M.J.: Weighting of features in content-based filtering with entropy and dependence measures. Int. J. Comput. Intell. Syst. 7(1), 80–89 (2014)

7. Dellarocas, C.: Immunizing online reputation reporting systems against unfair ratings and discriminatory behavior. In: Proceedings of the 2nd ACM Conference on Electronic Commerce, pp. 150–157. ACM (2000)

8. Desrosiers, C., Karypis, G.: A comprehensive survey of neighborhood-based recommendation methods. In: Ricci, F., Rokach, L., Shapira, B., Kantor, P.B. (eds.) Recommender Systems Handbook, pp. 107–144. Springer, New York (2011)

9. Ekstrand, M.D., Riedl, J.T., Konstan, J.A.: Collaborative filtering recommender systems. Found. Trends Hum. Comput. Interact. 4(2), 81–173 (2011)

10. Espinilla, M., Montero, J., Rodríguez, J.: Computational intelligence in decision making. Int. J. Comput. Intell. Syst. 7(SUPPL.1), 1–5 (2014)

11. Gunawardana, A., Shani, G.: A survey of accuracy evaluation metrics of recommendation tasks. J. Mach. Learn. Res. 10, 2935–2962 (2009)

12. Gunes, I., Kaleli, C., Bilge, A., Polat, H.: Shilling attacks against recommender systems: a comprehensive survey. Artif. Intell. Rev. 42(4), 767–799 (2014)

13. Konstan, J.A., Riedl, J.: Recommender systems: from algorithms to user experience. User Model. User-Adap. Inter. 22(1–2), 101–123 (2012)

14. Li, B., Chen, L., Zhu, X., Zhang, C.: Noisy but non-malicious user detection in social recommender systems. World Wide Web 16(5–6), 677–699 (2013)

15. Martínez, L., Herrera, F.: An overview on the 2-tuple linguistic model for computing with words in decision making: extensions, applications and challenges. Inf. Sci. 207(1), 1–18 (2012)

16. Martínez, L., Barranco, M.J., Pérez, L.G., Espinilla, M.: A knowledge based recommender system with multigranular linguistic information. Int. J. Comput. Intell. Syst. 1(3), 225–236 (2008)

17. Martínez, L., Pérez, L.G., Barranco, M.: A multigranular linguistic content-based recommendation model: research articles. Int. J. Intell. Syst. 22(5), 419–434 (2007)

18. Mobasher, B., Burke, R., Bhaumik, R., Williams, C.: Toward trustworthy recommender systems: an analysis of attack models and algorithm robustness. ACM Trans. Internet Technol. 7(4), Article 23 (2007)

19. Noguera, J., Barranco, M., Segura, R., Martínez, L.: A mobile 3D GIS hybrid recommender system for tourism. Inf. Sci. 215, 37–52 (2012)

20. O'Mahony, M.P., Hurley, N.J., Silvestre, G.: Detecting noise in recommender system databases. In: Proceedings of the 11th International Conference on Intelligent User Interfaces, pp. 109–115. ACM (2006)

21. Pazzani, M., Billsus, D.: Content-based recommendation systems. Adaptive Web 4321, 325–341 (2007)

22. Pham, H.X., Jung, J.J.: Preference-based user rating correction process for interactive recommendation systems. Multimedia Tools Appl. 65(1), 119–132 (2013)

23. Pilászy, I., Tikk, D.: Recommending new movies: even a few ratings are more valuable than metadata. In: Proceedings of the third ACM Conference on Recommender Systems, pp. 93–100. ACM (2009)

24. Quesada, F.J., Palomares, I., Martínez, L.: Managing experts behavior in large-scale consensus reaching processes with uninorm aggregation operators. Appl. Soft Comput. **35**, 873–887 (2015)
25. Rodríguez, R., Espinilla, M., Sánchez, P., Martínez, L.: Using linguistic incomplete preference relations to cold start recommendations. Internet Res. **20**(3), 296–315 (2010)
26. Rodríguez, R.M., Labella, Á., Martínez, L.: An overview on fuzzy modelling of complex linguistic preferences in decision making. Int. J. Comput. Intell. Syst. **9**, 81–94 (2016)
27. Vozalis, M.G., Margaritis, K.G.: Using SVD and demographic data for the enhancement of generalized Collaborative Filtering. Inf. Sci. **177**(15), 3017–3037 (2007)
28. Xiao, B., Benbasat, I.: E-commerce product recommendation agents: use, characteristics, and impact. Manage. Inf. Syst. Q. **31**(1), 137–209 (2007)
29. Toledo, R.Y., Mota, Y.C.: An e-learning collaborative filtering approach to suggest problems to solve in programming online judges. Int. J. Distance Educ. Technol. **12**(2), 51–65 (2014)
30. Toledo, R.Y., Mota, Y.C., Martínez, L.: Correcting noisy ratings in collaborative recommender systems. Knowl. Based Syst. **76**, 96–108 (2015)
31. Toledo, R.Y., Castro, J., Martínez, L.: A fuzzy model for managing natural noise in recommender systems. Appl. Soft Comput. **40**, 187–198 (2016)

Applications of Natural Computing

Realization of Periodic Functions by Self-stabilizing Population Protocols with Synchronous Handshakes

Anissa Lamani$^{(\boxtimes)}$ and Masafumi Yamashita

Department of Informatics, Kyushu University, Fukuoka, Japan
anissa.lamani@gmail.com

Abstract. We consider in the following the problem of realizing periodic functions by a collection of finite state-agents that cooperate by interacting with each other. More formally, given a periodic non-negative integer function f that maps the set of non-negative integers $\mathbf{N}$ to itself, we aim in this paper at designing a distributed protocol with a state set Q and a subset $S \subseteq Q$, such that, for any initial configuration C_0, with probability 1, there are a time instant t_0 and a constant $d \in \mathbf{N}$ satisfying $f(t + d) = \nu_S(C_t)$ for all $t \geq t_0$, where $\nu_S(C)$ is the number of agents with a state in S in a configuration C. The model that we consider is a variant of the population protocol (PP) model in which we assume that each agent is involved in an interaction at each time instant t, hence the notion of synchronous handshakes. These additional assumptions on the model are necessary to solve the considered problem. We also assume that the interacting pairs are matched uniformly at random.

Keywords: Self-organizing systems · Self-stabilization · Clock synchronization · Oscillators · Group construction · Population protocol · Uniform scheduler

1 Introduction

The food hunting of army ants, the synchronized flashing of fireflies..., these remarkable self-organized behaviors observed in biological systems have intrigued a lot of researchers and a lot of investigations have been initiated to understand these autonomous and self-organized behaviors to implement them in artificial distributed systems.

In a typical artificial distributed system, its global behavior is controlled by its distributed elements, each of which determines its behavior depending only on its local view (i.e., local snapshot of the system). The wider views the elements have, the more delicately the global behavior can be controlled, needless to say; or equivalently, the narrower views they have, the more disorderly the distributed system would behave (at least in the worst case). Note that if no communication (direct or indirect) is allowed then obviously coordination is impossible to achieve. The extreme case is then when a distributed element

© Springer International Publishing AG 2016
C. Martín-Vide et al. (Eds.): TPNC 2016, LNCS 10071, pp. 21–33, 2016.
DOI: 10.1007/978-3-319-49001-4_2

is completely isolated from the other elements, and changes its (local) state when it happens to interact with another element. In this paper, provided this extreme case and assuming an arbitrary initial state of the system (i.e., in a self-stabilizing manner), we examine what is necessary to control the distributed system and emerge a global behavior. Specifically, we examine the contribution of synchrony to have the system behave orderly. Self-stabilization is an important feature in distributed computing. It is more challenging to achieve as the system must retrieve, by itself, a correct behavior starting from any possible initial configuration. This permits to tolerate transient faults.

The closest model to our setting is the population protocol (PP) model that was introduced by Angluin et al. [1] to model a collection of finite-state agents that interact with each other in order to accomplish a common task [6]. Computations in PPs are performed through pairwise interactions i.e., when two agents interact, they exchange their local information and update their state according to a common protocol. The interaction pattern is assumed to be unpredictable i.e., each agent has no control on the agents it interact with. Hence, it is assumed that there is an external entity, called scheduler, which is in charge of selecting the pairs of agents for an interaction. Remark that the definition of PP is general enough to represent not only artificial distributed systems as sensor networks but also natural distributed systems as animal populations and chemical reactions.

Let $\mathbf{N}$ be the set of non-negative integers. Given a periodic non-negative integer function $f : \mathbf{N} \to \mathbf{N}$ with a period τ i.e., $f(t + \tau) = f(t)$ for all $t \in \mathbf{N}$. We present in this paper, a population protocol with a state set Q and a subset $S \subseteq Q$, such that, for any initial configuration C_0, with probability 1, there are a time instant t_0 and a constant $d \in \mathbf{N}$ satisfying $f(t + d) = \nu_S(C_t)$ for all $t \geq t_0$, where $\nu_S(C)$ is the number of agents with a state in S in a configuration C. That is, we aim at realizing the function f by counting the number of agents in a given set of states S. In other words, our target is to design a protocol to completely control, in a distributed manner, the number of agents with a state in S to represent f. Remark that if we allow a scheduler that may not invite some agents to interact at some time t, the problem becomes unsolvable even for a simplest problem instance. For example, define a function f_τ by $f_\tau(t) = n$ if t mod $\tau = 0$ (where n is the size of the population), and $f_\tau(t) = 0$, otherwise. Since the agents can only update their states when they are involved in an interaction, provided that there are at least three agents in the population, there is no PP that realizes f_τ, since all agents must participate in an interaction to update their states and reach a configuration C such that $\nu_S(C) = n$ from a configuration C' in which $\nu_S(C') = 0$ (after convergence). We thus consider a variant of PP in which we assume that every agent is part of an interaction at each instant.

To solve our problem, we also need to consider the self-stabilizing clock synchronization problem. Clock synchronization is one of the important features in distributed computing as it provides a form of logical clock that could be used to solve several distributed problems. The problem has been widely investigated in the context of distributed computing [3,6,9]. Under the PP model, the problem was recently addressed in [4] where it has been shown that in the case where the agents have only a constant number of states, the self-stabilizing synchronization problem is impossible to solve, even if the agents know their covering time, which is the minimum number of transitions for them to have met with each other agent with certainty. A self-stabilizing population protocol is then proposed to solve the phase synchronization problem. In the proposed solution, an unlimited resource station called *Base Station* is used to provide an infinite repetition of phases, $0, 1, \ldots, \tau - 1$ and ensure that any agent i does not execute phase $x + 1 \pmod{\tau}$ before all the agents have executed phase $x \pmod{\tau}$ i.e., there are time instants in which the clock values of the agents are not all the same. In this paper, provided our scheduler, we propose a solution for the self-stabilizing synchronization problem using a constant number of states.

Most of the problems investigated in PPs consider the computational power of the model and hence are static. So far, only few investigations have considered *dynamic* problems: in [2], a self-stabilizing token circulation protocol on rings with a pre-selected leader was proposed. In [5], both the self-stabilizing mutual exclusion and the group mutual exclusion problems were considered. In [10], the authors investigated the convergence time and the threshold effects exhibited by Lotka-Volterra-type protocols. In a companion paper [8], the authors investigated the problem of realizing a (digitized) sine curve in a self-stabilizing manner. Under a deterministic scheduler which is adversarial, they showed that the problem is at least as difficult as the self-stabilizing leader election problem, and hence (by [7]) at least n states are necessary to solve the problem.

2   Preliminaries

We consider a collection $A = \{0, 1, \ldots, n - 1\}$ of identical (anonymous) finite-state agents that interact with each other in order to cooperate and solve a given problem. Computations are performed through pairwise interactions i.e., when two agents interact, they exchange their information and update their states according to a common deterministic protocol $P = (Q, \delta)$, where Q is a finite set of states (of an agent) and δ is a transition function $(Q \times Q) \to (Q \times Q)$ that specifies the result of each interaction; if two agents in A with states p and p' interact at time t, their states at $t+1$ will be q and q', where $(q, q') = \delta(p, p')$. We assume that each agent is able to interact with any other agent in the population.

Let $p_i \in Q$ be the state of an agent $i \in A$. The n-tuple $C = (p_1, p_2, \ldots, p_n)$ of states where each entry p_i corresponds to the state of the agent i, describes the global state of the population, and is called a *configuration*. We frequently regard C as a mapping $A \to Q$ such that $C(i) = p_i$ for all $i \in A$. Once an interaction pattern has been given to a configuration C, the configuration C' at the next time instant is naturally constructed from C as follows: for each pair (i, j) of agents in the interaction pattern, we replace p_i and p_j in C with q_i and q_j, where $(q_i, q_j) = \delta(p_i, p_j)$. In this paper, we distinguish the *initiator* and the *responder* in δ, so that $\delta(p_i, p_j) = (q_i, q_j)$ *may not* imply $\delta(p_j, p_i) = (q_j, q_i)$.

Unlike the classical model of PP, we assume that at each instant t, each agent is part of an interaction, we hence assume that n is even. The scheduler, in charge of creating a maximum matching on all the agents, is assumed to be probabilistic and uniform i.e., the pairs of agents are matched uniformly at random.

Let $P = (Q, \delta)$ and C be the set of all possible configurations of P, respectively. Given a configuration $C \in C$ and an interaction pattern, i.e., a set of interactions (i.e., disjoint pairs of agents) $R = \{(i_1, j_1), (i_2, j_2), \ldots, (i_m, j_m)\}$, we say that C' yields from C via R, denoted by $C \xrightarrow{R} C'$, if for all $k = 1, 2, \ldots, m$, $(C'(i_k), C'(j_k)) = \delta(C(i_k), C(j_k))$, and otherwise, if $i \notin \{i_k, j_k : 1 \leq k \leq m\}$, $C'(i) = C(i)$ holds. Let C_t and R_t be respectively the configuration and the interaction pattern on C_t at time t. An execution $\mathcal{E}$ of a protocol P can be represented by a sequence of configurations and interaction patterns $(C_0, R_0, C_1, R_1, \ldots)$ such that for all $t \geq 0$, $C_t \xrightarrow{R_t} C_{t+1}$. Recall that R_t is produced by the scheduler. Since this paper assumes that each agent is part of an interaction and n is even, $|R_t| = n/2$ for any t. By $C \xrightarrow{*} C'$, we denote the fact that a configuration C' is reachable from C after a finite number of transitions.

Let $\mathbf{N}$ be the set of non-negative integers. For any configuration C and a subset of states S, $\nu_S(C)$ denotes the number of agents with a state $p \in S$ in C. Suppose that f is a periodic non-negative integer function $f : \mathbf{N} \to \mathbf{N}$ with a period τ, i.e., $f(t+\tau) = f(t)$ for all $t \in \mathbf{N}$. This paper investigates the problem of designing a protocol P that *realizes* f (in a self-stabilizing manner). Formally, a protocol $P = (Q, \delta)$ and a subset S of Q are looked for, that eventually realizes f, regardless of its initial configuration C_0, in the following sense: for any execution $\mathcal{E} : C_0, C_1, \ldots$, there are a time instant t_0 and a constant d $(0 \leq d \leq \tau)$ satisfying $f(t + d) = \nu_S(C_t)$ for all $t \geq t_0$ *with probability 1*.

To achieve our goal, we first present a protocol τ-CLK that implements a self-synchronized clock using τ states and then use it to design a protocol PO_h, called a primitive oscillator that realizes a primitive periodic function h whose period is τ and range is $\{0, n\}$. We next explain how to execute a set of primitive oscillators in parallel in such a way as to satisfy prescribed offsets between them, assuming that the agents that participate in different oscillators are disjoint, although they interact to synchronize their executions. Since a periodic function f is represented by the sum of a set of primitive periodic functions h_i with range $\{0, n_i\}$, the problem of designing a protocol that realizes f is reduced to the group construction problem to assign each agent to a group g_i in such a way that each group g_i eventually accommodates n_i agents (to run primitive oscillators PO_{h_i}). The group construction problem for one group is trivial. The general group construction problem can be reduced to the problem for n groups, each consisting of one agent. We present first a protocol for solving the general group construction problem that requires $\Omega(n)$ states. Aiming at the reduction of the space complexity, we next present a heuristic protocol to approximately construct m groups of size $n_0, \ldots, n_{m-1}$ respectively, using $m \cdot c \cdot max\{b_1, \ldots, b_{m-1}\}$ states, where c is a small constant larger than 5 and $b_k = n_k/n_0 \in \mathbf{N}$ for $k = 1, 2, \ldots, m-1$.

3   Clock Synchronizers and Primitive Oscillators

3.1   Self-stabilizing Clock Synchronization

In this section, we first formulate the self-stabilizing clock synchronization problem taking care of the fact that the scheduler is probabilistic, and show that there is a self-stabilizing clock synchronization protocol that solves the problem. A protocol $P = (T_\tau, \delta_\tau)$, where $T_\tau = \{0, 1, \ldots, \tau - 1\}$, is said to be a self-stabilizing modulo τ clock synchronization protocol if for any execution $\mathcal{E} : C_0, C_1, \ldots$ starting from any initial configuration $C_0 \in \mathcal{C}$, with probability 1, there are a time instant $t_0 \in \mathbf{N}$ and an integer $d \ (\geq -t_0)$ satisfying $\nu_{\{(t+d) \mod \tau\}}(C_t) = n$ for all $t (\geq t_0)$. Consider the following protocol τ-CLK.

Protocol 1. τ-CLK: Self-stabilizing Modulo τ Clock Synchonizer

$\delta(x, y) = ((min(x, y) + 1) \mod \tau, (min(x, y) + 1) \mod \tau)$

Theorem 1. *Protocol τ-CLK is a self-stabilizing modulo τ clock synchronization protocol.*

Proof. Let $\mathcal{E} : C_0, C_1, \ldots$ be any execution starting from any initial configuration C_0. Once it reaches a configuration C_t such that $\nu_{\{(t+d) \mod \tau\}}(C_t) = n$, by the assumption on the scheduler, no matter what maximum matching is proposed as the interaction pattern, $\nu_{\{(t+d+1) \mod \tau\}}(C_{t+1}) = n$ holds. Thus it suffices to show that, with probability 1, there is a time instant t such that $\nu_{\{t'\}}(C_t) = n$ holds for some $t' \in T_\tau$.

Since the case of $\tau = 1$ is trivial, we assume that $\tau \geq 2$. Consider a directed graph $\mathcal{G} = (\mathcal{C}, E)$ representing the transition relation between configurations, i.e., $(C, C') \in E$ if and only if $C \xrightarrow{R} C'$ via some interaction pattern R, which implies that when the current configuration is C, the next configuration is C' with a positive probability. Let $\mathcal{C}^* = \{C : \nu_{\{t\}}(C) = n \text{ for some } t \in T_\tau\}$. Thanks to the theory of finite state Markov chain, in order to show that, with probability 1, there is a time instant t such that $\nu_{\{t'\}}(C_t) = n$ holds for some t', it is sufficient to show that for any $C \in \mathcal{C}$, there is a $C' \in \mathcal{C}^*$ that is reachable from C in $\mathcal{G}$. We show this fact in the following.

For any $C \in \mathcal{C}$, let $Z_C = \{t \in T_\tau : \nu_{\{t\}}(C) = 0\}$, which is the set of states $t \in T_\tau$ that does not appear in C. By definition, $C \in \mathcal{C}^*$ if and only if $|Z_C| = \tau - 1$. We show that for any $C \notin \mathcal{C}^*$ there is a configuration C' reachable from C in $\mathcal{G}$ such that $|Z_C| < |Z_{C'}|$.

First consider the case in which $|Z_C| = 0$. Recall that n is even and thus $n/2$ is a natural number. If $\nu_{\{\tau-1\}}(C) \leq n/2$, there is a maximum matching R that matches every agent with state $\tau - 1$ to an agent with a different state, and by definition $0 \in Z_{C'}$, where $C \xrightarrow{R} C'$, since an agent with 0 emerges in C' if and only if two agents with state $\tau - 1$ interact in C.

Suppose otherwise that $\nu_{\{\tau-1\}}(C) \geq n/2+1$, which implies that $\nu_{\{\tau-2\}}(C) \leq n/2 - 1$. Consider a maximum matching R that matches every agent with state $q_{\tau-1}$ to an agent with the same state; if $\nu_{\{\tau-1\}}(C)$ is odd, then R matches the remaining one to an agent with state 0. Then $\nu_{\{\tau-1\}}(C') \leq n/2$, where $C \xrightarrow{R} C'$, since $\nu_{\{\tau-1\}}(C') \leq \nu_{\{\tau-2\}}(C) + 1 \leq n/2$. A configuration C'' such that $0 \in Z_{C''}$ is reachable from C in $\mathcal{G}$.

Next, consider the case in which $|Z_C| > 0$. Let R be any interaction pattern in C and C' the configuration such that $C \xrightarrow{R} C'$. Observe that if $\nu_{\{t\}}(C) = 0$ then $\nu_{\{(t+1) \bmod \tau\}}(C') = 0$, and hence $|Z_C| \leq |Z_{C'}|$ holds. Assume first that $\nu_{\tau-1}(C) > 0$, if $\nu_{\{\tau-1\}}(C) \leq n/2$, then we can easily find C' such that $|Z_C| < |Z_{C'}|$ holds. Otherwise if $\nu_{\{\tau-1\}}(C) \geq n/2+1$, by a similar argument as above, we can show that there is a path from C to C' in G, such that $0 < \nu_{\{\tau-1\}}(C') \leq n/2$ holds.

By contrast, assume that $\nu_{\tau-1}(C) = 0$. We show that after at most τ steps, $\nu_{\tau-1}(C') > 0$, where $C \to C'$. Let consider the smallest $t \in [0, \tau - 2]$ such that $\nu_t(C) > 0$ (for all $t' = 0, 1, \ldots, t - 1$, $\nu_{t'}(C) = 0$). Note that $\nu_{t+1}(C') > 0$. If $\nu_{\tau-1}(C') = 0$ then again $\nu_{t+2}(C'') > 0$ where $C' \to C''$. By repeating the same reasoning, after at most τ steps, $\nu_{\tau-1}(C^-) > 0$ where $C \xrightarrow{*} C^-$. We retrieve the cases discussed above.

3.2   Primitive Oscillators

Let $\alpha = (\iota_a, \iota_p, \iota_d, \iota_\ell)$ be a tuple of four parameters representing respectively *amplitude*, *period*, *delay* and *length* where $0 \leq \iota_d \leq \iota_p$. By f_α, we denote a function with period ι_p defined as follows: $f_\alpha(t) = \iota_a$ if $\iota_d \leq t(\bmod \iota_p) \leq \iota_d + \iota_\ell - 1$, and $f_\alpha(t) = 0$, otherwise.

Figure 1 illustrates a part of f_α, where $\alpha = (5, 10, 6, 4)$. That is, for example, $f_\alpha(x) = 0$ when $x = 0, 1, \ldots, 5$, and $f_\alpha(x) = 5$ when $x = 6, 7, 8, 9$. We call such a function (f_α) *primitive (periodic) function*. Note that a constant function is also a primitive function.

In Fig. 1, f_α is presented as a continuous trapezoidal function to emphasize the shape of the oscillations, however, recall that, in reality, f_α is a discontinuous step function.

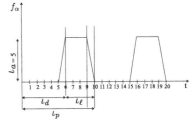

Fig. 1. A primitive (periodic) function f_α, where $\alpha = (5, 10, 6, 4)$

A pair of protocol $P = (Q, \delta)$ and a subset S of Q is said to be a *primitive oscillator* if it realizes a primitive function f_α: For any execution $\mathcal{E} : C_0, C_1, \ldots$ starting from any initial configuration $C_0 \in \mathcal{C}$, with probability 1, there are a time instant $t_0 \in \mathbf{N}$ and an integer $d \ (\geq -t_0)$ satisfying $\nu_S(C_{t+d}) = f(t)$ for all $t(\geq t_0)$.

Given $\alpha = (n, \tau, \iota_d, \iota_\ell)$, let $T_{\iota_d, \iota_\ell} = \{\iota_d, \iota_d + 1, \ldots, \iota_d + \iota_\ell - 1\}$. Then, the pair $PO_\alpha = (\tau\text{-CLK}, T_{\iota_d, \iota_\ell})$ is a primitive oscillator for f_α, by the next corollary.

Corollary 2. *Let f be any periodic function with period τ that takes a value in $\{0, n\}$. Then there is a state set $S_f \subseteq Q_\tau$ such that τ-CLK with S_f realizes f.*

Proof. Letting $S_f = \{t \bmod \tau : f(t) = n\}$, τ-CLK with S_f realizes f by definition.

4 Synchronization of Primitive Oscillators

In this section, we investigate how to synchronize several primitive oscillators, in order to satisfy prescribed offsets between them, assuming that the agents that participate in different oscillators are disjoint (i.e., they know to which group they belong), although they do interact to synchronize their executions. The *offset* is the difference, expressed in time, between the delays of two primitive oscillators referenced to the same point in time (see Fig. 2). In our case, the offset is expressed as the difference between the agents' clock values. We assume that the primitive oscillators have the same period, however, they might have different delays. Note that we can assume that the offset is positive without loss of generality, since we can order the primitive oscillators according to the predefined offsets.

To simplify the explanation of our protocol, we first focus on how to synchronize two primitive oscillators. Let PO_{α_k} ($k = 0, 1$) be two primitive oscillators for the set of agents A_k, where $\alpha_k = (n_k, \tau, \iota_{d_k}, \iota_{\ell_k})$ and $n_k = |A_k|$. Let o be the offset. Provided that $A_0 \cap A_1 = \emptyset$ and $|A_0 \cup A_1|$ is even, a protocol that works on $A = A_0 \cup A_1$ is looked for, such that for any execution $\mathcal{E} : C_0, C_1, \ldots$ starting from any initial configuration $C_0 \in \mathcal{C}$, with

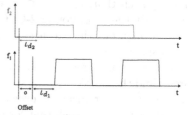

Fig. 2. Offset between two primitive oscillators

probability 1, there are a time instant $t_0 \in \mathbf{N}$ and integers d_0, d_1 ($\geq -t_0$) satisfying the following conditions: (1) $o = d_1 - d_0$, and (2) for $k = 0, 1$, $\nu_{S_k}(C_{t+d_k}) = f_{\alpha_k}(t)$ for all $t (\geq t_0)$, where S_k is the state set of PO_{α_k}, i.e., $PO_{\alpha_k} = (\tau\text{-CLK}, S_k)$. We call a protocol satisfying these conditions $\langle PO_{\alpha_0}, o, PO_{\alpha_1} \rangle$.

In the following, we present a protocol $P = (Q, \delta)$ and a subset S of Q that satisfy these conditions. First, the set of agents is $A = A_0 \cup A_1$, and the state set is $Q = G_2 \times Q_\tau$, where $G_2 = 0, 1$. An agent $i \in A$ is in state $(k, t) \in Q$ means that it belongs to group A_k and its local time is t. Note that in this section, agents do not change their group A_k, and we concentrate on the synchronization of their local times so that all members in the same group have the same time, while the difference of the local times in A_0 and A_1 is exactly o, provided that initially all members in A_k are in a state in $\{k\} \times T_\tau$, i.e., initially each agent correctly recognizes its group. Let $x = (k, r)$ and $x' = (k', r')$ be two states. The following protocol 2-CPO defines $(y, y') = \delta(x, x')$, where $y = (\ell, s)$ and $y' = (\ell', s')$. In the 2-CPO, δ_τ is the transition function of τ-CLK. Note that the description of 2-CPO presents the case in which $k = 0$ and $k' = 1$ holds (and the case in which $k = k'$ holds). Although omitted in 2-CPO, the other case in which $k = 1$ and $k' = 0$ should be defined symmetrically.

Protocol 2. 2-CPO: Coupling Two Primitive Oscillators

---

if $k = k'$ then   /* The agents are part of the same group. */
    $\ell = \ell' = k$ and $(s, s') = \delta_\tau(r, r')$
else /* The agents are part of different groups. */ ($k = 0$ and $k' = 1$) */
    if $(r + o)$ mod $\tau = r'$ then
        $\ell = k = 0$, $\ell' = k' = 1$, $s = (r + 1)$ mod τ and $s' = (r' + 1)$ mod τ
    else
        $\ell = k = 0$, $\ell' = k' = 1$, $s = (r + 1)$ mod τ and $s' = (r + o + 1)$ mod τ

Theorem 3. *The protocol defined by 2-CPO is indeed* $\langle PO_{\alpha_0}, o, PO_{\alpha_1} \rangle$, *provided that initially all agents in* A_k *have a state in* $\{k\} \times T_\tau$ *for* $k = 0, 1$.

Proof. Let $\mathcal{E} : C_0, C_1, \ldots$ be any execution starting from any initial configuration C_0 such that, for all $i \in A$, $C_0(i) = (0, t)$ for some $t \in T_\tau$ if and only if $i \in A_0$. By the definition of 2-CPO, the agents do not change their groups, and thus through out the execution, all members originally in A_0 (resp. A_1) are in A_0 (resp. A_1).

Observe that agents in A_1 cannot affect agents in A_0 (except to increment time), and the clocks (i.e., the second element t of state $(0, t)$) of agents in A_0 are eventually synchronized by executing τ-CLK.[1] That is, there is a time instant t_0 and a constant d such that for any $t \geq t_0$, all of their clocks show $r = (t + d)$ mod τ at C_t, with probability 1, by Theorem 1. All agents in A_1 also execute τ-CLK, but their clocks are not synchronized, unless all of their clocks show r' satisfying $r' = (r + o)$ mod τ at C_t. On the other hand, if there is a time instant $t > t_0$ at which the clock of each of the agents in A_1 at C_t shows time r' satisfying $r' = (r + o)$ mod τ, then the conditions for $\langle PO_{\alpha_0}, o, PO_{\alpha_1} \rangle$ hold.

Thus it suffices to show that there is a time instant $t \geq t_0$ at which all of their clocks are synchronized and show time r' satisfying $r' = (r + o)$ mod τ, with probability 1. Thanks again to the theory of finite state Markov chain, we follow the same argument as in the proof of Theorem 1. We define the graph $\mathcal{G}$ on the configuration space $\mathcal{C}$ of 2-CPO representing the transition of this protocol. Let $\mathcal{C}^*$ be the set of configurations corresponding to the desired configurations, and show that for all configuration $C \in \mathcal{C}$, there is a path to a configuration in $\mathcal{C}^*$. Let C be any configuration. Without loss of generality, we can assume that the clocks of all agents in A_0 are synchronized in C. If $n_0 \geq n_1$, then obviously there

---

[1] In spite that the size of A_0 may be odd, the clocks of agents in A_0 are eventually synchronized by executing τ-CLK, since every agent that interacts with an agent in different group increments its time, even if it does not interact with an agent in the same group.

is an interaction pattern R that matches all members in A_1 to members in A_0, and $C' \in C^*$ is reached from C via R, by the definition of 2-CPO.

Otherwise if $n_0 < n_1$, let Z_C be the set of agents i in A_1 whose clock in C satisfies $r' = (r + o) \mod \tau$. Consider an interaction pattern R defined as follows:

M1: Take a maximum matching among Z_C, so that every agent (except at most one, say i) matches to an agent in Z_C.

M2: Take a maximum matching between agents in A_0 and those in $A_1 \backslash Z_C(\cup\{i\})$ if there is such an i in M1.

M3: Take a maximum matching among the agents whose parters have not been determined in M1 and M2.

Let C' be a configuration reached from C via R. If all agents in A_1 can be matched by M1 and M2 (without using M3), then $C' \in C^*$.

Otherwise, by M1, $Z_C \backslash \{i\} \subseteq Z_{C'}$. Set $Z_{C'}$ also contains agents in A_1 that are matched with agents in A_0 by M2. Since $n_0 \geq 1$ and $|A_1| + |A_2|$ is even, $|Z_C| < |Z_{C'}|$. Thus there is a path from C to a configuration C'' at which all agents in A_2 can be matched by M1 and M2.

We extend this protocol to synchronize m primitive oscillators. Let PO_{α_k} ($k = 0, 1, \ldots, m-1$) be m primitive oscillators for the set of agents A_k, where $\alpha_k = (n_k, \tau, \iota_{d_k}, \iota_{\ell_k})$ and $n_k = |A_k|$. Let o_k ($k = 0, 1, \ldots, m-1$) be the offset between PO_{α_k} and $PO_{\alpha_{k+1}}$. Provided that A_k's are disjoint and $A = \cup_{0 \leq k \leq m-1} A_k$ is of even size, a protocol that works on A is looked for, such that for any execution $\mathcal{E} : C_0, C_1, \ldots$ starting from any initial configuration $C_0 \in \mathcal{C}$, with probability 1, there are a time instant $t_0 \in \mathbf{N}$ and integers d_k ($\geq -t_0$) for $k = 0, 1, \ldots, m-1$ satisfying the following conditions: (1) $o_k = d_{k+1} - d_k$ for $k = 0, 1, \ldots, m-2$, and (2) for $k = 0, 1, \ldots, m-1$, $\nu_{S_k}(C_{t+d_k}) = f_{\alpha_k}(t)$ for all $t (\geq t_0)$, where S_k is the state set of PO_{α_k}, i.e., $PO_{\alpha_k} = (\tau\text{-CLK}, S_k)$. We call a protocol satisfying these conditions $\langle PO_{\alpha_0}, o_0, PO_{\alpha_1}, o_1, \ldots, o_{m-2}, PO_{\alpha_{m-1}} \rangle$.

We present a protocol $P = (Q, \delta)$ and a subset S of Q that satisfies this condition. First, the set of agents is $A = \cup_{1 \leq k \leq m} A_k$, and the state set is $Q = G_m \times T_\tau$, where $G_m = \{0, 1, \ldots, m-1\}$. An agent $i \in A$ is in state $(k, t) \in Q$ means that it belongs to group A_k and its local time is t. We are concerned with synchronization so that all members in the same group have the same time, while the difference of the local times in A_k and A_h is exactly o_k if $h = k+1$, provided that initially all members in A_k are in a state in $\{k\} \times T_\tau$. Let $x = (k, r)$ and $x' = (k', r')$ be two states. The following protocol m-CPO defines $(y, y') = \delta(x, x')$, where $y = (\ell, s)$ and $y' = (\ell', s')$. In the m-CPO, δ_τ is the transition function of τ-CLK. Note that the description of m-CPO presents the case in which $k \leq k'$ holds. Although omitted in m-CPO, the other case in which $k > k'$ should be defined symmetrically.

Protocol 3. m-CPO: Coupling m Primitive Oscillators

---

if $k = k'$ then   /* The agents are part of the same group. */
    $\ell = \ell' = k$ and $(s, s') = \delta_\tau(r, r')$
else /* The agents are part of different groups. */ $(k < k')$ */
    if $(((r + o_k) \mod \tau = r') \vee (k + 1 < k'))$ then
        $\ell = k$, $\ell' = k'$, $s = (r + 1) \mod \tau$ and $s' = (r' + 1) \mod \tau$
    else
        $\ell = k$, $\ell' = k'$, $s = (r + 1) \mod \tau$ and $s' = (r + o_k + 1) \mod \tau$

By induction on m and using Theorem 3 the following theorem holds.

Theorem 4. *The protocol defined by m-CPO is indeed* $\langle PO_{\alpha_0}, o_0, PO_{\alpha_1}, o_1, \ldots,$ $o_{m-2}, PO_{\alpha_{m-1}} \rangle$, *provided that initially all agents in* A_k *have a state in* $\{k\} \times T_\tau$ *for* $k = 0, 1, \ldots, m - 1$.

For $k = 0, 1, \ldots \tau - 1$, by defining f_k as $f_k(t) = f(t)$ if $t(\mod \tau) = k$, we deduce the following:

Proposition 5. *Any periodic function* f *with period* τ *can be decomposed into* τ *primitive periodic functions* f_k *(k* $= 0, 1, \ldots \tau - 1$*) such that* $f(t) = \sum_{0 \le k \le \tau - 1} f_k(t)$ *for all t.*

Let PO_k be the primitive oscillator for f_k in the decomposition of f in the proof of Proposition 5, for $k = 0, 1, \ldots, \tau - 1$. Define $P = (Q, \delta)$ as $\langle PO_0, o_0, PO_1, o_1, \ldots, o_{\tau-2}, PO_{\tau-1} \rangle$, where $o_k = 0$ for $k = 0, 1, \ldots, \tau - 2$, and δ is τ-CPO. Let $S = \{(k, k)) : k = 0, 1, \ldots, \tau - 1\} \subseteq Q$.

Corollary 6. *Let* C_0 *be any configuration such that for any* $k = 0, 1, \ldots, \tau - 1$, $|\{i : C_0(i) = (k, t)$ *for some* $t \in T_\tau\}| = f(k)$ *holds. Then* P *with* S *realizes* f *from* C_0 *with probability 1.*

Now, the remaining task is to reach a configuration C, starting from any configuration C_0, that satisfies the initial condition in Corollary 6, which is the theme of the next section.

5   Self-stabilizing Group Composition

Given a number of groups $G_m = \{0, 1, \ldots, m - 1\}$ along with their respective sizes $\{n_0, n_1, \ldots, n_{m-1}\}$, a protocol is said to solve the self-stabilizing group construction problem if it ensures that given a population of size $n = \sum_{i=0}^{m-1} n_i$, starting from an arbitrary configuration $C_0 \in \mathcal{C}$, the population is eventually divided into m groups of sizes $n_0, n_1, \ldots, n_{m-1}$, respectively.

• **Accurate Solution.** We first present a protocol $P = (G_n, \delta_n)$, denoted n-GC, with the state set $G_n = \{0, 1, \ldots, n - 1\}$ that solves the group construction problem for n groups, each of size 1. The idea behind n-GC is the same as the one used in the protocol proposed in [7], which is used for the leader election and ensures that starting from an arbitrary configuration $C_0 \in \mathcal{C}$, in any execution $\mathcal{E} : C_0, C_1, \ldots$, there is a time instant $t_0 \in \mathbf{N}$ from which each agent has a unique state. Transition function δ_n is given below.

Protocol 4. n-GC: Self-stabilizing n-Group Constructor

---

if $(r \neq r')$ then $\delta_n(r, r') = (r, r')$
else $\delta_n(r, r') = (r, (r+1) \mod n)$

By the definition of the n-GC, we can state the following proposition:

Proposition 7. *Protocol n-GC is a self-stabilizing group construction protocol.*

Corollary 8. *The (general) self-stabilizing group construction problem is solvable by using n-GC.*

Proof. Let n_k $(k = 0, 1, \ldots, m-1)$ be the size of Group k. We assume that an agent i is in Group k if its state ℓ satisfies $\sum_{j=0}^{k-1} n_j \leq \ell < \sum_{j=0}^{k} n_j$. Then by Proposition 7, the corollary holds.

Note that n-GC correctly works under a deterministic scheduler, and after the convergence, agents never change the group to which they belong. The (only) drawback however is the size n of state set G_n.

By Theorem 4 and Corollaries 6 and 8, we can construct a protocol that realizes f with probability 1, by applying the fair merge technique. Hence,

Theorem 9. *Any periodic function f is realizable using $(n + \tau)$ states.*

As a note, in the special case where $m = 2$ and $n_0 = n_1$, it is possible to solve accurately the group construction problem using only two states per agent. However, agents change their groups infinitely often and hence, the solution cannot be used directly in our case since the agents need to stay long enough in their group to insure the synchronization of their clocks.

• Heuristic Protocol. Aiming at solving the self-stabilizing group construction problem using a smaller number of states, we propose in the following a heuristic protocol $P = (Q, \delta)$, denoted HGC, that approximately solves the group construction problem. It is a heuristic in that we do not have a formal proof that it indeed approximately solves the problem, with probability 1. Some simulations have been performed that show the possible convergence of the protocol, however, the stabilization time is extremely long.

Let $n_0, n_1, \ldots, n_{m-1}$ be the sizes of the groups, and assume that they are sorted in the increasing order without loss of generality, i.e., $n_k \leq n_{k+1}$ for $k = 0, 1, \ldots, m-2$. Protocol HGC assumes $n_0 | n_j$ for all j. Let $B = \{b_1, b_2, \ldots, b_{m-1}\}$, where $n_k = b_k \cdot n_0$. Let $c \in \mathbf{N}$ be a small constant (compared with n) greater than 5. The state of agent $i \in A$ is (k, t), where $k \in \{0, 1, \ldots, m - 1\}$ is the current group the agent belongs to, and $t \in \{0, 1, \ldots, c \cdot b_k - 1\}$ indicates its *local progress*. Protocol HGC defines $(y, y') = \delta(x, x')$, where $x = (k, r)$, $x' = (k', r')$, $y = (\ell, s)$ and $y' = (\ell', s')$.

Protocol 5. HGC: Heuristic Group Constructor

---

if $k = k'$ then   /* The agents are part of the same group. */
   if $r = r' = c \cdot b_k$ then $\ell = (k + 1) \mod m$, $s = 0$ and $y' = y$
   else
      if $r < c \cdot b_k$ then $\ell = k$, $s = r + 1$ and $y' = x'$
      if $r' < c \cdot b_{k'}$ then $y = x$, $\ell' = k'$ and $s' = r' + 1$
else /* The agents are part of different groups. */
   $\ell = k$, $s = 0$, $\ell' = k'$ and $s' = 0$

To understand the idea of Protocol HGC, assume that $n_0 = n_1 = \ldots = n_{m-1}$ and thus $b_k = 1$ for all $k = 1, 2, \ldots, m - 1$. In order for an agent i to change its group k to $((k+1) \mod m)$, agent i needs to interact $c \cdot b_k = c$ consecutive times with an agent in the same group. That is, for any sufficiently large population, as long as the difference in the group sizes is too large, there would be agents who change their groups, which eventually leads a configuration to an equilibrium state in which the size of each group is approximately the same.

As a final note, since the agents may change their group during the execution of HGC, in order to realize a given function f using the fair merge of m-CPO and HGC, we need to make sure that when an agent updates its group, it also updates its clock value to adjust it to the new offset. That is, when an agent interacts, it first executes the actions of m-CPO (assume that the new computed clock value is s) and then executes the actions of HGC. If by executing HGC, it changes the group it belongs to, it also updates its clock value to respect the offset o (if any). That is, its new clock value is updated to $(s + o) \mod \tau$.

6   Conclusion

In this paper, we have investigated the problem of realizing a periodic function f assuming a variant of the PP model in which each agent is part of an interaction at each time instant and the interacting pairs are chosen uniformly at random.

Several open problems arise from this work: (1) The problem of designing a memory efficient self-stabilizing protocol that solves the group construction problem under our setting remains open. That is, our group construction protocol is based on n-GC which requires n states, independently of the actual specification. Provided that the number of groups is $m = o(n)$, is it possible to solve the problem in $O(m)$ space?. Observe that by using less than n states, agents need to change their group infinitely often (since initially, all agents might have the same state). Hence, for our implementation, we also need to ensure that agents stay in a given group long enough to allow the stabilization of the primitive oscillators. (2) While protocol HGC seems to achieve the desired goal from the different simulations performed, its formal analysis remains open. More precisely, is it possible to estimate the "approximation ratio" of HGC?. (3) We have assumed that every agent is part of an interaction at each time instant, this assumption is necessary to represent accurately a given periodic function f. If we relax the specification and allow an approximation of the periodic function f, we may choose a weaker scheduler that chooses $1 \le p < n/2$ pairs of agents for an interaction. It will be then challenging to investigate the impact of the degree of synchrony (number of interactions at each instant), on the considered problem.

References

1. Angluin, D., Aspnes, J., Diamadi, Z., Fischer, M.J., Peralta, R.: Computation in networks of passively mobile finite-state sensors. In: PODC, pp. 290–299 (2004)
2. Angluin, D., Aspnes, J., Fischer, M.J., Jiang, H.: Self-stabilizing population protocols. TAAS, 3(4), 13:1–13:28 (2008)
3. Awerbuch, B., Kutten, S., Mansour, Y., Patt-Shamir, B., Varghese, G.: A time-optimal self-stabilizing synchronizer using A phase clock. IEEE Trans. Dependable Secure Comput. 4(3), 180–190 (2007)
4. Beauquier, J., Burman, J.: Self-stabilizing synchronization in mobile sensor networks with covering. In: Rajaraman, R., Moscibroda, T., Dunkels, A., Scaglione, A. (eds.) DCOSS 2010. LNCS, vol. 6131, pp. 362–378. Springer, Heidelberg (2010). doi:10.1007/978-3-642-13651-1_26
5. Beauquier, J., Burman, J.: Self-stabilizing mutual exclusion and group mutual exclusion for population protocols with covering. In: Fernàndez Anta, A., Lipari, G., Roy, M. (eds.) OPODIS 2011. LNCS, vol. 7109, pp. 235–250. Springer, Heidelberg (2011). doi:10.1007/978-3-642-25873-2_17
6. Boulinier, C., Petit, F., Villain, V.: When graph theory helps self-stabilization. In: PODC, pp. 150–159 (2004)
7. Cai, S., Izumi, T., Wada, K.: How to prove impossibility under global fairness: on space complexity of self-stabilizing leader election on a population protocol model. Theory Comput. Syst. 50(3), 433–445 (2012)
8. Cooper, C., Lamani, A., Viglietta, G., Yamashita, M., Yamauchi, Y.: Constructing self-stabilizing oscillators in population protocols. In: Pelc, A., Schwarzmann, A.A. (eds.) SSS 2015. LNCS, vol. 9212, pp. 187–200. Springer, Heidelberg (2015). doi:10.1007/978-3-319-21741-3_13
9. Couvreur, J., Francez, N., Gouda, M.G.: Asynchronous unison (extended abstract). In: ICDCS, pp. 486–493 (1992)
10. Czyzowicz, J., Gąsieniec, L., Kosowski, A., Kranakis, E., Spirakis, P.G., Uznański, P.: On convergence and threshold properties of discrete Lotka-Volterra population protocols. In: Halldórsson, M.M., Iwama, K., Kobayashi, N., Speckmann, B. (eds.) ICALP 2015. LNCS, vol. 9134, pp. 393–405. Springer, Heidelberg (2015). doi:10.1007/978-3-662-47672-7_32

Localized Load Balancing in RFID Systems

Ahnaf Munir[1], Md Sakhawat Hossen[1], and Salimur Choudhury[2(✉)]

[1] Islamic University of Technology, Dhaka, Bangladesh
{ahnaf,sakhawat}@iut-dhaka.edu
[2] Algoma University, Sault Ste. Marie, ON, Canada
salimur.choudhury@algomau.ca

Abstract. Radio Frequency Identification (RFID) technology consists of uniquely identifiable and inexpensive tags as well as readers that monitor these tags with the help of radio frequency signal. Balancing the load of tags among the readers in a multi-reader RFID system is an important issue to successfully collect data from all the tags. In this paper we try to minimize the reading time of the readers by distributing the tags among the readers in the RFID system. We introduce a Cellular Automaton (CA) based localized load balancing algorithm to transfer tags from highly loaded readers to readers with lower number of tags associated with them. Our simulation results exhibit that our algorithm outperforms the existing algorithm.

Keywords: RFID · Readers · Tags · Load balancing · Reading time · Cellular automata · Fairness index

1 Introduction

Radio Frequency Identification (RFID) is a wireless technology which is being widely used in various real life applications including wireless identification, tracking, supply chain management, access control and security, temperature logging, patient and children identification and monitoring etc. Scalability and affordability have made it widely recognized and important technology for 'Internet of Things' [9,10]. A RFID system generally contains a large number of tags (transponders) and one or a few readers (transceivers). The tags are usually passive with limited energy to store and maintain limited amount of information. The tags can also respond to queries made by the readers. A reader is capable of interrogating the tags to read the stored information. A reader can only interrogate the tags that are within its interrogation range. It can also actively decide to ignore a tag that is within its proximity. Unlike many other identification systems such as bar-code systems, optical character recognition systems, biometrics etc., the readers in RFID systems require no line-of-sight communication with tags that are within its interrogation range. Due to the significantly higher number of tags compared to readers in a RFID system, most of the readers have numerous tags within their interrogation range. When a reader sends out a query, multiple tags may reply simultaneously and thus cancel each other out.

© Springer International Publishing AG 2016
C. Martín-Vide et al. (Eds.): TPNC 2016, LNCS 10071, pp. 34–45, 2016.
DOI: 10.1007/978-3-319-49001-4_3

This causes a delay in the reading time of the tags. Although many anti-collision protocols [3,17,18,22,24] have been developed to prevent such collisions, they cannot ensure short tag reading time. This is because in most of the multi-reader RFID systems, the readers usually do not cooperate with other. The tags within the interrogation range of multiple readers are read by all the readers. If the readers were able to communicate with each other then this redundant information gathering could be avoided hence greatly improve the tag reading times of the readers. Xie *et al.* [23] propose a distributed algorithm to balance the load of the readers so that each tag is interrogated by only one reader in a dense environment. Hence, it makes the tag reading much faster.

In this paper we address the same fast reading problem by representing it as a load balancing problem with the goal to distribute the tags among the readers as uniformly as possible. We develop a cellular automaton (CA) based improved algorithm that uses local information to achieve this goal. The advantage of using CA based algorithms is that they are strictly localized. To the best of our knowledge, we propose the first CA based strictly localized solution for this problem. Simulation results show that our algorithm outperforms the existing algorithm [23] in terms of load balancing. In a localized solution, algorithms might need to go through different iterations. Through simulation we find that our algorithm require fewer iterations compared to the existing algorithm [23]. The rest of the paper is organized as follows. Section 2 briefly introduces CA. Work related to the fast reading problem are discussed in Sect. 3. The system model and the problem statement are discussed in Sect. 4. Detailed description of our proposed algorithm can be found in Sect. 5. Simulation results are presented in Sect. 6 while concluding remarks are given in Sect. 7.

2   Cellular Automata

A CA is a biologically inspired model that has been widely used to model different physical systems [6,7]. A CA consists of a collection of cells on a grid whose state evolves at discrete time steps according to the rules based on the states of the neighboring cells. A two-dimensional CA can be defined as a quadruple, $A = (C, S, \delta, N)$ where C is the grid. The elements that compose this grid are called cells. S is the finite set of possible states of the cells, δ is the transition rule of the automaton and N is the neighborhood of the cell. At time t, each cell of C is assigned a state of S. The state of a cell $c \in C$, at time $t + 1$, is determined by the transition function δ depending on the current state of c and the states of cells in the neighborhood of c at time t. If all the adjacent cells are considered as neighbors, then it is called a Moore neighborhood. The Moore neighbors at radius 1 and radius 2 are shown in Fig. 1. Here the neighbors at radius 1 are marked as 'a' while the neighbors at radius 2 are marked as 'b'. In a typical CA, all the cells synchronously verify the states of their neighbors and change their states accordingly. More detail on CAs can be found in [13].

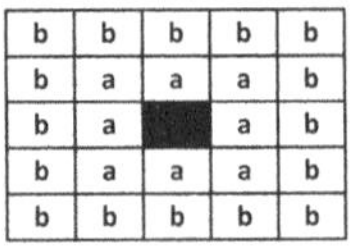

Fig. 1. Radius 1 and radius 2 Moore neighbors.

3 Related Work

A wide range of anti-collision protocols have been developed to improve the performance of RFID systems. There are mainly two classes of anti-collision protocols: (i) tree based protocols and (ii) ALOHA based protocols. The tree based protocols [3,17] are deterministic models and use either binary tree or query trees. They split the set of tags of a reader into smaller subsets until each subset contains a single tag. The identifier of the subset is used to uniquely identify the tags. Each subset with multiple tags is represented by an inner node in the tree while a leaf node represent a subset with a single tag. The identification delay is high in these protocols. On the other hand, the ALOHA base protocols are probabilistic as the tags have to randomly chose a time slot in the query frame sent by the reader [18,22]. The ALOHA based protocols do not completely ensure the prevention of collision. In these protocols, a specific reader may not be identified for a long time leading to 'tag starvation'. Approximating the number of tags present in a RFID system is a key problem that many anti-collision protocols face as they cannot correctly select the frame length. Estimating the cardinality of the tags in the interrogation region of a reader is discussed in [4]. They introduce an algorithm that uses bitmap and hash function to develop a replication-intensive estimation protocol which is helpful when multiple readers are present in the network. Here tags do not need to be uniquely identified and there is no need for any anti-collision protocols in order to estimate the number of tags to a certain degree of accuracy.

A transmission control strategy for a common class of RFID multiple access schemes has been suggested in [12]. It is built on earlier work based on Bayesian broadcast strategies but adopts it for the RFID domain. It estimates the cardinality of tags based on the number of idle slots in framed ALOHA. Two unified estimation algorithms having complementary properties are presented in [19]. The unified simple estimator proposes three estimators and provides a high level of accuracy, while the unified probabilistic estimator uses probabilistic framed ALOHA protocol that has a running-time independent of the size of the estimated tag set, for a given level of accuracy. Imbalanced tag distribution is a common scenario in RFID systems with multiple readers. This creates further challenges in achieving fast reading time which are not addressed properly in the literature. Imbalanced topologies commonly occur in warehouses, supermarkets, intelligent airports etc. Qunfeng *et al.* [20] suggests a probabilistic distributed algorithm that uses min-max tag count assignment to balance the tag loads in these topologies. Both load balancing and redundant reader elimination problem are jointly considered in [8]. It stores load information about the current reader in the memory of each of the tags and updates it in each time step. This is however, an impractical solution for very large scale RFID systems.

A fuzzy logic control-based load balancing agent for distributed RFID systems is considered in [16]. The proposed agent predicts data volume of an edge M/W and evaluates workload of the edge M/W by fuzzy logic control. In order to maintain stable workload, the agent migrates overload to other under-loaded edge M/Ws or requests data reallocation to other overloaded edge M/Ws according to the dynamic RFID load balancing algorithm. Eliminating redundant readers can make the reading faster (as it eliminates unnecessary readers) if after eliminating redundant readers, the load of the readers are quite similar. Several centralized and localized solutions are proposed to eliminate redundant readers in RFID systems [1,2,14,15]. Recently, a CA based redundant reader elimination technique has been proposed too [21]. However, these algorithms do not guarantee anything on the load of each reader. Xie et al. [23] introduce a distributed load balancing algorithm for addressing the fast reading problem. To compare the fairness of the loads among readers in the network they use a metric called fairness index which was first introduced in [5]. According to their algorithm, in a single time period, each reader determines its neighboring readers. Then the reader iterates through each neighbor reader and checks whether a neighbor has less number of associated tags than itself. If so, then the reader transfers a certain fraction of the tags ($0 \leq \alpha \leq 1$) to that neighbor reader. Each reader continues to do this until either the fairness index of the reader reaches a certain threshold or the transfer of tags does not have any effect on the fairness index. Dong et al. propose a centralized optimal load balancing algorithm for RFID readers using maximum flow algorithm [11].

4   System Model and Problem Statement

We consider a RFID system with a large number of tags and multiple readers. An example of the system is shown in Fig. 2. Here the numbers 1–6 are the readers while the small black circles represent the tags. The tags in the system are considered to be passive. A passive tag does not have any external power source and processing power. They generate power from the signal sent by the reader. When a reader sends a signal to a tag, the tag sends back the information it contains in its memory. This kind of passive tags are less expensive. So they are extensively used in different applications.

We consider two dimensional grid deployment where each cell can contain multiple tags and maximum of one reader. The reader is capable of reading all the tags in its interrogation range which we mean the interrogating radius in this paper. It can also decide whether it should monitor a tag in its region or not. All the readers in the grid together form a reader network where readers can cooperate and communicate with each other. We assume that at any given time a tag is associated with only a single reader. Initially, if a tag is within the interrogation range of multiple readers then it can be randomly assigned to any

Fig. 2. Model of a multi-reader RFID system.

of them and this assignment can not assure that the load of all readers in the network are mostly even. The time taken by each reader to read any of its tags is constant. As a result, total time taken to read data from all of the tags depends on the total number of tags assigned to that particular reader. To achieve a fast tag reading, the feasible objective is to minimize the maximum reading time of any reader in the multi reader RFID system. Therefore the fast reading problem can be represented as a load-balancing problem with the goal of distributing the tags among the readers to minimize the maximum load of readers. This can be expressed as:

$$minimize, maximum(w_1, w_2, ..., w_n)$$

$$where, w_i = |S_i|$$

where S_i denotes the associated tag set of reader r_i and w_i denotes the number of tags in S_i. If a reader in the multi-reader RFID system is associated with a large number of tags, then it tries to transfer a fraction of its tags to other readers which can interrogate those tags (i.e. tags are within the interrogation range of those readers).

5   Algorithm

5.1   Algorithm Metric

To evaluate the fairness of the load-balancing algorithm we use similar fairness index used in [5]. The fairness index can be used to determine the load distribution fairness in a certain area of the RFID system or the entire RFID system. If $w = (w_1, w_2, ..., w_n)$ be the load vector of the RFID system then the fairness index of the system can be expressed as follows:

$$fairness\_index = \frac{(\sum_{i=1}^{n} w_i)^2}{n \sum_{i=1}^{n} w_i^2}.$$

The value of fairness index is bounded within 0 to 1 with a higher value indicating a better fairness. If the fairness index is 1 then the load distribution is completely fair. In this case, each reader is associated with a equal number of tags. If the load distribution is completely unfair then the fairness index will be $\frac{1}{n}$. Here all tags will be associated with a single reader. Our intention is to improve the fairness index for a overall RFID network. However, in a localized solution, each reader can only communicate with its own neighbors and by exchanging the load information, it can only calculate the fairness index in its own locality. Please note that, the optimal solution for minimizing the maximum load of a reader does not always guarantee the optimal fairness index.

5.2   Proposed Algorithm

We model the problem using CA where each cell can have both reader and tag. A cell can have either one reader or none. However, there is no such restrictions on the number of tags. The description of the algorithm (Algorithm 1) is given below:

State representation: The status of each tag represents the reader which is currently interrogating the tag. A tag can be in the interrogating radius of maximum 9 readers. The state of the tag represents the direction of that reader (shown in Fig. 3). For example, if the tag is currently being interrogated by a reader which is in the same cell, then the state is "C". A reader's status represents its current load (the number of tags is currently assigned to it).

NW	N	NE
W	C	E
SW	S	SE

Fig. 3. Positions of interrogating readers for a tag.

Neighborhood: Each reader can communicate with its neighboring readers to exchange the load information. It can also identify which tags are shared with those neighbors. We consider communication radius 2 for readers. A reader can read and write contents on the tag. A tag can only be assigned to a reader if it falls within the interrogation radius of that particular reader. We consider two interrogation ranges for each reader (radius 1 and 2). The details of these parameters are discussed later in the simulation result section.

Transition Rules: Initially a random number of readers and tags are deployed in the network. Each tag is randomly assigned to any of its interrogating readers. Hence, the state of readers and tags are updated accordingly. Now at the next time period, each reader does the following steps (steps are shown in Algorithm 1):

1. (lines 2–11) It calculates its own load (by checking the states of the tags which are in its interrogating radius) and the load of its neighboring readers (from the state description of each reader) as well to determine the fairness index of its own neighborhood (radius 2).
2. (lines 12–22) For each neighboring reader and tag, the reader checks whether transferring the tag to that neighbor can improve the fairness index of its neighborhood. If it improves, then it updates the state of that tag. A reader can locate

the position of that neighboring reader (where it is transferring the tag) in terms of that tag. For example, if any reader is transferring the tag to a neighboring reader which is in the NW corner of the tag, then it updates NW as the status of that tag.

3. Once a reader finishes step 2 for each neighboring readers and interrogating tags, it repeats step 1 and 2 again in the next time period. It is to be noted that a reader's own load might have been changed at this time period due to the tag transfer from its neighboring readers. This new load information can only be updated at the next time period as all readers are working in parallel at any given period of time, t and new state information of each readers and tags can only be observed at $t + 1$.

Algorithm 1. CA Load Balancing Rules for Readers in RFID Systems

---

1: **procedure** ALGORITHM(State Changes in Reader with Time) ▷ States of a reader at $t + 1$ from t
2:    **for** each R_i in readers **do**   ▷ at any time period, t each reader runs the same rules in parallel.
3:      $load_i \leftarrow 0$. ▷ reader is updating its current load based on the status of tags
4:      **for** each interrogating tags T_k **do**
5:         **if** getStatus(T_k) $== R_i$ **then**
6:            $load_i \leftarrow load_i + 1$
7:         **end if**
8:      **end for**
9:      **for** each R_j in neighboringReader **do**
10:         $getStatus(R_j)$ ▷ load information of each reader can be found from their status.
11:      **end for**
12:      $fairnessIndex \leftarrow localFairnessIndex(R_i)$
13:      **for** each R_j in neighboring Reader **do**   ▷ the reader checks whether transferring any of its tag to a neighboring reader will improve the local fairness index.
14:         **for** each common tag (t) between the reader (R_i) and the neighboring reader (R_j) **do**
15:            **if** getStatus(t) $= R_i$ **then**
16:               **if** updatedLocalFairnessIndex $(L_i - 1, L_j + 1)$ >fairnessIndex **then**
17:                  $getStatus(t, R_j)$ ▷ updating the status of the tag with the new reader's direction.
18:                  $L_i \leftarrow L_i - 1$ ▷ locally updated the load information which might not be the completely
19:               **end if**
20:            **end if**
21:         **end for**
22:      **end for**
23:    **end for**
24: **end procedure**

When readers implement these rules in parallel, initially overall system fairness index might drop down a little. However, from our simulation, we find that, after few time periods the overall fairness index of the system improves a lot and all readers become stable (no more tag transfers are needed). The details of simulation results (fairness index improvement and the number of required time steps) are discussed in the following section.

6   Simulation Results

We compare our proposed algorithm with the load-balancing tag assignment algorithm (LBTA) which is proposed in [23]. We name our algorithm as "Cellular Automaton based Load Balancing Algorithm" (CALBA) and implement both algorithms in Python. We consider various scenarios with different grid sizes, different number of readers and tags, different interrogation and communication radius. In all cases, readers and tags are deployed randomly in the network and each tag is initially assigned to any of its interrogating readers. We also compare our results with the centralized maximum flow algorithm proposed in [11]. All simulations results show the average of 20 runs.

In LBTA, readers use a diffusion parameter (α, where $0 \leq \alpha \leq 1$) to migrate a fraction of its current load to its neighboring readers. According to LBTA, if the loads of two neighboring readers (i and j) are w_i and w_j ($w_i > w_j$) and the number of common tags between them are S_{ij} where $S_{ij} > \alpha * (w_i - w_j)$, then reader i can transfer $\alpha * (w_i - w_j)$ to reader j. The results of the algorithm varied with different α values which is one of the major shortcomings of LBTA. Moreover the algorithm does not explicitly identify the exact tags those should be migrated. It just finds out the number of tags that can be migrated.

The communication complexity of CALBA is almost similar to LBTA. However, we can avoid the reader to reader communication completely by writing more information in tags. In that case, each reader just writes down its presence with its total current load to all tags which are within its interrogating radius and other readers can take that information from those tags to compute the solution. However, we do not want to put much burden into tags as read/write operations are quite expensive. Hence we also choose to communicate among readers. We consider various α for the comparison purposes and find that our algorithm performs better than LBTA algorithms in terms of overall fairness index and the number of iterations required to reach that index. Moreover, in terms of fairness index sometimes our algorithm performs better than the centralized algorithm. It shows that CA based algorithms are good candidates to solve this type of load balancing problem. Table 1 shows the comparison results among LBTA, CALBA and the centralized algorithm in terms of fairness index and the maximum reading time. We consider reader to reader communication radius 2 and interrogation radius 1 for various numbers of grid sizes, readers and tags.

We also consider various diffusion parameters for LBTA and find that no specific diffusion parameter constantly performs well. It seems that diffusion parameters 0.5 and 0.7 overall perform better compared to others. However, overall our algorithm performs $\approx 4\%$ better than LBTA which is quite significant in large RFID systems. Moreover, CALBA provides results faster than LBTA. We also compare algorithms for reader to reader communication radius 2 and interrogation radius 2. The comparison results are shown in Table 2. It is to be noted that the performance of our algorithm is not as good as the previous case (interrogation radius 2). This is due to the fact that, in the case of interrogation radius 2, a tag might have readers which are in two opposite directions and can not communicate. Thus, the tag can not be migrated between these two readers to improve the fairness index. However, still CALBA performs $\approx 2\%$ better than LBTA.

Table 1. Comparison of Fairness Index and the maximum reading time for Interrogation Radius 1

Grid size	Readers	Tags	Algorithms		Initial fairness index	Iterations	Final fairness index	Maximum reading time
70×70	3500	7000	LBTA	$\alpha = 0.3$	0.66	2	0.77	5.5
				$\alpha = 0.5$		5	**0.89**	5.2
				$\alpha = 0.7$		6	0.88	6.2
			CALBA			5	**0.94**	3.4
			Max Flow			N/A	**0.93**	2.8
60 × 60	2500	5000	LBTA	$\alpha = 0.3$	0.65	2	0.80	6.5
				$\alpha = 0.5$		5	**0.89**	4.9
				$\alpha = 0.7$		6	0.89	5.6
			CALBA			4	**0.94**	3.3
			Max Flow			N/A	**0.92**	2.8
50 × 50	2000	4000	LBTA	$\alpha = 0.3$	0.66	2	0.79	5.2
				$\alpha = 0.5$		5	**0.91**	3.8
				$\alpha = 0.7$		7	0.90	5.0
			CALBA			5	**0.94**	3.2
			Max Flow			N/A	**0.94**	2.5
40 × 40	1200	2400	LBTA	$\alpha = 0.3$	0.66	2	0.78	5.6
				$\alpha = 0.5$		5	**0.91**	3.95
				$\alpha = 0.7$		7	0.90	4.0
			CALBA			4	**0.95**	3.2
			Max Flow			N/A	**0.92**	3.05
30 × 30	700	1500	LBTA	$\alpha = 0.3$	0.65	2	0.79	5.8
				$\alpha = 0.5$		5	**0.91**	4.6
				$\alpha = 0.7$		7	0.90	4.8
			CALBA			5	**0.94**	3.6
			Max Flow			N/A	**0.93**	3.4

Table 2. Comparison of fairness index and the maximum reading time with interrogation radius 2

Grid Size	Readers	Tags	Algorithms		Initial fairness index	Iterations	Final fairness index	Maximum reading time
70 × 70	3500	7000	LBTA	$\alpha = 0.3$	0.66	2	0.80	5.2
				$\alpha = 0.5$		6	**0.94**	4.9
				$\alpha = 0.7$		8	0.94	4.65
			CALBA			5	**0.95**	3.3
			MaxFlow			N/A	**0.95**	2.5
60 × 60	2500	5000	LBTA	$\alpha = 0.3$	0.65	2	0.80	4.67
				$\alpha = 0.5$		6	**0.94**	4.1
				$\alpha = 0.7$		6	0.94	4.0
			CALBA			5	**0.95**	3.65
			MaxFlow			N/A	**0.93**	2.05
50 × 50	2000	4000	LBTA	$\alpha = 0.3$	0.66	2	0.81	4.8
				$\alpha = 0.5$		7	0.94	3.9
				$\alpha = 0.7$		7	**0.94**	4.6
			CALBA			4	**0.95**	3.2
			MaxFlow			N/A	**0.92**	2.3
40×40	1200	2400	LBTA	$\alpha = 0.3$	0.65	2	0.81	4.8
				$\alpha = 0.5$		5	**0.94**	4.0
				$\alpha = 0.7$		7	0.94	4.05
			CALBA			4	**0.96**	3.3
			MaxFlow			N/A	**0.94**	2.6
30×30	700	1500	LBTA	$\alpha = 0.3$	0.67	2	0.83	4.6
				$\alpha = 0.5$		9	**0.93**	3.7
				$\alpha = 0.7$		11	0.93	3.5
			CALBA			6	**0.95**	3.3
			MaxFlow			N/A	**0.91**	3.0

7   Conclusion

In this paper we develop a cellular automaton based localized algorithm to address the load balancing problem of RFID systems. Our algorithm considers the spatial constrains of the readers and is suitable for the systems with multiple readers. We do extensive simulations and evaluate the performance of our algorithm by comparing the results with the existing algorithms. Simulation results show that our algorithm gives better results in a better time compared to the existing localized algorithm and even sometimes performs better than the centralized algorithm. In future, we plan to implement and compare both algorithms in a parallel programming platform, for example, in Compute Unified Device Architecture (CUDA).

References

1. Ali, K., Alsalih, W., Hassanein, H.: Set-cover approximation algorithms for load-aware readers placement in rfid networks. In: 2011 IEEE International Conference on Communications (ICC), pp. 1–6, June 2011
2. Ali, K., Hassanein, H.S., Alsalih, W.: Using neighbor and tag estimations for redundant reader eliminations in rfid networks. In: 2011 IEEE Wireless Communications and Networking Conference, pp. 832–837, March 2011
3. Capetanakis, J.: Tree algorithms for packet broadcast channels. IEEE Trans. Inf. Theory **25**(5), 505–515 (1979)
4. Chen, Q., Hoilun, N., Yunhao, L.: Cardinality estimation for large-scale rfid systems. In: Sixth Annual IEEE International Conference on Pervasive Computing and Communications (PerCom), pp. 30–39 (2008)
5. Chiu, D., Jain, R.: Analysis of the increase and decrease algorithms for congestion avoidance in computer networks. Comput. Netw. ISDN Syst. **17**(1), 1–14 (1989)
6. Choudhury, S.: Cellular automaton based algorithms for wireless sensor networks. Canadian theses (2012)
7. Choudhury, S., Salomaa, K., Akl, S.G.: Cellular automaton-based algorithms for the dispersion of mobile wireless sensor networks. Int. J. Parallel Emergent Distrib. Syst. **29**(2), 147–177 (2014)
8. Dhas, V.G., Muthukaruppan, R., Balakrishnan, K., Ganesan, R.: Optimal Solution for RFID Load Balancing. In: Meghanathan, N., Boumerdassi, S., Chaki, N., Nagamalai, D. (eds.) ASUC/NeCoM/VLSI/WeST/WiMoN -2010. CCIS, vol. 90, pp. 41–49. Springer, Heidelberg (2010). doi:10.1007/978-3-642-14493-6_5
9. Dominikus, S.: Medassist - a privacy preserving application using rfid tags. In: IEEE International Conference on RFID-Technologies and Applications (RFID-TA), pp. 370–375 (2011)
10. Dong, C., Guiran, C., Jiajia, L., Jie, J.: Study on the interconnection architecture and access technology for internet of things. In: International Conference on Computer Science and Service System (CSSS), pp. 1744–1748 (2011)
11. Dong, Q., Shukla, A., Shrivastava, V., Agrawal, D., Banerjee, S., Kar, K.: Load balancing in large-scale rfid systems. In: IEEE INFOCOM 2007–26th IEEE International Conference on Computer Communications, pp. 2281–2285, May 2007
12. Floerkemeier, C.: Transmission control scheme for fast rfid object identification. In: Fourth Annual IEEE International Conference on Pervasive Computing and Communications Workshops (PerCom Workshops 2006), pp. 457–462 (2006)
13. Garzon, M.: Models of Massive Parallelism: Analysis of Cellular Automata and Neural Networks. Springer, Heidelberg (1995)
14. Hsu, C.H., Chen, Y.M., Yang, C.T.: A layered optimization approach for redundant reader elimination in wireless rfid networks. In: The 2nd IEEE Asia-Pacific Service Computing Conference, pp. 138–145, December 2007
15. Irfan, N., Yagoub, M.C.E., Hettak, K.: Redundant reader elimination approaches for RFID networks. In: Kamel, M., Karray, F., Gueaieb, W., Khamis, A. (eds.) AIS 2011. LNCS (LNAI), vol. 6752, pp. 396–405. Springer, Heidelberg (2011). doi:10.1007/978-3-642-21538-4_39
16. Jang, S., Lee, J.: Fuzzy logic control-based load balancing agent for distributed RFID systems. In: Huang, D.-S., et al. (eds.) ICIC 2008. LNCS, vol. 5226, pp. 653–660. Springer, Heidelberg (2008)
17. Jihoon, M., Wonjun, L.: Adaptive splitting protocols for rfid tag collision arbitration. In: 7th ACM International Symposium on Mobile Ad Hoc Networking and Computing, Florence, Italy (2006)

18. Lawrence, G.: Aloha packet system with and without slots and capture. In: ACM-SIGCOMM Computer Communication Review, vol. 5, pp. 28–42, April 1975
19. Murali, K., Thyaga, N.: Fast and reliable estimation schemes in rfid systems. In: 12th Annual International Conference on Mobile Computing and Networking, Los Angeles, CA, USA (2006)
20. Qunfeng, D., Shukla, A., Shrivastava, V., Agrawal, D., Banerjee, S., Kar, K.: Load balancing in large-scale rfid systems. In: IEEE INFOCOM 2007–26th IEEE International Conference on Computer Communications, pp. 2281–2285, May 2007
21. Rashid, N., Choudhury, S., Salomaa, K.: CARRE: cellular automaton based redundant readers elimination in RFID networks. In: 2016 IEEE International Conference on Communications, ICC 2016, Kuala Lumpur, Malaysia, 22–27 May 2016, pp. 1–6 (2016)
22. Vinod, N., Lixin, G.: Energy-aware tag anti-collision protocols for rfid systems. In: Fifth IEEE International Conference on Pervasive Computing and Communications, pp. 23–36, March 2007
23. Xie, K., Cao, J., Wen, J.: Distributed load-balancing algorithm for fast tag reading. Int. J. Parallel Emergent Distrib. Syst. **28**(5), 434–448 (2012)
24. Yoon, W., Vaidya, N.: Rfid reader collision problem: performance analysis and medium access. Wireless Communications and Mobile Computing, pp. 1–24, April 2010

The Fuel-Efficient Platooning of Heavy Duty Vehicles by Mathematical Programming and Genetic Algorithm

Abtin Nourmohammadzadeh[(✉)] and Sven Hartmann

Department of Informatics, Clausthal University of Technology,
Clausthal-Zellerfeld, Germany
{abtin.nourmohammadzadeh,sven.hartmann}@tu.clausthal.de
https://www.in.tu-clausthal.de/

Abstract. As fuel accounts for a significant proportion of the total operational cost of heavy duty vehicles (HDVs) and to alleviate the environmental impacts, companies are seeking for novel practical methods to reduce fuel consumption. Platooning is an effective approach in which a string of HDVs driving close behind each other is formed. This reduces the aerodynamic drag leading to a reduction in the overall resistive force on vehicles which can provide an amount of fuel-saving in each of the following vehicles. These trivial reductions result in a considerable decrease in the total fuel consumption corresponding to all the vehicles. In this paper, we propose a mathematical model for the fuel-efficient platooning problem with a deadline for each vehicle (truck) to reach its destination by then. We create a graph partly based on the German road network considering only 20 important cities and solve 50 instances including 10 to 50 trucks. The small samples are solved by the LINDO solver in real time but as the problem has a high computational complexity, a Genetic Algorithm is applied to obtain fast solutions of a good quality for larger instances. The final results show a satisfactory fuel-saving in all of the cases.

Keywords: HDV platooning · Fuel saving · Mathematical programming · Genetic algorithm

1 Introduction

Due to strong economical and environmental reasons, transportation companies try to reduce the fuel consumption of their heavy duty vehicles (HDVs). This is because of the fact that the fuel cost constitutes about 30 % of the life-cycle operational expenses of an HDV (Schittler 2003 [14]). Furthermore, vehicles account for a considerable 20 % of total carbon emissions of which a quarter comes from HDVs (Schroten et al. 2012 [15]). Hence, a reduction in HDVs' fuel consumption results in a significant economical profit as well as achieving the absolutely important goal of environmental protection.

Such significant aims can only be realised with the aid of novel effective approaches. Platooning is a promising approach which focuses on reducing the

© Springer International Publishing AG 2016
C. Martín-Vide et al. (Eds.): TPNC 2016, LNCS 10071, pp. 46–57, 2016.
DOI: 10.1007/978-3-319-49001-4_4

Fig. 1. An example platoon: vehicles drive all at the same speed (v) and with the same distance (d) from each other.

aerodynamic drag or resistive force on vehicles by forming a string of vehicles driving together behind each other as it is shown in Fig. 1. Depending on the speed of HDVs (v) and the distances between them (d), the normal fuel consumption of every trailing truck can be reduced based on a saving factor because it drives in the slip stream of another vehicle driving ahead. Safety issues must be considered by forming a platoon since HDVs are driving at close distances from each other.

Platoons do not take shape spontaneously on a road network, in other words, we cannot simply send HDVs (trucks) on their way hoping to make platoons. Given a set of trucks with their origins, destinations, deadlines and the fuel saving factor of platooning as well as the road network's topology as the inputs, we need to determine a fuel efficient route and travelling times for each truck as the outputs of this problem. If it is beneficial, trucks should deviate from their shortest path and take a detour in order to join a platoon. For some trucks, it might be worthwhile to stop and wait for other trucks at some steps on their route, whereas for some others it could be more efficient to keep travelling alone.

Thus, we need to employ some high-level decision making approaches which are capable of assisting the navigation systems of trucks to form platoons on a large scale and calculate optimal routes of each HDV based on the chosen routes for other HDVs. Thanks recent improvements in computing power, the implementation of the platooning concept for real cases has become possible, although the idea was initially presented in 1966 by Levine and Athans [10].

Up to now, only a few attempts have been made to optimally form HDV platoons to minimise the fuel consumption and most of the researches have assumed that the platoons have been already formed and focused on the maintenance and safe manoeuvring of them.

In this research, we aim at proposing practical and efficient approaches to deal with the HDV platooning problem of various sizes. We create a simple graph partly based on the road network in Germany, but only consisting of 20 important cities and shortest routes between them. Firstly, we present a mixed-integer zero-one mathematical model considering a deadline for each HDV to reach its destination. Secondly, as this problem is NP-hard (Kammer 2013 [7], Larsson et al. 2015 [9]), and difficult to be solved in large scale in real time, a genetic algorithm (GA) approach with a novel encoding system for solutions based on the elimination of impractical routes, is presented.

The structure of this paper is organised as follows: In Sect. 2, we review some previous researches into vehicle platooning. Section 3 contains our mathematical formulations for the problem and the related descriptions. The proposed solution methodology is explained in Sect. 4. Section 5 covers, firstly, the explanation of the created road network and our test problems, then, the main results of the mathematical programming and GA are presented and compared. Finally, in Sect. 6, we draw the conclusions of our paper and give some recommendations for future research in this field.

2   Previous Works

As already mentioned, the most of conducted researches have not addressed the formation of platoons and they have mainly involved safety and technological issues. As some examples, see Bergenhem et al. 2012 [3], Linsenmayer & Dimarogonas 2015 [12], Kianfar et al. 2015 [8], Alam et al. 2015 [2], Davis 2013 [4], Omae et al. 2012 [13], Kaku et al. 2012 [6], and Wang et al. 2005 [16].

Only a small number of works have dealt with the fuel-efficient platoon formation. Liang 2014 [11] addresses this problem by dividing the overall complex transport system into manageable layers and focuses on adjusting vehicles' speeds through catch-up coordination. Larsson et al. 2015 [9] propose an integer linear programming model where deadlines of trucks are not taken into account. They prove that the problem is an NP-hard one, even in the case that the road network graph is planar. Two heuristics with a local search are applied to the problem and their performance is compared with the optimal solutions on the German Autobahn road network.

Kammer 2013 [7] presents a comprehensive mathematical formulation and a global solution approach for the problem. A locally distributed approach is applied to the problem due to an exponential increase in its computational complexity. Moreover, he investigates the influence of the number of trucks on the total fuel savings and examines the effect of limiting the maximum travel time of trucks.

The review of the related literature shows that there is a need for further research into fuel-optimal platooning because the previous attempts in this field are few and new efficient and fast approaches are required.

3   Mathematical Model

In this section, we present our mathematical model. Firstly, the assumptions that the model is built based on are explained, then, we introduce the notations used in the model, and finally, in the last subsection, the mathematical formulations are given and described.

3.1   Assumptions

Our model is built based on the below assumptions:

– The HDVs (trucks) are all the same in terms of size and specifications.
– The trucks drive all at the same speed.

- For simplicity, as most of the previous works, we assume that there is no fuel saving for the leading truck of a platoon and all the trailing trucks benefit from the same fuel saving rate (factor).
- Unlike most of the previous works, we consider a deadline for each truck to be in its destination by then.
- Platoons are shaped in an undirected graph representing a road network. The graph consists of some nodes and some edges between them. The length of all the edges or the distance between any two connected nodes is considered to be the same.
- The unit fuel cost per edge is considered to be 1, as it does not effect the validity of solutions and the objective function can be multiplied by the real unit fuel cost to obtain the real total cost.
- We define our time unit to be the time required for each truck to traverse an edge.

3.2 Notations

The notation used in the model are as below:

Sets

A	The set of all trucks (HDVs)
G	The set of all nodes of the road network graph
E	The set of all available edges between the nodes
T	The set of time periods of an equal length

Inputs

e_{ij}	The edge between node i and node j
s_a	Starting node of truck a
d_a	Destination node of truck a
η	Fuel reduction factor for a trailing truck in the platoon
t_{max}^a	The deadline or due date of truck a to reach its destination no later than then

Variables

$x_{t,ij}^a$	Binary variable=1, if truck a is travelling along edge e_{ij} between time steps t and $t+1$; otherwise it is= 0
$\delta_{t,ij}$	Auxiliary binary variable=0, if no trucks traverse edge e_{ij} between time steps t and $t+1$
$c_{t,ij}$	Fuel cost that is incurred on edge e_{ij} between time steps t and $t+1$

3.3 Formulations

Based on the above mentioned assumptions and notations, our mathematical model is presented as follows:

Objective

$$Min\ Z = \sum_t \sum_{e_{ij} \in E} c_{ij,t} \tag{1}$$

Subject to

$$\sum_{t=0}^{t_{max}^a - 1} \sum_{e_{s_a j} \in E} x_{t,s_a j}^a = 1 \quad \forall a \in A \tag{2}$$

$$\sum_{e_{hi} \in E} x_{t,hi}^a - \sum_{e_{ij} \in E} x_{t+1,ij}^a = 0 \quad \forall a \in A; i \in G - \{s_a, d_a\}; t \in \{0, ..., t_{max}^a - 1\} \tag{3}$$

$$\sum_{t=0}^{t_{max}^a - 1} \sum_{e_{jd_a} \in E} x_{t,jd_a}^a = 1 \quad \forall a \in A \tag{4}$$

$$x_{t,ij}^a = 0 \quad \forall a \in A; i, j \in G; e_{ij} \in E; t \geq t_{max}^a \tag{5}$$

$$\delta_{t,ij} \leq \sum_a x_{t,ij}^a \quad \forall i, j \in G; e_{ij} \in E; t \in T \tag{6}$$

$$c_{t,ij} = \sum_a x_{t,ij}^a - \delta_{t,ij} \eta (\sum_a x_{t,ij}^a - 1) \quad \forall i, j \in G; e_{ij} \in E; t \in T \tag{7}$$

$$x_{t,ij}^a, \delta_{t,ij} \in \{0, 1\} \quad \forall a \in A; i, j \in G; t \in T. \tag{8}$$

Equation (1) is the objective function of our problem consisting of the sum of all truck fuel cost incurring on all edges during every time period.

Constraints (2)–(4) are responsible for node balancing. They ensure that trucks leave their starting node early enough, then, prevent them from being lost or created in a node, and finally, force them to reach their destination no later than their deadline. No movement of trucks after their deadline is guaranteed by Eq. (5). Constraint (6) sets the auxiliary variable $\delta_{t,ij}$ to be used in the next constraint. Constraint (7) calculates the cost incurred on each edge during each time period. $\delta_{t,ij}$ is used here to ensure that the cost of an edge during a specific period is zero if no trucks travel along it. Lastly, binary values for $x_{t,ij}^a$, $\delta_{t,ij}$ are ensured by constraint (8).

4   Solution Approach

In this section, our solution methodology is explained in two subsections. Firstly, the strategy of eliminating long and useless routes of trucks, and secondly, our main solution approach, which is a GA is described.

4.1 Pruning

To reduce the computational complexity of our problem, it is absolutely important to analyse all the feasible routes of each truck from its origin to destination in order to realise where it is worthwhile for a truck to drive in a platoon and for which routes platooning does not make sense based on the fuel reduction factor η and the route length. Feasible routes for this examination are those whose shortest required traversing time allows the vehicle to reach its destination by the deadline.

We describe the pruning procedure of impractical routes by a simple example shown in Fig. 2. Assume that a truck locating at its origin shown as node S, is going to drive to its destination D. There are two alternative routes: a, which is the shortest path, and b. The lengths of these routes are l_a and l_b. To analyse if choosing the longer path (b) is worth it in the case of platooning, we can do the calculation: $(1 - \eta)l_b \leq l_a$

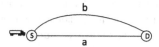

Fig. 2. Analysing the longer path: if the relation $(1 - \eta)l_b \leq l_a$ is not true for path b then it is ignored and not considered as a potential route for platooning.

The above calculation is based on the optimistic assumption of maximum saving that there is a platooning opportunity on the entire longer path which is not always the case because platoons can usually be formed only on a part of the path. Therefore, after finding all the different feasible routes, we can find the shortest path and easily ignore those of others that do not satisfy the above relation.

4.2 Genetic Algorithm

By applying the above pruning strategy, we have for each truck a set of alternative feasible routes on which platooning can be worthwhile. For example, if there are m possible paths (routes) for truck i after pruning, we have the set $R_i = \{1, 2, ..., m\}$ where paths are sorted based on their length, so the first path is always the shortest one. The encoding structure of a feasible solution can be a string of chosen paths from the first to the last truck as shown in Fig. 3. The example shows a solution (chromosome representation) for a platooning problem consisting of 10 trucks. In this example the first, second, third, fifth, ninth and tenth truck drive on their shortest path, whereas the forth, sixth and eighth truck drive on their second path but the seventh on its third path.

Now that we have a chromosome representation of solutions, we can use the genetic algorithm (GA) procedure to search for better solutions in the feasible space. GA is an effective evolutionary optimisation algorithm which works with

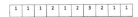

Fig. 3. An example chromosome: each cell contains the label of the chosen path for the corresponding vehicle from the ordered list of feasible paths that it can take.

a population of chromosomes or solutions in each iteration. GA tries to improve the fitness or quality of solutions in the population, iteration by iteration. We present a brief explanation of our applied GA but for more general details the interested readers are referred to the book of Haupt and Haupt 2004 [5].

The steps of the employed GA are as follows:

1. Initialise a random population of *npop* solutions and evaluate the objective function of each based on the maximum achievable platooning by respecting the deadlines of vehicles. Based on this, the traversing time of each edge of the path that the corresponding chromosome shows is determined.
2. Choose a subset of the population with the size *pcross* × *npop* (*pcross* is the crossover rate) based on the fitness by the roulette wheel method (see [5]). They are used as parents to perform the crossover operation and produce new solutions. For crossover, we choose a random cell (gene) along the parent chromosomes and exchange the cells between them based on it to have two new solutions. The crossover procedure is shown in Fig. 4. It is worth noting that if a big route number is placed in a cell of a chromosome resulted from crossover which is infeasible for the corresponding truck, this value will be then changed to the biggest available path label of the truck.
3. Choose another subset of the population with the size *pmutat* ∗ *npop* (*pmutat* is the mutation rate) to perform the mutation operation. For mutation a random cell is chosen along the chromosomes and the value inside that cell is randomly changed to another possible value.
4. Merge the current population with the individuals resulted from crossover and mutation. Sort the merged population based on the fitness and choose the *npop* best chromosomes (individuals) of it to be sent to the next iteration as the new population.
5. If the termination criterion of the algorithm is met stop; otherwise go to Step 2.

Fig. 4. An example of crossover

5 Computational Experiments

This section consists of explaining our road network graph and presenting as well as comparing the results.

5.1 Road Network Graph

In this research, we try to use a road network graph which is created based on the location of some cities in Germany. Thus, 20 important cities are chosen as the main nodes and only the shortest roads between them are considered. This undirected graph is shown in Fig. 5. The shortest distances between cities are found on Google map [1] and they are divided to equal parts by placing an auxiliary node in approximately every 40 Km to produce edges of the same length according to our model. Distances are approximated and are not their exact real values.

It must be pointed out that this simple graph do not reflect the real Autobahn network in Germany and there are so many alternative cities and roads which are not considered.

The resulted graph has altogether 137 nodes (the cities+auxiliary nodes) and 152 edges. We generate instances with 10, 20, 30, 40 and 50 trucks by assigning a random origin and destination to each truck from the 20 cities of our graph. The fuel reduction factor η is assumed to be 10 % for any trailing truck like most of the previous works. The deadlines of trucks are randomly given in an interval of [shortest path time, shortest path time+25]. The total number of time periods is considered to be $T = \max_a(t^a_{max})$.

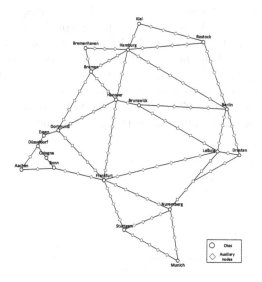

Fig. 5. The considered graph of road network

5.2   Results and Comparisons

As mentioned, we aim at applying our approaches to problems of 5 different sizes from 10 to 50 trucks. Concerning the fact that random start and end cities of trucks can effect the difficulty and final solution of the problems and to evaluate the performance of the solution methodologies with more samples, we generate 10 different test problems for each of the 5 sizes. So 50 problems are solved altogether. All computational experiments of this paper are executed on a computer with an Intel(R) Core(TM) i7, 3.10 GHz CPU and 16 GB of RAM.

The samples are firstly solved through the presented mathematical model by the LINDO solver in the GAMS platform. Once again all of the instances are solved by our proposed GA which is implemented in MATLAB.

For our problem, the amount of fuel saving is absolutely important. This is the difference between the initial case that trucks are driving separately on their shortest path without any platooning and the best found platooning solution. Furthermore, the computation time, which is the elapsed time that the method requires to reach its final or best solution, is also significant, because we seek to find a platooning solution in a reasonable time.

The percentage of the fuel saving by LINDO and GA applied to 10 instances for each size are shown by box plots in Figs. 6 and 7, respectively. Similarly, the solution times of the methods are depicted by Figs. 8 and 9. In addition, the average fuel saving and computation time of LINDO and GA are illustrated in Figs. 10 and 11.

Due to an exponential increase in the solution time by growing the problem size, solving problems containing 30 trucks and more within the solver time limit becomes impossible and the LINDO results are only obtainable for the problems with 10 and 20 trucks.

As it is evident for the test instances with 10 trucks, the exact optimal solutions with LINDO can be reached in some reasonable times. The obtained fuel savings range from 1.05 % to 1.98 % with an average of 1.63 %. On the other hand, GA is able to find the same solutions in 7 of the cases in much shorter times with an average saving of 1.5 %. For the instances with 20 trucks, the solver time grows very sharply, whereas the GA time does not considerably increase and stays in the range of 23.07 to 38.21 s. The GA finds in 60 % of cases the optimal solution and in the other cases the difference between the solutions of

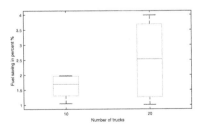

Fig. 6. Percentage of fuel saving by LINDO applied to 10 instances for each size

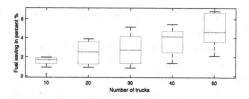

Fig. 7. Percentage of fuel saving by GA applied to 10 instances for each size

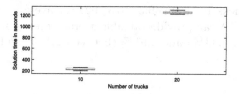

Fig. 8. Solution times by LINDO

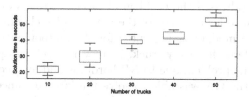

Fig. 9. Solution times by GA

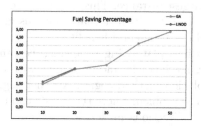

Fig. 10. Average fuel saving percentages of the approaches

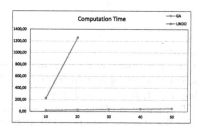

Fig. 11. Average computation time of the approaches in seconds

the approaches is very small. The obtained average saving by the two methods are 2.5 % and 2.45 %, respectively.

As the problem size increases to 30, the solver becomes unable to solve any of the instances even within a long time limit set at 90 min. Thus, for these instances, we present only the output of our GA, which are obtained in very short time of almost 38.5 s on average. The GA resulted in platooning solutions with fuel saving between 0.85 % and 5.16 % with an average of 2.73 %. Finally, while the solution times rage only from 37.88 to 46.82 s (on average 42.58) for instances with 40 trucks and from 49.37 to 57.62 s (on average 53.59) for instances with 50 trucks, our GA can provide valuable average fuel saving of about 3.71 % (between 1.34 % and 5.43 %) and 4.91 % (between 2.10 % and 6.82 %) for these sizes, respectively.

6   Conclusion and Future Research

In this paper, we addressed the problem of forming groups of HDVs or trucks to drive together in order to decrease the amount of fuel consumption. A non-linear mathematical model was presented for the platooning problem in which a deadline is considered for every truck. Moreover, a GA was proposed to solve large instances of the problem due to NP-hardness and long computation time. We observed that the GA was able to solve the large instances in a relatively short time, while the exact solver had problem when solving instances with 30 trucks and more. The results show an average reduction of almost 5 % in fuel consumption with the largest instance. This percentage of saving may seem low but we should pay attention to the fact that even this amount can result in a large total financial and environmental benefit.

For further research into platooning problems, we can recommend dealing with instances including more trucks and on graphs with more nodes and edges by other appropriate solution methodologies. Another suggestion is to consider the dynamic version of the problem where the inputs can change as time passes. These two recommended directions make the research conform more with the reality.

References

1. http://www.maps.google.com
2. Alam, A., Mårtensson, J., Johansson, K.H.: Control engineering practice experimental evaluation of decentralized cooperative cruise control for heavy-duty vehicle platooning. Control Eng. Pract. **38**, 11–25 (2015)
3. Bergenhem, C., Hedin, E., Skarin, D.: Vehicle-to-vehicle communication for a platooning system. Procedia Soc. Behav. Sci. **48**, 1222–1233 (2012)
4. Davis, L.C.: The effects of mechanical response on the dynamics and string stability of a platoon of adaptive cruise control vehicles. Phys. A **392**(17), 3798–3805 (2013)
5. Haupt, R.L., Haupt, S.E.: Haupt Practical Genetic Algorithms. Wiley InterScience Electronic Collection. Wiley, Chichester (2004)

6. Kaku, A., Mukai, M., Kawabe, T.: A centralized control system for ecological vehicle platooning using linear quadratic regulator theory. Artif. Life Robot. **17**(1), 70–74 (2012)
7. Kammer, C.: Coordinated heavy truck platoon routing using global and locally distributed approaches. Master's Degree Project, KTH Electrical Engineering, Stockholm, Sweden, April 2013
8. Kianfar, R., Falcone, P., Fredriksson, J.: A control matching model predictive control approach to string stable vehicle platooning. Control Eng. Pract. **45**, 163–173 (2015)
9. Larsson, E., Sennton, G., Larson, J.: The vehicle platooning problem: computational complexity and heuristics. Transp. Res. Part C **60**, 258–277 (2015)
10. Levine, W., Athans, M.: On the optimal error regulation of a string of moving vehicles. IEEE Trans. Autom. Control **11**(3), 355–361 (1966)
11. Liang, K.-Y.: Coordination and routing for fuel-efficient heavy-duty vehicle platoon formation. Licentiate Thesis in Electrical Eng., Stockholm, Sweden (2014)
12. Linsenmayer, S., Dimarogonas, D.V.: Event-triggered control for vehicle platooning. In 2015 American Control Conference, pp. 3101–3106, July 2015
13. Omae, M., Honma, N., Usami, K.: Flexible and energy-saving platooning control using a two-layer controller. Int. J. Intell. Transp. Syst. Res. **10**(3), 115–126 (2012)
14. Schittler, M.: State-of-the-art and emerging truck engine technologies for optimized performance, emissions and life cycle costs. In: 9th Diesel Emissions Reduction Conference, Rhode Island, USA, August 2003
15. Schroten, A., Warringa, G., Bles, M.: Marginal abatement cost curves for heavy duty vehicles. In: Background Report. CE Delft, Delft (2012)
16. Wang, D., Pham, M., Phampt, C.T.: Simulation study of vehicle platooning maneuvers with full-state tracking control. In: Simulation Study of Vehicle Platooning Maneuvers with Full-State Tracking Control, pp. 539–548 (2005)

How to Implement a Random Bisection Cut

Itaru Ueda[1]([✉]), Akihiro Nishimura[1], Yu-ichi Hayashi[2], Takaaki Mizuki[3], and Hideaki Sone[3]

[1] Graduate School of Information Sciences, Tohoku University,
6-3-09 Aramaki-Aza-Aoba, Aoba, Sendai 980-8579, Japan
{itaru.ueda.t6,akihiro.nishimura.p3}@dc.tohoku.ac.jp
[2] Faculty of Engineering, Tohoku Gakuin University,
1-13-1 Chuo, Tagajo, Miyagi 985-8537, Japan
[3] Cyberscience Center, Tohoku University,
6-3 Aramaki-Aza-Aoba, Aoba, Sendai 980-8578, Japan
tm-paper+cardsebi@g-mail.tohoku-university.jp

Abstract. By using a deck of cards, it is possible to realize a secure computation. In particular, since a new shuffling operation, called a random bisection cut, was devised in 2009, many efficient protocols have been designed. The shuffle functions in the following manner. A sequence of cards is bisected, and the two halves are swapped randomly. This results in two possible cases, depending on whether the two halves of the card sequence are swapped or not. Because there are only two possibilities when a random bisection cut is performed, it has been suggested that information regarding the result of the shuffle could sometimes be leaked visually. Thus, in this paper we propose some methods for implementing a random bisection cut without leaking such information.

Keywords: Cryptography · Card-based protocols · Real-life hands-on cryptography · Secure multi-party computations

1 Introduction

It is known that by using a deck of cards, we can realize secure computations. For example, consider a secure AND computation of bits $a \in \{0,1\}$ and $b \in \{0,1\}$, i.e., assume that we would only like to know the value of $a \wedge b$. By utilizing a black card ♣ and a red card ♡, we can represent the value of a bit as follows:

$$ ♣♡ = 0, \quad ♡♣ = 1. $$

According to this encoding, each of the input bits a and b can be represented by two face-down cards of different colors:

$$ \underbrace{?\,?}_{a}\,\underbrace{?\,?}_{b}. $$

A pair of face-down cards (such as in the above example) is called *a commitment*. That is, the two cards on the left constitute a commitment to a, and the two

© Springer International Publishing AG 2016
C. Martín-Vide et al. (Eds.): TPNC 2016, LNCS 10071, pp. 58–69, 2016.
DOI: 10.1007/978-3-319-49001-4_5

cards on the right constitute a commitment to b. As in this example, the cards we use are either black cards ♣ or red cards ♡, whose backs are assumed to be identical ?. As shown in Table 1, many protocols have been designed to perform a secure AND computation, among which we now introduce the Mizuki-Sone AND protocol [10], designed in 2009. Given commitments to inputs a and b along with two additional cards ♣♡, the protocol works as follows.

Table 1. Some of committed AND protocols

	# of colors	# of cards	Type of shuffle	Avg. # of trials
Crépeau and Kilian [2]	4	10	RC	6
Niemi and Renvall [12]	2	12	RC	2.5
Stiglic [15]	2	8	RC	2
Mizuki and Sone [10]	2	6	RBC	1

RC: Random Cut, RBC: Random Bisection Cut.

1. A commitment to 0 is placed between the two input commitments:

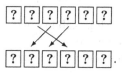

2. Rearrange the sequence order as follows:

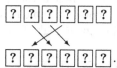

3. Apply *a random bisection cut*:

$$\left[\boxed{?}\boxed{?}\boxed{?} \,\Big\|\, \boxed{?}\boxed{?}\boxed{?} \right] \to \boxed{?}\boxed{?}\boxed{?}\boxed{?}\boxed{?}\boxed{?}.$$

A random bisection cut is a shuffling operation that bisects a sequence of cards and swaps the two halves randomly. Therefore, the shuffle results in two possible cases, depending on whether the two halves are swapped or not, each with a probability of 1/2.

4. Rearrange the sequence order as follows:

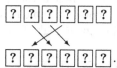

5. Turn over the two left-most cards. Then, we are able to obtain a commitment to $a \wedge b$ as follows:

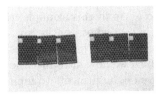

(a) Bisect a sequence of cards   (b) Shuffle the two halves

Fig. 1. Execution of a random bisection cut

Although we omit an explanation regarding the correctness and secrecy of this protocol, one can confirm that it outputs a commitment to $a \wedge b$ using six cards after one execution of the random bisection cut [10]. (A protocol such as this that outputs commitments is called a *committed protocol.*)

In practice, humans can perform a random bisection cut by shuffling the two halves after bisecting a given sequence of cards, as illustrated in Fig. 1. Thus, given a sequence of six cards

$$\underset{\begin{matrix}1 & 2 & 3 & 4 & 5 & 6\end{matrix}}{\boxed{?}\,\boxed{?}\,\boxed{?}\,\boxed{?}\,\boxed{?}\,\boxed{?}},$$

a random bisection cut results in

$$\underset{\begin{matrix}1 & 2 & 3 & 4 & 5 & 6\end{matrix}}{\boxed{?}\,\boxed{?}\,\boxed{?}\,\boxed{?}\,\boxed{?}\,\boxed{?}} \text{ or } \underset{\begin{matrix}4 & 5 & 6 & 1 & 2 & 3\end{matrix}}{\boxed{?}\,\boxed{?}\,\boxed{?}\,\boxed{?}\,\boxed{?}\,\boxed{?}},$$

with a probability of $1/2$ for each possibility, where the numbers attached to the cards are for the sake of convenience.

Following the computational model formalized in [4,8], this random bisection cut can be described as follows:

$$(\mathsf{shuffle}, \{\mathsf{id}, (1\,4)(2\,5)(3\,6)\}),$$

where id represents the identity permutation, and an expression such as $(1\,4)$ represents a cyclic permutation. Therefore, id indicates that the two halves are not swapped, and the permutation $(1\,4)(2\,5)(3\,6)$ indicates that the two halves are swapped. Historically, random bisection cuts first appeared when a six-card AND protocol was designed in 2009 [10]. Even before that, some committed AND protocols had been designed. These earlier protocols employed the *random cut* as a shuffling operation, as shown in Table 1. A random cut refers to a cyclic shuffling operation. For example, given eight face-down cards

$$\underset{\begin{matrix}1 & 2 & 3 & 4 & 5 & 6 & 7 & 8\end{matrix}}{\boxed{?}\,\boxed{?}\,\boxed{?}\,\boxed{?}\,\boxed{?}\,\boxed{?}\,\boxed{?}\,\boxed{?}},$$

a random cut results in one of the following eight cases, each with a probability of $1/8$:

$$\underset{\begin{matrix}1 & 2 & 3 & 4 & 5 & 6 & 7 & 8\end{matrix}}{\boxed{?}\,\boxed{?}\,\boxed{?}\,\boxed{?}\,\boxed{?}\,\boxed{?}\,\boxed{?}\,\boxed{?}}, \underset{\begin{matrix}2 & 3 & 4 & 5 & 6 & 7 & 8 & 1\end{matrix}}{\boxed{?}\,\boxed{?}\,\boxed{?}\,\boxed{?}\,\boxed{?}\,\boxed{?}\,\boxed{?}\,\boxed{?}}, \cdots, \underset{\begin{matrix}8 & 1 & 2 & 3 & 4 & 5 & 6 & 7\end{matrix}}{\boxed{?}\,\boxed{?}\,\boxed{?}\,\boxed{?}\,\boxed{?}\,\boxed{?}\,\boxed{?}\,\boxed{?}}.$$

Therefore by following the computational model in [4,8], we can similarly describe the random cut as

$$(\text{shuffle}, \{\text{id}, \pi, \pi^2, \pi^3, \pi^4, \pi^5, \pi^6, \pi^7\}),$$

where $\pi = (8\,7\,6\,5\,4\,3\,2\,1)$.

Table 2. Some other protocols

	# of colors	# of cards	Type of shuffle	Avg. # of trials
Non-committed AND Protocols				
den Boer [1]	2	5	RC	1
Mizuki et al. [7]	2	4	RBC	1
Committed XOR Protocols				
Crépeau-Kilian [2]	4	14	RC	6
Mizuki et al. [11]	2	10	RC	2
Mizuki and Sone [10]	2	4	RBC	1

As seen in Table 1, committed AND computations have become more efficient by virtue of the introduction of the random bisection cut in 2009. This introduction also provided the additional benefit that we were able to improve the efficiency of non-committed AND computations and committed XOR computations, as detailed in Table 2. In addition, further efficient protocols have been designed using random bisection cuts [3,5,6,13,14].

As explained above, *card-based protocols* are intended in practice to be executed by humans, who would like to actually perform secure computations using a real deck of cards. Hence, when we execute a card-based protocol, it is expected that all players gather at the same physical location, and perform operations such as shuffles in public, as in the case of ordinary card games [9].

In order to implement a random cut in such a situation, it is sufficient that each player cuts a sequence of face-down cards in turn until all players are satisfied with the result. Indeed, we note that in practice it is relatively easy to implement a random cut such that nobody is able to determine the result of the shuffle at all. We will discuss this further in Sect. 4.

Meanwhile, when we execute a random bisection cut in reality, as illustrated in Fig. 1, there exists a concern that the result of the shuffle may leak, because there are only two possibilities, i.e., the two halves of the card sequence are swapped or not. Therefore, this paper provides some methods for executing a random bisection cut securely.

This paper is composed as follows. In Sect. 2, we present some methods for implementing a random bisection cut using auxiliary tools. In Sect. 3, we propose methods to reduce the execution of a random bisection cut to the execution of random cuts using dummy cards. In Sect. 4, we discuss implementations of the random cut, and confirm through a basic experiment that humans are able to implement random cuts securely, implying that random bisection cuts can also be implemented securely.

2 Executing a Random Bisection Cut Using Auxiliary Tools

In this section, we provide methods for implementing a random bisection cut by using auxiliary tools that consist of everyday objects.

2.1 The Use of Paper Clips, Envelopes, or Boxes

When players operate a random bisection cut, if they are not familiar with playing cards and have difficulty shuffling the two halves such that each half stays together, as in Fig. 1(b), then they may want to secure each half using paper clips or envelopes [7, 10]. By using these auxiliary tools, we are able to fix each of the two halves together as shown in Fig. 2. Following this, it suffices to swap the two bundles of cards randomly.

However, as explained in Sect. 1, the result of the shuffle could be revealed when we execute a random bisection cut in public. That is, someone may count how many times the two bundles are swapped. To avoid such a leak of information, one solution is that each player shuffles the two bundles behind his/her back or under a table, so that other players cannot see whether the two bundles are swapped or not. In this case, it may be preferable to use envelopes or boxes (as illustrated in Fig. 3) rather than paper clips, to avoid malicious actions.

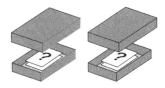

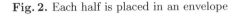

Fig. 2. Each half is placed in an envelope   **Fig. 3.** Each half is placed in a box

However, as mentioned in Sect. 1, it is desirable for all actions to be performed in front of all players and/or third parties publicly. Therefore, in Sects. 2.2 and 3 we present implementations of random bisection cuts where every action can be performed completely in public.

(a) Separator and two halves

(b) One half is placed on the separator

(c) The pile consisting of one half and the separator is flipped

(d) The other half is placed on the pile

Fig. 4. Setup for spinning throw

2.2 The Use of a Separator Card and Rubber Band

In this subsection, we present a novel method of performing a random bisection cut using a separator card with a rubber band. Both sides of the separator (as shown in the middle of Fig. 4(a)) must be indistinguishable.

The method works as follows. First, a sequence of cards is bisected, with one half placed on the separator, as shown in Fig. 4(b). Second, the pile consisting of one half and the separator is turned over, as in Fig. 4(c)[1]. Third, the other half is placed on the pile, as shown in Fig. 4(d), and these are fixed together using a rubber band, to prevent the cards from scattering. Next, the pile is thrown in a spinning manner (as illustrated in Fig. 5). We call this action a *spinning throw*. After the pile is caught, we are completely unsure of which half is on the top. Finally, the rubber band is removed, and the actions described in Fig. 4 are undone in reverse order, from (d) to (a). In this manner, we can conduct a random bisection cut securely.

(a) Hold the pile of cards

(b) Throw the pile like a coin

Fig. 5. A spinning throw

3 Executing a Random Bisection Cut Using Dummy Cards

In this section, we propose methods for reducing the execution of a random bisection cut to the execution of random cuts using dummy cards.

---

[1] The separator prevents information regarding the color of cards from being leaked.

It is assumed throughout this section that we want to apply a random bisection cut to a sequence of $2n$ cards, where $n \geq 2$:

$$\left[\; \overbrace{?\;?\;\cdots\;?}^{n \text{ cards}}\;\Big|\;\overbrace{?\;?\;\cdots\;?}^{n \text{ cards}}\;\right].$$

3.1 The Use of Cards of Other Colors

Here, as dummy cards we use cards whose backs are ? and faces are different from ♣ and ♡, namely ◇ or ♠. Specifically, we use $2s$ ◇ and $2t$ ♠ cards, where $s, t \geq 1$. That is, we have a total of $2(s + t)$ additional cards.

By using such dummy cards, we are able to implement a random bisection cut as follows.

1. Place dummy cards with their faces down, as follows:

$$\overbrace{?\;?\;\cdots\;?}^{\text{dummy cards}}\;\overbrace{?\;?\;\cdots\;?}^{n \text{ cards}}\;\overbrace{?\;?\;\cdots\;?}^{\text{dummy cards}}\;\overbrace{?\;?\;\cdots\;?}^{n \text{ cards}},$$

where the dummy cards are arranged as below:

$$\overbrace{?\;?\;\cdots\;?}^{s \text{ cards}}\;\overbrace{?\;?\;\cdots\;?}^{t \text{ cards}}.$$
$$\;\;◇\;\;◇\;\;\;\;\;◇\;\;♠\;\;♠\;\;\;\;\;♠$$

2. Apply a random cut:

$$\langle\; ?\;?\;\cdots\;?\;?\;?\;\cdots\;?\;?\;?\;\cdots\;?\;?\;?\;\cdots\;?\;\rangle.$$

3. Turn over the left-most card.
   (a) If the face-up card is ◇, then turn over cards forward (in the right-hand direction) until t ♠ cards appear. Now, we have determined the positions of all of the dummy cards, and hence we can remove them all:

$$\overbrace{◇\;\cdots\;◇}\;\overbrace{♠\;\cdots\;♠}^{t \text{ cards}}\;\overbrace{?\;\cdots\;?}^{n \text{ cards}}\;\overbrace{◇\;\cdots\;♠}^{s+t \text{ cards}}\;\overbrace{?\;\cdots\;?}^{n \text{ cards}}\;◇\;\cdots\;◇.$$

   (b) If the face-up card is ♠, then turn over cards backward (aside from cyclic rotations) until s ◇ cards appear. Now, we have determined the positions of all of the dummy cards, and hence we can remove them all:

$$♠\;\cdots\;♠\;\overbrace{?\;\cdots\;?}^{n \text{ cards}}\;\overbrace{◇\;\cdots\;♠}^{s+t \text{ cards}}\;\overbrace{?\;\cdots\;?}^{n \text{ cards}}\;\overbrace{◇\;\cdots\;◇}^{s \text{ cards}}\;♠\;\cdots\;♠.$$

   (c) If the face-up card is ♣ or ♡, then turn it over again and return to Step 2.

In this manner, after all of the dummy cards are removed, a random bisection cut has been completed.

In Step 3, the probability that either (a) or (b) occurs is $(s+t)/(n+s+t)$. Therefore, we are able to implement a random bisection cut using $2(s+t)$ dummy cards after an average of $(n+s+t)/(s+t)$ executions of the random cut.

This method of discarding dummy cards was first devised by Crépeau and Kilian [2], when they proposed some random permutation generating protocols. Here, we have adopted their idea.

Regarding the parameters s and t, there is a trade-off between the number of required cards and the average number of executions of the random cut. For example, if we want to implement the Mizuki-Sone six-card AND protocol [10] with an average number of two random cuts, then we require six additional dummy cards, and hence this requires more cards than Stiglic's eight-card AND protocol [15] (although the former might have the advantage that it is simpler to understand its correctness).

Moreover, we can select the parameters as $s = 1$ and $t = 0$, i.e., the above method works even with only two ◇ dummy cards (and no ♠ cards).

3.2 Utilizing Vertical Asymmetricity of the Backs of Cards

In Sect. 3.1, we required additional types of cards to reduce the execution of a random bisection cut to the execution of random cuts. On the other hand, in this section we do not use such additional cards, but rather employ the same cards that we have used before (♣ and ♡) as dummy cards.

Our method works as follows. We exploit the vertical asymmetricity of the backs of cards ?. Because the back is asymmetric, it can be seen as either ? or ¿, depending on the setting. Now, we describe how to implement a random bisection cut by executing a random cut with $2m$ additional dummy cards, where $m \geq 1$. (Here, any cards of type ♡ or ♣ can be used as dummy cards.)

1. Arrange the $2m$ additional dummy cards with their upsides facing down, as follows:

$$\overbrace{\boxed{¿}\,\boxed{¿}\cdots\boxed{¿}}^{m\text{ cards}}\,\overbrace{\boxed{?}\,\boxed{?}\cdots\boxed{?}}^{n\text{ cards}}\,\overbrace{\boxed{¿}\,\boxed{¿}\cdots\boxed{¿}}^{m\text{ cards}}\,\overbrace{\boxed{?}\,\boxed{?}\cdots\boxed{?}}^{n\text{ cards}}.$$

2. Apply a random cut:

$$\langle\,\boxed{?}\,\boxed{?}\cdots\boxed{?}\,\boxed{¿}\,\boxed{¿}\cdots\boxed{¿}\,\boxed{?}\,\boxed{?}\cdots\boxed{?}\,\boxed{¿}\,\boxed{¿}\cdots\boxed{¿}\,\rangle.$$

3. Cyclically shift the first several cards to the rightmost positions, without changing their order, so that the first card will be a dummy card:

$$\boxed{?}\cdots\boxed{?}\,\boxed{¿}\cdots\boxed{¿}\,\boxed{?}\cdots\boxed{?}\,\boxed{¿}\cdots\boxed{¿}\,\boxed{?}\cdots\boxed{?}$$

$$\downarrow$$

$$\overbrace{\boxed{¿}\,\boxed{¿}\cdots\boxed{¿}}^{m\text{ cards}}\,\overbrace{\boxed{?}\,\boxed{?}\cdots\boxed{?}}^{n\text{ cards}}\,\overbrace{\boxed{¿}\,\boxed{¿}\cdots\boxed{¿}}^{m\text{ cards}}\,\overbrace{\boxed{?}\,\boxed{?}\cdots\boxed{?}}^{n\text{ cards}}.$$

4. Remove all dummy cards:

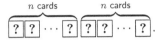

In this manner, by using $2m$ additional cards and executing one random cut, we are able to implement a random bisection cut. For example, the Mizuki-Sone six-card AND protocol [10] can be implemented with one random cut by adding two additional cards.

In this method, we must apply a random cut to cards that have asymmetric backs, and hence information regarding the result of the shuffle could be leaked more easily than with cards that have identical backs.

Taking this into account, we will discuss secure implementations of the random cut in the next section.

4   Secrecy of Implementations of the Random Cut

In Sect. 3, we proposed some methods for reducing the execution of a random bisection cut to the execution of random cuts. In general, it is believed that a random cut can be securely implemented by humans. To support this belief, we discuss the secure implementation of a random cut by performing a shuffle with a real deck of cards. Specifically, in Sect. 4.1 we point out that a naive implementation is not secure, and then propose a secure implementation that we call the "Hindu cut." In Sect. 4.2, we demonstrate that the "Hindu cut" is in fact a secure implementation of a random cut by conducting a basic experiment.

4.1   Discussion Regarding Implementations

Because a random cut consists of a cyclic shuffle, its simple implementation proceeds as in Fig. 6: some cards (or a card) are taken from the top of the pile, and then moved to the bottom of the pile (this is called a *cut*). At every cut, we should change the number of cards that are to be moved. To verify whether this simple implementation is secure, we conducted an experiment.

We asked eleven students in our laboratory to observe one author executing a simple implementation of a random cut with a pile of eight cards. We then asked them to track a specific card.

While most of the participants were unable to recognize the location of the targeted card and gave up guessing, three participants were able to follow the move and track the specific card with a high probability. Therefore, in the presence of people who are capable of following the cutting move, such a simple implementation is not secure.

Thus, we require an alternative secure implementation of the random cut. The three participants who were able to break the simple implementation informed us that they could visually observe how many cards were moved at every cut, and summed up the numbers. Hence, the key consideration is how to

Fig. 6. Simple execution of a random cut

make it impossible for people to count the number of cards moved during every cut.

One idea is to move cards from the bottom to the top of the pile instead of moving them from the top to the bottom when executing a cut operation. By doing so, it becomes difficult to recognize the number of cards that have been moved. Moreover, if the positions of the cards are out of alignment, as in Fig. 6, then it is possible to easily recognize the number of cards moved. Therefore, we should ensure that cards are not out of alignment when we execute cut operations.

Based on this idea, we found that a variation of the so-called Hindu shuffle (shown in Fig. 7) is effective for preventing the cut operation from being revealed (we call this the *Hindu cut*). In fact, the three participants mentioned above were unable to guess the specific cards, and hence they all gave up following the implementation of a Hindu cut.

Fig. 7. Execution of a "Hindu cut"   **Fig. 8.** A card sequence including two upside-down cards

Next, in order to verify the security of the Hindu cut, we conducted another experiment based on the method presented in Sect. 3.2, which exploits the vertical asymmetricity of the backs of cards. That is, we placed two cards (out of eight) with their upsides down and applied a Hindu cut, as illustrated in Fig. 8. Clearly, these upside-down cards are advantageous to people who wish to track the move. Furthermore, we asked the participants to guess the location of a specific upside-down dummy card out of the two. (There are only two possibilities after the shuffle, by virtue of the two upside-down cards.) As a result, even the three participants mentioned above gave up guessing the specific dummy card.

4.2 Confirming the Security of the Hindu Cut

In order to confirm the security of the Hindu cut more, we requested 72 participants (as shown in Table 3) who came to the Sone-Mizuki laboratory booth

Table 3. Number of examinees

# of partic-ipants	Ratio of male and female (M:F)
72	62 : 10

Table 4. Result of our experiment

Choice	# of answers
(1) I have no idea	64
(2) Definitely, it must be A	5
(3) Definitely, it must be B	3

in the Open Campus of Tohoku University in 2016, to watch a movie depicting the execution of a Hindu cut. In the movie, we employ the same sequence of cards as in Sect. 4.1. We arranged two upside-down cards, named A and B, and applied a Hindu cut. The time taken for the execution was 30 s, and the movie can be found at https://youtu.be/Zm-IpuOobIY. Following the Hindu cut, we asked every participant whether he/she could determine which card was the left upside-down card with certainty. Each participant was asked to choose his/her answer from the following three options.

1. I have no idea[2].
2. Definitely, it must be A.
3. Definitely, it must be B.

The result is presented in Table 4. Most of the participants submitted the answer (1), whereas five people gave the answer (2), and three gave the answer (3)[3]. For the participants whose answers were (2) or (3), we requested that they watch additional movies and answer again, in order to rule out wild guesses. As a result, none of the participants were able to answer correctly for all of the five movies that we had prepared.

Thus, we can conclude that the Hindu cut is an effective method for implementing a random cut securely, although we recognize that a more careful and wide ranging investigation is still required.

5   Conclusion

The random bisection cut has played an important role in improving card-based protocols. However, implementation issues have not previously been discussed. Therefore, in this paper we have proposed some novel methods for implementing the random bisection cut, and demonstrated that humans are able to implement it in practice.

Acknowledgments. We thank the anonymous referees, whose comments have helped us to improve the presentation of the paper. We would like to offer our special thanks to Kohei Yamaguchi, who provided an excellent implementation of the random bisection cut, the spinning throw, as introduced in Sect. 2.2. In addition, we are grateful to all

---

[2] If a participant could not track the move with confidence, then he/she is assumed not to have any motivation to reveal secret information from the result of the shuffle.

[3] We note that the correct answer was B.

members of the Sone-Mizuki laboratory in Tohoku University, who cooperated with our experiment in Sect. 4. This work was supported by JSPS KAKENHI Grant Number 26330001.

References

1. den Boer, B.: More efficient match-making and satisfiability: the five card trick. In: Quisquater, J.J., Vandewalle, J. (eds.) Advances in Cryptology – EUROCRYPT '89. LNCS, vol. 434, pp. 208–217. Springer, Berlin Heidelberg (1990)
2. Crépeau, C., Kilian, J.: Discreet solitary games. In: Stinson, D.R. (ed.) CRYPTO 1993. LNCS, vol. 773, pp. 319–330. Springer, Heidelberg (1994). doi:10.1007/3-540-48329-2_27
3. Ishikawa, R., Chida, E., Mizuki, T.: Efficient card-based protocols for generating a hidden random permutation without fixed points. In: Calude, C.S., Dinneen, M.J. (eds.) UCNC 2015. LNCS, vol. 9252, pp. 215–226. Springer, Heidelberg (2015). doi:10.1007/978-3-319-21819-9_16
4. Koch, A., Walzer, S., Härtel, K.: Card-based cryptographic protocols using a minimal number of cards. In: Iwata, T., Cheon, J.H. (eds.) ASIACRYPT 2015. LNCS, vol. 9452, pp. 783–807. Springer, Heidelberg (2015). doi:10.1007/978-3-662-48797-6_32
5. Mizuki, T.: Card-based protocols for securely computing the conjunction of multiple variables. Theor. Comput. Sci. **622**, 34–44 (2016)
6. Mizuki, T., Asiedu, I.K., Sone, H.: Voting with a logarithmic number of cards. In: Mauri, G., Dennunzio, A., Manzoni, L., Porreca, A.E. (eds.) UCNC 2013. LNCS, vol. 7956, pp. 162–173. Springer, Heidelberg (2013). doi:10.1007/978-3-642-39074-6_16
7. Mizuki, T., Kumamoto, M., Sone, H.: The five-card trick can be done with four cards. In: Wang, X., Sako, K. (eds.) ASIACRYPT 2012. LNCS, vol. 7658, pp. 598–606. Springer, Heidelberg (2012). doi:10.1007/978-3-642-34961-4_36
8. Mizuki, T., Shizuya, H.: A formalization of card-based cryptographic protocols via abstract machine. Int. J. Inf. Secur. **13**(1), 15–23 (2014)
9. Mizuki, T., Shizuya, H.: Practical card-based cryptography. In: Ferro, A., Luccio, F., Widmayer, P. (eds.) Fun with Algorithms. LNCS, vol. 8496, pp. 313–324. Springer, Heidelberg (2014)
10. Mizuki, T., Sone, H.: Six-card secure AND and four-card secure XOR. In: Deng, X., Hopcroft, J.E., Xue, J. (eds.) FAW 2009. LNCS, vol. 5598, pp. 358–369. Springer, Heidelberg (2009). doi:10.1007/978-3-642-02270-8_36
11. Mizuki, T., Uchiike, F., Sone, H.: Securely computing XOR with 10 cards. Aust. J. Combinatorics **36**, 279–293 (2006)
12. Niemi, V., Renvall, A.: Secure multiparty computations without computers. Theor. Comput. Sci. **191**(1–2), 173–183 (1998)
13. Nishida, T., Hayashi, Y., Mizuki, T., Hideaki, S.: Securely computing three-input functions with eight cards. IEICE Trans. Fundam. Electron. Commun. Comput. Sci. **98**(6), 1145–1152 (2015)
14. Nishida, T., Hayashi, Y., Mizuki, T., Sone, H.: Card-based protocols for any boolean function. In: Jain, R., Jain, S., Stephan, F. (eds.) TAMC 2015. LNCS, vol. 9076, pp. 110–121. Springer, Heidelberg (2015). doi:10.1007/978-3-319-17142-5_11
15. Stiglic, A.: Computations with a deck of cards. Theor. Comput. Sci. **259**(1–2), 671–678 (2001)

Evolutionary Computation

A Discrete Artificial Bee Colony Algorithm Based on Similarity for Graph Coloring Problems

Kui Chen[1](✉) and Hitoshi Kanoh[2]

[1] Department of Computer Science,
Graduate School of Systems and Information Engineering,
University of Tsukuba, Tsukuba, Japan
chen@kslab.cs.tsukuba.ac.jp
[2] Division of Information Engineering, Faculty of Engineering,
Information and Systems, University of Tsukuba, Tsukuba, Japan
kanoh@cs.tsukuba.ac.jp

Abstract. In this paper, a novel non-hybrid discrete artificial bee colony (ABC) algorithm is proposed for solving planar graph coloring problems. The original ABC intends to handle only continuous optimization problems. To apply ABC to discrete problems, the original ABC operators need to be redefined over discrete space. In this work, a new algorithm based on *Similarity* is introduced. Compared with HDPSO, the experiment shows that the proposed method matches the competitive results and obtains higher success rate and lower average evaluation times when solving planar graph coloring problems.

Keywords: Artificial bee colony · Graph coloring problem · Swarm intelligence · Combinatorial optimization

1 Introduction

Graph coloring problem (GCP) is a famous combinatorial optimization problem (COP). It states that given an undirected graph with n vertices and m edges, each vertex is assigned one of k colors so that none of the vertices connected with an edge have the same color. This problem belongs to a kind of NP-complete problems. Because of its simple definition, graph coloring problem is used to model many scheduling and resource allocation problems, such as examination scheduling.

Swarm intelligence is the collective behavior of decentralized, self-organized systems. It is inspired from biological system such as the collective behavior of birds, ants or fish for foraging and defending, and often consists of simple agents interacting locally with other individuals and with the environment. This concept is introduced into computer science by Gerardo Beni and Jing Wang [1] and has been successfully applied to many combinatorial optimization problems. For example, particle swarm optimization, which is proposed by Kennedy and

© Springer International Publishing AG 2016
C. Martín-Vide et al. (Eds.): TPNC 2016, LNCS 10071, pp. 73–84, 2016.
DOI: 10.1007/978-3-319-49001-4_6

Eberhart [2], has been extended to solve discrete optimization problems [3] such as graph coloring problem [4–7] and timetabling problem [8–10]. In addition, ant colony optimization obtains good results by solving Travelling-Salesman Problem (TSP) [11,12]. Finally, the Artificial Bee Colony (ABC) Algorithm proposed by Karaboga and Basturk [13] exhibits excellent results when solving flow shop scheduling problem [14,15] and graph coloring problem [16].

Artificial bee colony (ABC) algorithm is one of optimization algorithms in swarm intelligence. Original ABC is inspired by the intelligent behavior of honey bee swarm and recognized as a fast, reliable and efficient method for solving continuous optimization problems [17]. In recent years, original ABC has also been applied to solve discrete optimization problems such as graph coloring problem [16]. In [16], the proposed ABC algorithm is hybridized with a random walk with direction exploitation local search and obtains great performance. However, hybrid algorithms are generally designed for specific problems and their structures are more complicated. It is difficult to apply them to other combinatorial optimization problems.

In this paper, we propose a novel discrete ABC algorithm based on similarity to solve graph 3-coloring problems. Although hybrid ABC for graph coloring problem has been proposed [16], few general-use discrete ABC has been found. In the proposed method, we introduce *Similarity* and discretize the original ABC directly without hybrid algorithms. Our method is simple to implement and can be applied to other COPs readily.

The structure of this paper is as follows: first of all, the objective problem and related works are discussed in Sect. 2. Next, the proposed algorithm is described in detail in Sect. 3. Finally, in Sect. 4, the results of experiments are given and show that this approach is more effective than HDPSO.

2   Problem Description

2.1   Graph Coloring Problems

In graph theory, graph coloring problem can be defined as coloring the vertices of a given undirected graph with k colors such that no two adjacent vertices share the same color. This problem is a well-studied NP-hard problem that is often used to test the efficiency for many newly developed algorithms. In this paper, we focus on graph 3-coloring problems, namely $k = 3$.

Following the proposed method in [18], solvable problems with n vertices and m edges are generated as below:

1. Dividing vertices into three groups, each with $\frac{n}{3}$ vertices.
2. Creating m edges randomly between vertices in different groups.
3. Accepting the graph if there is no unconnected components.

We also define a constraint density:

$$d = \frac{m}{n} \tag{1}$$

Constraint density indicates the level of difficulty for a given graph. Hogg pointed out that the most difficult problems arise when d is between 2.0 and 2.5 because the loose constraints allow for more local optimal solutions [19].

Figure 1 presents an example of graph 3-coloring problem, along with a possible candidate solution. A candidate solution for GCP is represented as a $1 \times n$ color vector $\boldsymbol{x_i} = [x_{i1}, x_{i2}, x_{i3}, ..., x_{ij}, ..., x_{in}]$, where $x_{ij} \in \{0, 1, 2\}$. In our coding scheme, 0, 1 and 2 represent red(R), green(G) and blue(B) respectively. Based on this coding scheme, the solution of the graph in Fig. 1 can be expressed as $\boldsymbol{x_i} = [0, 0, 2, 1]$.

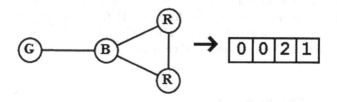

Fig. 1. An example of graph 3-coloring problem

To evaluate a candidate solution $\boldsymbol{x_i}$, we define *conflict* for each solution:

$$conflict_{jl} = \begin{cases} 1 & if \quad x_{ij} = x_{il} \wedge jl \in E(G) \\ 0 & otherwise \end{cases} \tag{2}$$

$$conflict(\boldsymbol{x_i}) = \frac{1}{2} \sum_{j=1}^{n} \sum_{l=1}^{n} conflict_{jl} \tag{3}$$

where $E(G)$ indicates the set of edges. Equation 2 states that if two adjacent vertices share the same color, the conflict between the two vertices is 1, otherwise 0. The total conflict of $\boldsymbol{x_i}$ is given by Eq. 3 obviously. Note that $\frac{1}{2}$ is indispensable for avoiding calculating the conflict of two vertices twice.

2.2 Original Artificial Bee Colony Algorithm

Original artificial bee colony (ABC) consists of three bee groups: employed bees, onlooker bees and scout bees. First of all, the employed bees explore the search space and discover food sources. In most cases, one food source is equivalent to a candidate solution. Next, onlooker bee evaluates food sources' information and selects a food source with a probability associated with its fitness. This probabilistic selection is essentially a roulette wheel selection which is described as below:

$$P_i = \frac{fit_i}{\sum_{j=1}^{N} fit_j} \tag{4}$$

where N is the swarm size and fit_i is the fitness value of the ith food source in the swarm. Obviously, the better the food source i is, the higher the probability of ith food source will be selected. Finally, if a food source cannot be improved over a predefined iteration number $limit$, then this food source is abandoned and replaced with a new random food source discovered by scout bee.

In order to produce a new candidate v_i food source from the old one x_i, ABC uses the following equation:

$$v_{il} = x_{il} + \phi \times (x_{il} - x_{jl}) \tag{5}$$

where $i, j \in \{1, 2, 3, ..., N\}$ and $l \in \{1, 2, 3, ..., n\}$ are randomly selected indexes. Although j is determined randomly, it has to be different from i. ϕ is a uniformly distributed random number generated from $[-1, 1]$. Once the new candidate food source v_i is generated, a greedy selection is applied. If the fitness of v_i is better than that of the old food source x_i, then replace x_i with v_i; otherwise keep x_i unchanged.

2.3 Discrete Swarm Algorithms

In this section, we review swarm algorithms to solve discrete optimization problems with reference to literature [3].

PSO: Particle swarm optimization (PSO), which is proposed by Kennedy and Eberhart [2], is a stochastic search algorithm inspired by the coordinated movement of fish schools and bird flocks. Though PSO is designed for solving continuous problems, it has been extended to solve discrete optimization problems [3]. Sigmoid function is used to calculate the trajectory in binary search space to solve Knapsack problem (KP) [20,21]. By applying Smallest Position Value (SPV) method, a discrete PSO is used to solve flow shop scheduling problem [22]. Some hybrid methods are also used with PSO to solve graph coloring problem [5].

FA: Firefly algorithm (FA), which is proposed by Yang [23], is inspired by the flashing behaviour of fireflies. The first FA for combinatorial optimization is proposed by Sayadi et al. [24]. In this case, Sigmoid function is applied to each component of the real-valued vector for updating the fireflies' position. The Sigmoid function is also used to transform the values form real to binary for Knapsack problem [25] and feature selection [26]. Fister et al. apply Random Key method in FA to solve graph 3-coloring problems and Random Key method converts the real values to discrete values [27].

CSA: Cuckoo search algorithm (CSA) is an optimization algorithm developed by Yang and Deb in 2009 [28]. It is inspired by the obligate brood parasitism of some cuckoo species by laying their eggs in the nests of other host birds. By applying Nearest Integer method to modify Levy Flights from continuous values to discrete values, CSA can be used to solve a scheduling problem for a flexible manufacturing system [29]. A discrete binary CSA is also proposed to solve Knapsack problem by using Sigmoid function [30].

2.4 Related Works

HDPSO: PSO with Transition Probability Based on Hamming Distance (HDPSO) is a non-hybrid discrete PSO algorithm proposed by Takuya Aoki [7]. To compare the positions of particles, the Hamming distance is introduced as the distance among particles. Then, to take into account the internal relationship between colors in one particles, three relevant transition probabilities are calculated: P_{rand}, P_{pbest} and P_{gbest}. Finally, each component in a particle is updated according to these probabilities. The basic updating strategy of HDPSO is shown below:

Pseudo-code of HDPSO updating strategy for one particle x_i

```
procedure update-position(xi)
    for j = 1 to N
        Generate random number r in [0,1];
        if r <= Prand
            xi[j] = random color;
        else if r <= Prand + Ppbest
            xi[j] = pbest[i][j];
        else
            xi[j] = gbest[j];
        end if
    end for
end procedure
```

Experiment on graph 3-coloring problem shows that HDPSO is an efficient method and can obtain better result than GA. However, when the size of graph becomes large, the performance of HDPSO turns to be worse.

Hybrid ABC: Hybrid ABC (HABC) proposed by Izotok Fister [16] is also used to solve graph 3-coloring problems. In this algorithm, original ABC is hybridized with random walk with direction exploitation (RWDE) local search. Compared with hybrid evolutionary algorithm (HEA) and EA-SAW, experiment shows that HABC matches the competitive results. However, though Hybrid ABC outperforms the original ABC, it is designed for solving graph 3-coloring problems only and difficult to be applied to other discrete optimization problems.

3 Proposed Method

3.1 Objective Function

The objective function is measured by:

$$fitness(x_i) = 1 - \frac{conflict(x_i)}{m} \qquad (6)$$

where x_i is a candidate solution and m is the edge number of graph. $conflict(x_i)$ represents the number of conflicts of x_i, which is given by Eq. 3.

If there is no such two adjacent vertices that are assigned the same color, i.e. $conflict(\boldsymbol{x}_i) = 0$, the objective function converges to optimal value 1 and the candidate solution becomes the optimal solution.

3.2 Similarity

In original ABC, the employed bees and onlooker bees generate a new candidate solution from $\boldsymbol{x}_i$ by randomly choosing a neighbor solution $\boldsymbol{x}_j$ and invoking Eq. 5. However, in the proposed method, instead of choosing a neighbor randomly, we select a neighbor solution which is *similar* to $\boldsymbol{x}_i$. The *Similarity* describes the similar degree between two solutions $\boldsymbol{x}_i$ and $\boldsymbol{x}_j$. It is defined as:

$$hd = H(\boldsymbol{x}_i, \boldsymbol{x}_j) \tag{7}$$

$$Similarity = 1 - rn * \frac{hd}{n} \tag{8}$$

where hd indicates the Hamming distance between $\boldsymbol{x}_i$ and $\boldsymbol{x}_j$ and n is the vertex number of graph. To increase some randomness, a uniformly distributed random number rn from interval $[0, 1]$ is introduced in Eq. 8.

HDPSO also introduces *Similarity*. It is defined as below:

$$Similarity = 1 - \frac{hd}{n} \tag{9}$$

Note that there is no such rn in Eq. 9. By adding rn in our implementation, the search range is extended properly and more candidate solutions can take part in the improvement of current solution $\boldsymbol{x}_i$.

3.3 Updating Strategy

Only such $\boldsymbol{x}_j$ that is similar to $\boldsymbol{x}_i$ will be selected as a neighbor and used to generate a new candidate solution $\boldsymbol{v}_i$. Once a neighbor solution $\boldsymbol{x}_j$ is determined, we randomly choose u components from $\boldsymbol{x}_j$ and replace the corresponding components of $\boldsymbol{x}_i$ by them. Note that if $u = 1$, the updating strategy is quite similar to the original ABC which modifies only one component at a time (see Eq. 5). The procedure of updating is as follows:

Pseudo-code of updating strategy

```
procedure update-strategy(swarm)
    for each solution xi in swarm
        vi = xi;
        randomly select a solution xj;
        calculate the Hamming distance between xi and xj;
        calculate the Similarity;
        generate a random number r in [0,1];
        if r < Similarity
            randomly choose u components from xj and
```

```
            replace the corresponding component of vi
            by them;
            if fitness(vi) > fitness(xi)
                replace xi by vi;
            else
                keep xi unchanged;
            end if
        end if
    end for
end procedure
```

3.4   Main Procedure

The main procedure of proposed method is exactly identical to the original ABC. Note that there is only one scout bee in the proposed method, which abandons a solution that can not be improved in a predefined iteration time *limit* and generates a new solution randomly. The main procedure is shown below:

Pseudo-code of main procedure

```
procedure proposed-ABC
    initialization;
    while (optimal solution is not found) and
    (loop time < max iteration times)
        send employed bees;
        send onlooker bees;
        send scount bee;
    end while
end procedure
```

4   Experiments

4.1   Parameter Dependence

Before comparing with other algorithms, we have to examine the dependence of the success rate on the parameters u and *limit* through experiments. Success rate expresses the ratio of the number of successfully finding the optimal solution from all runs. Using the method introduced in Sect. 2.1, 50 random graphs with 90 vertices ($n = 90$) are generated. The constraint density d is 2.5, which is the most difficult problem. Swarm size (N) is 200 and max iteration is 10000.

First of all, fixing u on 3, we test proposed method on these 50 random graphs using different *limit*. The result is shown by Fig. 2a.

Figure 2a demonstrates that the best success rate 86 % is obtained when *limit* = 90. We accept 90 as the optimal value of *limit*. Next, to get the optimal value of u, we fix *limit* on its optimal value 90 and examine the success rate on

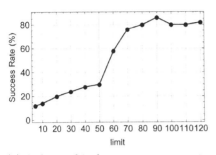

(a) Relationship between success rate and parameter *limit*

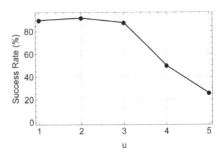

(b) Relationship between success rate and parameter u

Fig. 2. Optimization of parameters *limit* and u

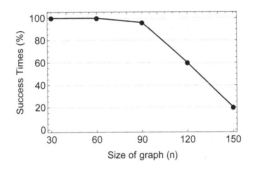

Fig. 3. Success rates by size of graph

these 50 random graphs with different u. The result is illustrated by Fig. 2b, and the best success rate 92 % arises when $u = 2$.

Finally, using the optimal values gained above, we investigate the success rate of proposed method on graphs with different size n. For each size, 100 trials are executed at constraint density $d = 2.5$. The success rates are shown by Fig. 3.

Table 1. Experiment conditions

	Proposed Method	HDPSO
Swarm size	200	200
Max iteration	10000	10000
w	0.05	–
c_1	7.0	–
c_2	0.03	–
limit	–	90
u	–	2

The success rate of proposed method is excellent when $n = 30, 60, 90$. Even when $n = 150$, the size of graph is large, we also obtain 20 % success rate.

4.2   Comparative Study

The proposed algorithm is compared with HDPSO on different constraint density d to evaluate its performance. The two algorithms are compared according to two measures: success rate, which has been defined above, and average evaluation

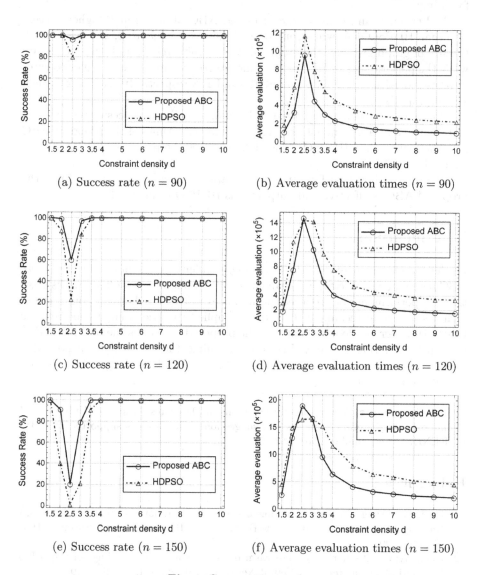

(a) Success rate ($n = 90$)

(b) Average evaluation times ($n = 90$)

(c) Success rate ($n = 120$)

(d) Average evaluation times ($n = 120$)

(e) Success rate ($n = 150$)

(f) Average evaluation times ($n = 150$)

Fig. 4. Comparative study

times of objective function to solution, which reflects the efficiency of a particular algorithm.

The parameters are listed in Table 1. The value of parameters w, c_1 and c_2 for the HDPSO are taken from [7]. For the sake of fairness, 100 independent runs are observed for each d because of the stochastic nature of both algorithms. The results are shown by Fig. 4.

Figure 4 is divided into 6 diagrams according to graph size and the two measures, i.e. success rate and average evaluation times. We can observe the following:

As Fig. 4a, b and c show, the proposed ABC obtains much higher success rate than HDPSO does when constraint density d is equal to 2, 2.5 and 3. With the size of graph growing, the proposed ABC retains relatively high success rate while the performance of HDPSO becomes worse. For example, the success rates of proposed ABC and HDPSO are 20 % and 1 % respectively for $d = 2.5$ when size of graph is 150.

On the other hand, as Fig. 4b, d and f show, even if the success rates are both 100 % when d is larger than 4, the average evaluation times of the proposed ABC are much lower than HDPSO. That demonstrates the proposed ABC are much faster than HDPSO.

The results show that for both success rate and average evaluation times, the proposed ABC is effective and outperforms HDPSO dramatically.

5   Conclusion

In this paper, we solve graph 3-coloring problems using non-hybrid discrete ABC based on *Similarity*. Experiments on 100 randomly generated graphs show that the performance of proposed method is excellent. Furthermore, our method includes a general technique that can be applied to various large-scale real-life COPs. However, we do not claim that the proposed method is the best method to solve graph coloring problems. In our forthcoming study, we will make a detailed comparison with other optimization algorithms such as Firefly algorithm, Cuckoo algorithm and so on.

Acknowledgments. The authors wish to thank Dr. Claus Aranha of University of Tsukuba for his helpful comments and suggestions. This work is supported by JSPS KAKENHI Grant Number 15K00296.

References

1. Beni, G., Wang, J.: Swarm intelligence in cellular robotic systems. Robots and Biological Systems: Towards a New Bionics?, vol. 102, pp. 703–712. Springer, Heidelberg (1993)
2. Kennedy, J., Eberhart Particle swarm optimization. In: Proceedings of the IEEE International Conference on Neural Networks, vol. 4, pp. 1942–1948 (1995)

3. Krause, J., Cordeirol, J., Parpinelli, R.S., Heitor S.L.: A survey of swarm algorithms applied to discrete optimization problems. Swarm Intelligence and Bio-Inspired Computation, pp. 169–191 (2013)
4. Cui, G., Qin, L., Liu, S., Wang, Y., Zhang, X., Cao, X.: Modified PSO algorithm for solving planar graph coloring problem. Progress Nat. Sci. **18**, 353–357 (2008)
5. Hsu, L.-Y., Fan, P., Horng, S.-J., Khurram, M., Wang, Y.-R., Run, R.-S., Lai, J.-L., Chan, R.-J.: MTPSO algorithm for solving planar graph coloring problem. Expert Syst. Appl. **38**, 5525–5531 (2001)
6. Zhang, K., Zhu, W., Liu, J., He, J.: Discrete particle swarm optimization algorithm for solving graph coloring problem. In: 10th International Conference Bio-Inspired Computing - Theories and Applications, pp. 643–652 (2015)
7. Aoki, T., Aranha, C., Kanoh, H.: PSO algorithm with transition probability based on hamming distance for graph coloring problem. In: IEEE International Conference on Systems, Man, and Cybernetics, pp. 1956–1961 (2015)
8. Qu, R., Burke, E.K.: Hybridizations within a graph-based hyper-heuristic framework for University timetabling problems. J. Oper. Res. Soc. **60**, 1273–1285 (2009)
9. Fen, H.S., Safaai, D., Hashim, M., Zaiton, S.: University course timetable planning using hybrid particle swarm optimization. In: Proceedings of the first ACM/SIGEVO Summit on Genetic and Evolutionary Computation, pp. 239–246 (2009)
10. Kanoh, H., Chen, S.: Particle swarm optimization with transition probability for timetabling problems. In: Tomassini, M., Antonioni, A., Daolio, F., Buesser, P. (eds.) ICANNGA 2013. LNCS, vol. 7824, pp. 256–265. Springer, Heidelberg (2013). doi:10.1007/978-3-642-37213-1_27
11. Dorigo, M., Stutzle, T.: Ant Colony Optimization. MIT Press, Cambridge (2004)
12. Kanoh, H., Ochiai, J.: Solving time-dependent traveling salesman problems using ant colony optimization based on predicted traffic. In: International Symposium on Distributed Computing and Artificial Intelligence, Advances in Intelligent and Soft Computing, vol. 151, pp. 25–32 (2012)
13. Karaboga, D., Basturk, B., Owerful, A.: Efficient algorithm for numerical function optimization: artificial bee colony (ABC) algorithm. J. Global Optim. **39**, 459–471 (2007)
14. Pan, Q.K., Tasgetiren, M.F., Suganthan, P.N., Chua, T.J.: A discrete artificial bee colony algorithm for the lot-streaming flow shop scheduling problem. Inf. Sci. **181**(12), 2455–2468 (2011)
15. Tasgetiren, M.F., Pan, Q.K., Suganthan, P.N., Chen, A.H.-L.: A discrete artificial bee colony algorithm for the total flowtime minimization and permutation flow shops. Inf. Sci. **181**(16), 3459–3475 (2011)
16. Fister Jr., I., Fister, I., Brest, J.: A hybrid artificial bee colony algorithm for graph 3-coloring. Swarm Evol. Comput. **7269**, 66–74 (2012)
17. Karaboga, D., Basturk, A.: A survey: algorithms simulating bee swarm intelligence. Artif. Intell. Rev. **31**(1–4), 61–85 (2009)
18. Minton, S., Johnston, M.D., Philips, A.B., Laird, P.: Minimizing conflicts: a heuristic repair mehod for constraint-satisfaction and scheduling problems. Artif. Intell. **58**, 161–205 (1992)
19. Hogg, T., Williams, C.: The hardest constraint problems, a double phase transition. Artif. Intell. **69**(1–2), 359–377 (1994)
20. Deep, K., Bansal, J.C.: A socio-cognitive particle swarm optimization for multi-dimentional knapsack problem. In: First International Conference on Emerging Trends in Engineering an Technology, pp. 355–360 (2008)

21. Shen, X., Li, Y., Chen, C., Yang, J., Zhang, D.: Greedy continuous particle swarm optimization algorithm for the knapsack problems. Int. J. Comput. Appl. Technol. **44**(2), 137–144 (2012)
22. Ucar, H., Tasgetiren, M.F.: A particle swarm optimization algorithm for permutation flow shop sequencing problem with the number of tardy jobs criterion. In: 5th International Symposium on Intelligent Manufacturing Systems, pp. 237–250 (2006)
23. Algorithms, S., Yang, X.S.: Firefly algorithm for multimodal optimization. Found. Appl. **5792**, 169–178 (2009)
24. Sayadi, M.K., Ramezanian, R., Ghaffari-Nasab, N.: A discrete firefly meta-heuristic with local search for makespan minimization in permutation flow shop scheduling problems. Int. J. Ind. Eng. Comput. **1**(1), 1–10 (2010)
25. Palit, S., Sinha, S.N., Molla, M.A., Khanra, A., Kule, M.: A cryptanalytic attack on the knapsack cryptosystem using binary firefly algorithm. In: 2nd International Conference on Computer and Communication Technology, pp. 428–432 (2011)
26. Banati, H., Bajaj, M.: Firefly based feature selection approach. Int. J. Comput. Sci. Issues **8**(4), 73–480 (2011)
27. Fister, I., Yang, X.S., Fister, I., Brest, J.: Memetic firefly algorithm for combinatorial optimization. In: 5th International Conference on Bioinspired Optimization Methods and Their Applications, pp. 75–86 (2012)
28. Yang, X.S., Deb, S.: Cuckoo search via levy flights. In: World Congress on Nature and Biologically Inspired Computing, pp. 210–214 (2009)
29. Burnwal, S., Deb, S.: Scheduling optimization of flexible manufacuring system using cuckoo search-based approach. Int. J. Adv. Manuf. Technol. **64**(5), 951–959 (2013)
30. Gherboudj, A., Layeb, A., Chikhi, S.: Solving 0–1 knapsack problems by a discrete binary version of cuckoo search algorithm. Int. J. Bio-Inspired Comput. **4**(4), 229–236 (2012)

A Multi-objective Evolutionary Approach to Pareto Optimal Model Trees. A Preliminary Study

Marcin Czajkowski[✉] and Marek Kretowski

Faculty of Computer Science, Bialystok University of Technology,
Wiejska 45a, 15-351 Bialystok, Poland
{m.czajkowski,m.kretowski}@pb.edu.pl

Abstract. Decision tree induction is inherently a multi-objective task. However, most of the conventional learning algorithms can only deal with a single-objective that may possibly aggregate multiple objectives. This paper proposes the multi-objective evolutionary approach to Pareto optimal model trees. We developed a set of non-dominated model trees for a Global Model Tree framework using efficient sort and specialized selection. Performed study covers variants with two and three objectives that relate to the tree error and the tree comprehensibility. Pareto front generated by the GMT system allows the decision maker to select desired output model according to his preferences on the conflicting objectives. Experimental evaluation of the proposed approach is performed on three real-life datasets and is confronted with competitive model tree inducers.

Keywords: Data mining · Evolutionary algorithms · Model trees · Multi-objective optimization · Pareto optimality

1 Introduction

The most important role of data mining [10] is to reveal important and insightful information hidden in the data. Among various tools and algorithms that are able to effectively identify patterns within the data, the decision trees (DT)s [20] represent one of the most frequently applied prediction technique. Tree-based approaches are easy to understand, visualize, and interpret. Their similarity to the human reasoning process through the hierarchical tree structure, in which appropriate tests from consecutive nodes are sequentially applied, makes them a powerful tool [29] for data analysts.

Despite 50 years of research on DTs, there is still a space for the improvement [21], such as: the search for better structure, splits and leaves models; multi-objective optimization or efficient analysis of the cost-sensitive data. To help to resolve some of these issues, evolutionary algorithms (EA)s [23] are applied to DTs induction [2]. The strength of this approach lies in the global search for splits and predictions and results in simpler but still accurate trees in comparison to ones induced with greedy strategies [5].

© Springer International Publishing AG 2016
C. Martín-Vide et al. (Eds.): TPNC 2016, LNCS 10071, pp. 85–96, 2016.
DOI: 10.1007/978-3-319-49001-4_7

The objective of this paper is to allow the decision maker to select desired output model according to his preferences on tree comprehensibility and accuracy. The main contribution is a multi-objective evolutionary approach to Pareto optimal model trees. To the best of our knowledge, such study on multi-objective optimization for regression or model trees, surprisingly, has not yet been addressed in the literature. Despite the popularity of DTs, the topic has not yet been adequately explored even for classification trees.

In this work, we focus on the Global Model Tree (GMT) framework [5] that can be used for the evolutionary induction of different kinds of regression and model trees [6] and be applied in real-life applications [4]. We have extended the actual fitness function of the GMT system that applied weight-formula or lexicographic analysis with Pareto-based multi-objective optimization methodology. The efficient non-dominated sort (ENS) [31], archive list of non-dominated solutions as well as updated crowding functions were applied for the GMT system. We have also incorporated the knowledge about tree induction into the evolutionary search.

Experimental study was performed on three publicly available real-life datasets and covered two-objective: tree error and tree comprehensibility; and three-objective optimization: tree error, number of nodes and the number of attributes in regression models located in the leaves. We have also confronted obtained results with the competitive model tree inducers.

This paper is organized as follows. Section 2 provides a brief background and Sect. 3 describes in detail proposed Pareto optimal search for the GMT framework. Section 4 presents experimental validation of our approach on real-life datasets. In the last section, the paper is concluded and possible future works are outlined.

2   Background

In this section, we want to present some background information on DTs and the multi-objective optimization.

2.1   Decision Trees

Different variants of DTs [21] may be grouped according to the type of problem they are applied to, the way they are induced, or the type of their structure. In this paper, we focus on a model tree that can be seen as an extension of the typical regression tree [27] which, in turn, is considered as a variant of DT designed to approximate real-valued functions instead of being used for classification tasks. Although, regression and model trees are not as popular as classification trees, they are highly competitive with different machine learning algorithms [13].

In case of the simplest regression tree [3], each leaf is associated with a constant value, usually an average value of the target attribute. In the model tree, this value is replaced by a linear (or nonlinear) regression function. To predict the target value, a new tested instance is followed down the tree from a root node to a leaf using its attribute values to make routing decisions at each internal node. Next, the predicted value for the tested instance is evaluated based on a regression model in the leaf.

In this paper we study the evolutionary induced model trees; therefore, to go further, we must briefly describe the process of learning of DT based on the training set. The two most popular concepts for the DT induction are the top-down and global approaches. The first is based on a greedy procedure known as recursive partitioning [28]. In the top-down approach, the induction algorithm starts from the root node where the locally optimal split is searched according to the given optimality measure. Next, the training instances are redirected to the newly created nodes, and this process is repeated for each node until a stopping condition is met. Additionally, post-pruning [8] is usually applied after the induction to avoid the problem of over-fitting the training data. Inducing trees with the greedy strategy is fast and generally efficient but often produces only locally optimal solutions. One of the most popular representatives of top-down induced regression trees is Classification And Regression Tree (CART) [3]. As for the model trees, the M5 system [27] is the most recognized algorithm that induces a tree with multiple linear regression models in the leaves.

The global induction for the DTs limits the negative effects of locally optimal decisions. It simultaneously searches for the tree structure, tests in the internal nodes, and models in the leaves. This approach is mainly represented by systems based on an evolutionary search [2,5] and may reveal hidden regularities that are often undetectable by greedy methods. There are relatively fewer approaches for the evolutionary induction of regression and model trees than for the classification trees. Popular representatives of EA-based regression trees are: the TARGET system [9] that evolves a CART-like tree with basic genetic operators and a strongly typed GP (Genetic Programming) approach called STGP [14]. In case of globally induced model trees there is E-Motion [1] that is a counterpart of the M5 system and a GP approach called GPMCC [26] with nonlinear regression models in the leaves.

2.2 Multi-objective Optimization in the Decision Trees

Real-world optimization problems are usually characterized by multiple objectives which often conflict with each other. In case of the DT induction, it is advisable to maximize the predictive performance and the complexity of the output tree. A single evaluation measure may degrade the other measures; therefore, multi-objective optimization may present more acceptable overall results. In the context of DTs, a direct minimization of the prediction accuracy measured in the learning set usually leads to the over-fitting problem [8].

There are three popular multi-objective optimization strategies [2]: the weight formula, lexicographic analysis, and Pareto-dominance. The weight formula transforms a multi-objective problem into a single-objective one by constructing a single formula that contains all objectives. The main drawback of this strategy is the need to find adjusted weights for the measures. The lexicographic approach analyzes the objective values for the individuals one by one based on the priorities. This approach also requires defining thresholds; however, adding up non-commensurable measures, such as tree error and size, is not performed. In contrast to Pareto-dominance approach, both aforementioned solutions were already applied for evolutionary regression and model tree induction [1,5].

Pareto-dominance [25] searches not for one best solution, but rather for a group of solutions in such a way, that selecting any one of them in place of another will always sacrifice quality for at least one objective, while improving it for at least one other. Consider m conflicting objectives that need to be minimized simultaneously. A solution $\mathbf{A} = \{a_1, a_2, \ldots, a_m\}$ is said to dominate solution $\mathbf{B} = \{b_1, b_2, \ldots, b_m\}$ (symbolically denoted by $\mathbf{A} \prec \mathbf{B}$) if and only if:

$$(\mathbf{A} \prec \mathbf{B}) \Leftrightarrow (\forall i)(a_i \leq b_i) \wedge (\exists i)(a_i < b_i). \tag{1}$$

The Pareto optimal set is constituted only with solutions that are not dominated by any other solutions:

$$\{\mathbf{A} | \neg(\exists \mathbf{B}, \mathbf{B} \prec \mathbf{A})\}. \tag{2}$$

The set of all Pareto optimal solutions is referred to as the Pareto front. Next, these multiple alternative solutions are be presented to the decision maker for a consideration.

Although, Pareto optimal approach is popular in machine learning [17], it has not been explored for regression or model trees yet. However, in the literature we may find some attempts performed for classification trees. In [32] the author created Pareto optimal DTs to capture the trade-off between different types of misclassification errors in a cost-sensitive classification problem. Such multi-objective strategy was also applied [19] to top-down induced trees to minimize two objectives: classification error rate and the tree size (measured by the number of the tree nodes). Finally, the Pareto-optimality for greedy induced oblique DTs was investigated in [24]. The authors show that a inducer, that generates the most accurate trees does not necessarilly generate the smallest trees or the ones that are included in Pareto-optimal set.

3   Pareto-Optimal Search in GMT

In this section, we present a new multi-objective approach for evolutionary induced regression and model trees. At first, we briefly describe a system called Global Model Tree (GMT). Next, we illustrate how to efficiently adapt Pareto-based approach in the fitness function for GMT.

3.1   Global Model Tree

The general structure of the GMT system follows a typical EA framework [23] with an unstructured population and a generational selection. The GMT framework allows evolving all kinds of tree representations [6] e.g.: univariate, oblique, regression, model and mixed. In our description we focused on univariate model trees [5], however; our study can be easily adapted to the different types of trees.

Model trees are represented in their actual form as traditional univariate trees, so each split in the internal node is based on a single attribute. Each tree leaf contains a multiple linear regression model that is constructed with learning instances associated with that leaf. Tree-based representation requires developing specialized genetic operators corresponding to classical mutation and crossover. The GMT framework [5] offers several specialized variants that can modify the tree structure, tests in internal nodes, and models in the leaves.

Fitness function is one of the most important and sensitive element in the design of EA. It drives the evolutionary search process by measuring how good a single individual is in terms of meeting the problem objective. Currently there are two multi-objective optimization strategies implemented in the GMT: weight formula and lexicographic analysis. Among various weight formulas tested within the GMT system, the Bayesian information criterion (BIC) [30] has the highest performance with regression and model trees. The BMC is given by:

$$Fit_{BIC}(T) = -2 * ln(L(T)) + ln(n) * k(T), \qquad (3)$$

where $L(T)$ is the maximum of the likelihood function of the tree T, n is the number of observations in the data, and $k(T)$ is the number of model parameters in the tree. The log(likelihood) function $L(T)$ is typical for regression models and can be expressed as:

$$ln(L(T)) = -0.5n * [ln(2\pi) + ln(SS_e(T)/n) + 1], \qquad (4)$$

where $SS_e(T)$ is the sum of squared residuals of the tree T. In this measure of goodness of fit the term $k(T)$ can be viewed as a penalty for over-parametrization. It reflects the tree complexity which for regression trees equals to the number of nodes (denoted as $Q(T)$), where as for model trees it also includes the number of attributes in the linear models in the leaves (denoted as $W(T)$).

When the lexicographic analysis is applied in fitness evaluation, each pair of individuals is analyzed, in order of priorities, one of the measures: $SS_e(T)$, $Q(T)$ and $W(T)$. The first priority is set for the tree accuracy measure, next the number of terminal nodes to prevent overfitting and overgrown trees. The last measure $W(T)$ keeps the models in the leaves as simple as possible and also penalizes for over-parametrization.

The selection mechanism is based on the ranking linear selection [23] with the *elitist strategy*, which copies the best individual founded so far to the next population. Evolution terminates when the fitness of the best individual in the population does not improve during the fixed number of generations (default: 1000). In case of a slow convergence, maximum number of generations is also specified (default value: 10000), which limits the computation time.

3.2 Pareto-Based Approach for GMT

The main goal of the multi-objective optimization is to find a diverse set of Pareto-optimal solutions, which may provide insights into the trade-offs between

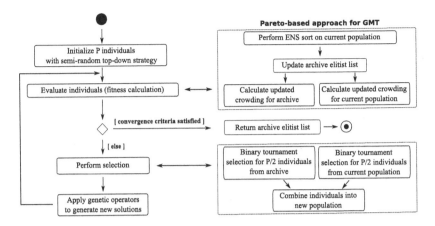

Fig. 1. General GMT schema together with proposed Pareto-based extension.

the objectives. Current GMT fitness functions: weight formula and lexicographic analysis yield only a limited subset of the solutions that may not even belong to the Pareto front.

Multiple EAs were developed to tackle the multi-objective optimization problems, in particular the search for a set of Pareto-optimal solutions [15]. Among various dominance comparison mechanisms, non-dominated sorting genetic algorithm NSGA-II [7] has been shown to be very effective. It showed fast convergence to the Pareto-optimal set, good spread of solutions and became a framework for many future algorithms.

In the GMT system, we have applied the basics of the NSGA-II workflow. Most of the elements like sorting strategy itself, crowding and elitism differ from the NSGA-II algorithm as they were specialized to fit more accurately to the problem of evolutionary model tree induction. Figure 1 shows the general GMT schema together with proposed Pareto-based extension.

In the first step, more recent search strategy called efficient non-dominated sorting strategy (ENS) [31] is applied. The reason why ENS was selected is due to its efficiency. Experimental evaluation of ENS showed that it outperforms other popular non-dominated sorting approaches especially for optimization problems having a small number of objectives which is here the case. The ENS algorithm is conceptually different from most existing non-dominated sorting methods. ENS determines the front each solution belongs to one by one, where typical non-dominated sorting approaches determine the front of all solutions on the same front as a whole. This way ENS avoids duplicate comparisons, since a solution to be assigned only needs to be compared with solutions that have already been assigned to the front.

In the second step of proposed extension (see Fig. 1) the archive fronts are updated. The NGSA-II approach maintains a population size set of non-dominated solutions that is later combined with the next population. However, in case of GMT, where population size is small (50 individuals), many interesting from the decision-maker point of view non-dominated solutions may be lost. Therefore, we have applied different strategy [33] that allows storing all non-dominated solutions investigated so far during the search. Solutions from Pareto front are stored in elitist list, which is updated each time a new solution from the current population dominates one in the list. Although, this operation is more computationally expensive, it is still acceptable as the Pareto front in case of GMT is not very large.

In proposed extension we also have adapted the updated crowding distance procedure [11]. The crowded comparison operator ($\prec_n$) helps ordering (ranking) the solutions. In NSGA-II the crowding-distance is used for diversity preservation and to maintain a well-spread Pareto front. The main improvement of the crowding distance calculation focuses on using unique fitnesses when two or more individuals share identical value. Such case in NSGA-II algorithm causes the crowding distance of the individual to either become null, or to depend on the individuals position within the Pareto front sequence.

Finally, proposed approach differs from NSGA-II in a way of creating a new population. In NSGA-II the archive and current population are merged into new population using the binary tournament as a selection method. Each solution is assigned a rank equals to its non-domination level (1 is the best level, 2 is the next-best level, and so on) and in case of a draw, crowding distance is considered. Due to storing the full list of non-dominated solutions in the archive, we have applied strategy proposed in [16]. We reserve a room for p elitist solutions in the next population (default: half of the population size P). In this strategy, $P - p$ solutions are selected from parents and newly created offspring and p solutions are selected from the stored elitist list. Both sets use the binary tournament as a selection method. The elitist solutions are scored with the crowding distance (as they all belong to a non-dominated set) and the current population is scored like in NSGA-II algorithm.

4   Experimental Validation

In this section, we perform a preliminary validation of proposed Pareto optimal extension. While evolving model trees one can distinguish three objectives that could to be minimized: prediction error measured with Root Mean Squared Error (RMSE), number of nodes and the number of attributes in regression models located in the leaves. The last two objectives are partially depended and may fall under one single-objective denoted as a tree comprehensibility. Thus, in performed experiments we present the results for the fitness function with 2 objectives where number of nodes and the attributes in models is summed; and with 3 objectives where all measures are analyzed separately.

To assess the performance of the proposed approach in solving real-life problems three real-life publicly available datasets from Louis Torgo repository [22] were analyzed: Abalone (4177 instances, 7 real-valued, 1 nominal attribute), Kinematics (8192, 8, 0) and Stock (950, 9, 0). Each dataset was divided into the training (66.6 %) and testing (33.4 %) set. In our experimental validation of

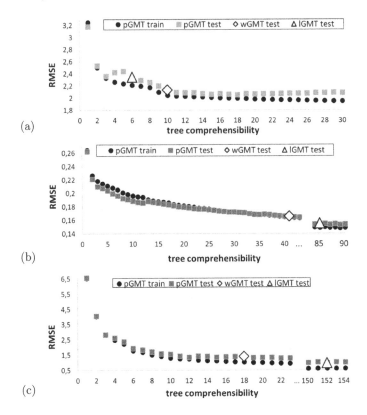

Fig. 2. Pareto front for GMT (pGMT) for 2 objectives on training and testing set of Abalone (a), Kinematics (b) and Stock (c). Results on testing set for GMT with weight (wGMT) and lexicographic (lGMT) fitness functions are also enclosed.

the proposed Pareto GMT (denoted in experiments as pGMT) we also enclosed the results for competitive systems. We have tested GMT with the weight fitness function (wGMT), GMT with the lexicographic fitness function (lGMT) and two popular top-down inducers: REP Tree (RT) that builds a regression tree and state-of-the-art model tree called M5 [27] which is the most adequate greedy counterpart of GMT.

Figure 2 shows the results achieved for the GMT system with different fitness functions. The Pareto front was achieved for bi-objective optimization problem that minimized the RMSE and the tree comprehensibility. One can observe, that for all tested dataset the GMT system with weight or lexicographic fitness functions managed to find non-dominated solutions, as they belong to the Pareto front. However, open question is if the induced trees by wGMT or lGMT will satisfy the decision maker. In case of the results for Abalone dataset (Fig. 2a) both wGMT and lGMT managed to find simple model trees with decent prediction performance. However, if the analyst wants to have slightly more accurate model, he might select trees with higher number of nodes/attributes. Opposite situation is for the Kinematics (wGMT and lGMT) and Stock (lGMT) datasets where they find accurate but complex prediction models which could be difficult to analyze and interpret. Although, the trade-off between prediction performance and tree comprehensibility can be partially managed by ad-hoc settings of the complexity term (wGMT) and thresholds (lGMT), there is no guarantee that founded solutions will belong to the Pareto front. With the proposed Pareto-based approach for GMT the decision maker can easily balance between the tree prediction performance and its comprehensibility, depending on the purpose of the analysis goals.

The Pareto front for three-objective optimization problem is illustrated in Fig. 3. For all datasets, one can see a trend that either induced trees are small but with large number of attributes, either large but with smaller number of the attributes. In all cases, more compact trees have higher prediction performance (smaller RMSE) than larger ones but with simpler models in the leaves. We can also observe, that the lGMT for Kinematics and Stock dataset finds solutions that do not belong to the Pareto front. The three-objective optimization enables obtaining more variants of the output trees, but it can also cause choosing right prediction more difficult.

Table 1 illustrates achieved results for evolutionary induced model trees with different fitness functions as well as popular greedy counterparts of GMT. For all datasets, three metrics are shown: RMSE on the testing set, number of nodes and number of attributes in regression models located in the leaves. One can observe that GMT variants induce much more comprehensible predictors with smaller number of nodes and less complex regression models in the leaves, which was also noticed in [5]. The RT algorithm induces only regression trees, thus the attribute metric does not apply.

In the real-life applications the predictive accuracy is usually considered more important than the comprehensibility of DT. Consider, for instance, two trees: T1 and T2 where T1 has 20 % smaller prediction error but also 20 % larger size. Most of the researches would clearly prefer the T1 over T2; however, the

Table 1. Performance results for evolutionary induced model trees with different fitness functions as well as popular greedy counterparts of GMT. Results for three solutions from the Pareto front (denoted as pGMT *) are also included.

Algorithm	Abalone			Kinematics			Stock		
	RMSE	nodes	attributes	RMSE	nodes	attributes	RMSE	nodes	attributes
wGMT	2.127	2.0	7.92	0.163	7.12	34.32	1.386	3.94	14.17
lGMT	2,341	1.0	5	0.154	9.7	74.5	0.935	41.4	111
M5	2.122	12.0	96	0.162	106	848	0.937	47	423
RT	2.223	291	-	0.194	819	-	1.469	137	-
pGMT 1*	2.359	1	2	0.184	2	13	1.531	3	8
pGMT 2*	2.102	2	9	0.174	4	25	0.928	31	38
pGMT 3*	2.079	3	12	0.149	17	116	0.782	61	121

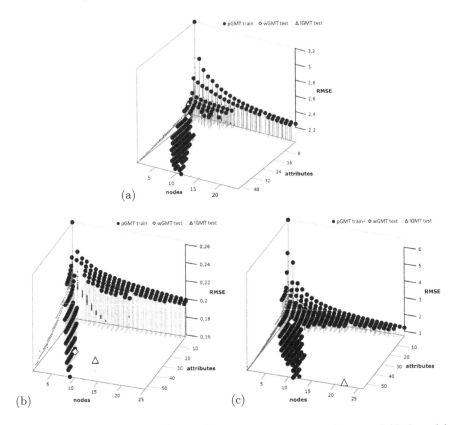

Fig. 3. Pareto front for GMT (pGMT) for 3 objectives on testing set of Abalone (a), Kinematics (b) and Stock (c). Results on testing set for GMT with weight (wGMT) and lexicographic (lGMT) fitness functions are also enclosed.

Pareto approach would consider that none of these two trees dominates the other. Therefore, in context of DT and the Pareto front, the weights preferences could be introduced to the multi-objective optimization [12].

5   Conclusion and Future Works

In the paper we propose a new fitness function to evolutionary induced regression and model trees. Preliminary experiments showed that our approach is capable of finding Pareto front for the GMT framework. Its a first step towards searching for efficient and easy to interpret Pareto optimal DTs. There are, however; still many open issues that need more research and clarification.

The impact of this new multi-objective optimization on the GMT performance need to be analyzed more deeply. The proposed approach increases the calculation time of each evolutionary loop and may affect the convergence of the EA. Additional efficiency improvements, especially in context of storing and preprocessing full list of non-dominated solutions need to be considered. Performance issue may also be partially mitigated with parallelization of the GPGPU approach for GMT [18].

Next issue that need to be resolved is the comprehensibility of the generated Pareto front. Currently, due to the size of the front and the number of possible trees, the decision maker may have problem to decide which predictor he should choose. Thus, more research need to be performed in context of limiting the output elitist front as well as improving the crowding function with aforementioned weights.

Acknowledgments. This project was funded by the Polish National Science Center and allocated on the basis of decision 2013/09/N/ST6/04083. The second author was supported by the grant S/WI/2/13 from Bialystok University of Technology founded by Ministry of Science and Higher Education.

References

1. Barros, R.C., Ruiz, D.D., Basgalupp, M.P.: Evolutionary model trees for handling continuous classes in machine learning. Inf. Sci. **181**(5), 954–971 (2011)
2. Barros, R.C., Basgalupp, M.P., de Carvalho, A.C.P.L.F., Freitas, A.A.: A survey of evolutionary algorithms for decision-tree induction. IEEE Trans. Syst. Man Cybern. Part C **42**(3), 291–312 (2012)
3. Breiman, L., Friedman, J., Olshen, R., Stone, C.: Classification and Regression Trees. Wadsworth and Brooks, Monterey (1984)
4. Czajkowski, M., Czerwonka, M., Kretowski, M.: Cost-sensitive global model trees applied to loan charge-off forecasting. Decis. Support Syst. **74**, 57–66 (2015)
5. Czajkowski, M., Kretowski, M.: Evolutionary induction of global model trees with specialized operators and memetic extensions. Inf. Sci. **288**, 153–173 (2014)
6. Czajkowski, M., Kretowski, M.: The role of decision tree representation in regression problems - an evolutionary perspective. Appl. Soft Comput. **48**, 458–475 (2016)
7. Deb, K., Pratap, A., Agarwal, S., Meyarivan, T.: A fast and elitist multiobjective genetic algorithm: NSGA-II. IEEE Trans. Evol. Comp. **6**(2), 182–197 (2002)
8. Esposito, F., Malerba, D., Semeraro, G.: A comparative analysis of methods for pruning decision trees. IEEE Trans. Pattern Anal. Mach. Intell. **19**(5), 476–491 (1997)
9. Fan, G., Gray, B.J.: Regression tree analysis using TARGET. J. Comput. Graph. Stat. **14**(1), 206–218 (2005)
10. Fayyad, U.M., Piatetsky-Shapiro, G., Smyth, P., Uthurusamy, R. (eds.): Advances in Knowledge Discovery and Data Mining. American Association for Artificial Intelligence, Menlo Park (1996)
11. Fortin, F.A., Parizeau, M.: Revisiting the nsga-ii crowding-distance computation. In: Proceedings of the 15th Annual Conference on Genetic and Evolutionary Computation, pp. 623–630. GECCO 2013. ACM, New York, NY, USA (2013)
12. Friedrich, T., Kroeger, T., Neumann, F.: Weighted preferences in evolutionary multi-objective optimization. Int. J. Mach. Learn. Cybern. **4**(2), 139–148 (2013)
13. Guzman, F.M.O., Valenzuela, O., Prieto, B., Saéz-Lara, M.J., Torres, C., Pomares, H., et al.: Comparing different machine learning and mathematical regression models to evaluate multiple sequence alignments. Neurocomputing **164**, 123–136 (2015)

14. Hazan, A., Ramirez, R., Maestre, E., Perez, A., Pertusa, A.: Modelling expressive performance: a regression tree approach based on strongly typed genetic programming. In: Rothlauf, F., et al. (eds.) EvoWorkshops 2006. LNCS, vol. 3907, pp. 676–687. Springer, Heidelberg (2006). doi:10.1007/11732242_64

15. Hiwa, S., Nishioka, M., Hiroyasu, T., Miki, M.: Novel search scheme for multi-objective evolutionary algorithms to obtain well-approximated and widely spread pareto solutions. Swarm Evol. Comput. **22**, 30–46 (2015). (Complete)

16. Ishibuchi, H., Murata, T.: A multi-objective genetic local search algorithm and its application to flowshop scheduling. IEEE Trans. Syst. Man Cybern. Part C **28**(3), 392–403 (1998). (Applications and Reviews)

17. Jin, Y., Sendhoff, B.: Pareto-based multiobjective machine learning: An overview and case studies. IEEE Trans. Syst. Man Cybern. Part C **38**(3), 397–415 (2008)

18. Jurczuk, K., Czajkowski, M., Kretowski, M.: Evolutionary induction of a decision tree for large scale data. a GOU-based approach. Soft Comput. doi:10.1007/s00500-016-2280-1 (in press, 2016)

19. Kim, D.E.: Structural risk minimization on decision trees using an evolutionary multiobjective optimization. In: Keijzer, M., O'Reilly, U.-M., Lucas, S., Costa, E., Soule, T. (eds.) EuroGP 2004. LNCS, vol. 3003, pp. 338–348. Springer, Heidelberg (2004). doi:10.1007/978-3-540-24650-3_32

20. Kotsiantis, S.B.: Decision trees: a recent overview. Artif. Intell. Rev. **39**(4), 261–283 (2013)

21. Loh, W.Y.: Fifty years of classification and regression trees. Int. Stat. Rev. **82**(3), 329–348 (2014)

22. Louis, T.: Regression data sets (2016). http://www.dcc.fc.up.pt/ltorgo/Regression/DataSets.html

23. Michalewicz, Z.: Genetic Algorithms + Data Structures = Evolution Programs, 2nd edn. Springer-Verlag, New York (1994)

24. Pangilinan, J., Janssens, G.: Pareto-optimality of oblique decision trees from evolutionary algorithms. J. Global Optim. **51**(2), 301–311 (2011)

25. Pappalardo, M.: Multiobjective optimization: a brief overview. In: Chinchuluun, A., Pardalos, P.M., Migdalas, A., Pitsoulis, L. (eds.) Pareto Optimality, Game Theory And Equilibria. Springer Optimization and Its Applications, vol. 17, pp. 517–528. Springer, Heidelberg (2008)

26. Potgieter, G., Engelbrecht, A.P.: Evolving model trees for mining data sets with continuous-valued classes. Expert Syst. Appl. **35**(4), 1513–1532 (2008)

27. Quinlan, J.R.: Learning with continuous classes. Proc. Aust. Joint Conf. Artif. Intell. **92**, 343–348 (1992). World Scientific, Singapore

28. Rokach, L., Maimon, O.: Top-down induction of decision trees classifiers - a survey. Trans. Sys. Man Cyber Part C **35**(4), 476–487 (2005)

29. Rokach, L., Maimon, O.: Data Mining with Decision Trees: Theroy and Applications. World Scientific Publishing Co. Inc., River Edge (2008)

30. Schwarz, G.: Estimating the dimension of a model. Ann. Statist. **6**(2), 461–464 (1978)

31. Zhang, X., Tian, Y., Cheng, R., Jin, Y.: An efficient approach to nondominated sorting for evolutionary multiobjective optimization. IEEE Trans. Evol. Comput. **19**(2), 201–213 (2015)

32. Zhao, H.: A multi-objective genetic programming approach to developing pareto optimal decision trees. Decis. Support Syst. **43**(3), 809–826 (2007)

33. Zitzler, E., Thiele, L.: Multiobjective evolutionary algorithms: A comparative case study and the strength pareto approach. IEEE Trans. Evol. Comp. **3**(4), 257–271 (1999)

A Sampling-Based Metaheuristic
for the Orienteering Problem with Stochastic
Travel Times

Vassilis Papapanagiotou, Roberto Montemanni[✉],
and Luca Maria Gambardella

IDSIA, Dalle Molle Institute for Artificial Intelligence, USI-SUPSI,
Manno-Lugano, Switzerland
{vassilis,roberto,luca}@idsia.ch

Abstract. In this paper we propose a new metaheuristic approach based on sampling for the Orienteering Problem with Stochastic Travel Times (OPSTS). As in many Stochastic Combinatorial Optimization Problems, the computational bottleneck of OPSTS is in the objective function evaluation. For this reason, this study is mainly devoted to the development and integration of on-purpose, sampling-based fast objective function evaluations into metaheuristic methods. In details, we show how a Variable Neighbourhood Search Metaheuristic can be enhanced by adopting such evaluators. Experimental results show that the new sampling-based method is faster than conventional methods for the given problem, and the improvement is particularly relevant for large-scale instances.

Keywords: Hybrid metaheuristics · Orienteering Problem with Stochastic Travel and Service Times · Variable Neighbourhood Search

1 Introduction

The Orienteering Problem with Stochastic Travel and Service Times is a Stochastic Combinatorial Optimization Problem (SCOP) where the objective is to select a subset of nodes to serve before a global deadline. When we serve a node as planned we get a reward, otherwise a penalty is incurred. Because part of OPSTS is to solve the Travelling Salesman Problem (TSP) a well-known NP-hard problem, OPSTS is also NP-hard. Because of its stochasticity, it's also very time consuming to find good quality solutions or even to compute the objective function. That is the reason that we resort to metaheuristics in order to achieve some good quality near-optimal solutions in a reasonable amount of time. Metaheuristics are general purpose methods for finding sufficiently good solutions but not necessarily optimal for hard optimization problems [18].

V. Papapanagiotou—Supported by the Swiss National Science Foundation through project 200020-156259/1: "Hybrid Sampling-based Metaheuristics for Stochastic Optimization Problems with Deadlines".

C. Martín-Vide et al. (Eds.): TPNC 2016, LNCS 10071, pp. 97–109, 2016.
DOI: 10.1007/978-3-319-49001-4_8

One of the most important components of any algorithm is the objective function which measures the quality of each solution produced. In OPSTS, as in other combinatorial optimization problems, the objective function is the most frequently called function of the algorithm. Furthermore, the objective function of Stochastic Combinatorial Optimization Problems (SCOPs) is usually either hard to compute as in [21] or very time consuming as in OPSTS. Therefore, it is well worth optimizing it.

The state-of-the art methods for many SCOPs use Monte Carlo Sampling to deal with the intricacies that SCOPs' objective functions introduce. Example of using sampling-based metaheuristics for SCOPs include [20] for the Stochastic Traveling Salesman Problem; [9,11,13], for the OPSTS, and [7] for the Mobile Facility Routing and Scheduling Problem. However, for OPSTS Monte Carlo Sampling tends to have large sampling error for particular parts of each solution [9,11] (see Sect. 4 for more details). To deal with this problem, we may combine analytical, sampling and deterministic evaluators for the objective function. These combinations produce different speed and error benefits. These characteristics of the hybrid evaluators like the ones proposed in [11] have positive effects in the quality of the final solutions found by metaheuristics.

In this paper, we consider novel hybrid sampling-based evaluators of the objective function of OPSTS and we design new experiments to examine their performance when coupled with a metaheuristic approach. Furthermore, we produce and test our metaheuristics on new large-scale datasets.

In Sect. 2 of the paper we examine the related work in the literature of SCOPs and OPSTS, in Sects. 3 and 4 we define the problem and the objective function evaluators. In Sect. 5 we examine the metaheuristic used. In Sect. 6, we present our experimental design and results, in Sect. 7 we state the conclusions of the paper.

2   Related Work

This section gives an overview of the state-of-the-art methods for approximating the objective functions of Stochastic Combinatorial Optimization Problems (SCOPS) using Monte Carlo Sampling.

There have been contributions in the Ant Colony Optimization domain. For example, in [5] the authors introduce the first Ant Colony System based on sampling. An application of S-ACO in a policy optimization problem in healthcare management can be found in [15]. S-ACO was further improved by ACO/F-Race proposed by Birattari et al. in [2] by combining S-ACO with a so called race algorithm. It is then applied to the Probabilistic Travelling Salesman problem.

In the Evolutionary Algorithms field, Yoshitomi and Yamaguchi [22] use a Genetic Algorithm for solving the stochastic job-shop scheduling problem. In their works the final solution is selected from the set of frequently visited solutions. An ant colony metaheuristic hybridized with local search and Monte Carlo sampling together an analytical approximation of the objective function can be found in Weyland et al. [19].

As far as the Orienteering Problem is concerned, an extensive survey can be found in [14]. The Orienteering Problem with Stochastic Travel and Service Times (OPSTS) treated in this paper was introduced in [3]. In that paper, the authors study special versions of the problem that can be solved optimally and present a Variable Neighborhood Search heuristic for the general problem.

Recently, Monte Carlo Sampling has been used to accelerate the computation of the objective function of the mobile facility routing and scheduling problem [7]. Additionally, hybrid evaluators for the OPSTS have been studied in isolation (without coupling them with any particular algorithm) in [9,11,12].

3   Problem Definition

In this section, we give the formal definition of OPSTS as it was introduced in [3].

We denote $N = \{1, \ldots, n\}$ a set of n customers with the depot being node 0. In OPSTS the aim of the problem is to select $M \subseteq N$, with M representing the set of customers to be served. There is a global deadline D for serving customers without a penalty. We assume that the graph is full and therefore there is an arc (i, j) for all $i, j \in M$. Servicing a customer $i \in M$ before the deadline results in a reward r_i otherwise a penalty e_i is incurred. Let $X_{i,j}$ be a non-negative random variable representing the travel time from node i to node j and S_i a random variable representing the service time of customer i. It is assumed that we know the probability distribution of $X_{i,j}$ $\forall i, j$ and that the service time S_i for the ith customer follows the same distribution as $X_{i-1,i}$ and can be added to the travel time $X_{i-1,i}$ and therefore need not be considered separately. In the experiments presented in Sect. 6, the probability distribution of the random variables will be a Γ distribution, for consistency with previous work [3]. Let the random variable A_i be the arrival time at customer i and $\bar{A}_i$ a realization of A_i. Now let $R(\bar{A}_i)$ be a function representing the reward earned at customer i when arriving to i at time $\bar{A}_i$. According to our definitions $R(\bar{A}_i) = r_i$ for $\bar{A}_i \leq D$, otherwise $R(\bar{A}_i) = -e_i$ (for $\bar{A}_i$).

A tour of the customers τ is defined as a sequence of customers $\in M$. The objective function of the problem is defined as the expected profit of the tour:

$$u(\tau) = \sum_{i \in \tau} [P(A_i \leq D)r_i - (1 - P(A_i \leq D))e_i] \qquad (1)$$

4   Objective Function Evaluators

As previously mentioned, in OPSTS the bottleneck of the computation when using metaheuristics is the objective function evaluation. By accelerating such a computation, while trying to preserve the approximation error low, we have several advantages including finding better solutions in a fixed amount of time and being able to apply metaheuristics on large datasets. In this section we present some evaluators that approximate the objective function of OPSTS in a fast way. The interested reader is referred to [11] for more insight and experimental evaluation of the different methods.

Analytical Evaluator (ANALYTICAL). This evaluator, which is used as our reference evaluator for the objective function of OPSTS is derived analytically from the expression of the objective function (1) and it is the one used in [3]. In the following we make the same assumptions as in [3] that the travel times $X_{i,j}$ are Γ distributed.

We let A_i be the arrival time at the node i. A_i will be the sum of the travel times $X_{j,k}$ of all (j, k) edges in the path from the depot to i. Since travel times are Γ distributed, A_i is the sum of Γ distributed variables. In [6], we can see an important property for our derivation, namely if Y_i follows a $\Gamma(k_i, \theta)$ distribution for $i = 1, 2, \cdots, N$ and all Y_i are independent then $\sum_{i=1}^{N}(Y_i) \sim \Gamma(\sum_{i=1}^{N}(k_i, \theta)$. This is the main property so that we can derive our analytical evaluator, and the same derivation can hold for other distributions if this property holds. By using this property, A_i can be approximated by the Γ function of the sum of all the travel times of all nodes j (k_j) before node i. We assume that $F_{k_i}(D)$ is the Cumulative Distribution Function (CDF) of A_i until the deadline D. In other words it is the probability that customer i is visited before the deadline ($P(A_i \leq D)$). To obtain k_i we sum all the arrival times k_j of the nodes on the path from the depot to i. Therefore now (1) can be computed in a closed form as follows:

$$u(\tau) = \sum_{i \in \tau}[F_{k_i}(D)r_i - (1 - F_{k_i}(D))e_i]$$

The analytical evaluator performance depends on the underlying distribution. In our paper the Γ distribution is used in order to compare with the seminal paper. In general, approximating distributions analytically will involve computation of integrals numerically, which usually can be outperformed by Monte Carlo techniques. For some distributions we might not even be able to derive an analytical approximation.

Monte Carlo Evaluator (MC). To compute the objective function (1) we must be able to compute $P(A_i \leq D)$. In this method we do it by using Monte Carlo Sampling. Firstly, we generate many different fully connected graphs (*scenarios*) with travel times – and consequently arrival times $\bar{A}_i$ at each node i – sampled according to the given travel time probability distributions. When a solution has to be evaluated, MC method computes the deterministic objective value of the solution for several scenarios (sampled according to the given distribution for travel times) and returns the average of the values of all the computations. The bottleneck of the MC method is the generation of random numbers of a specific distribution. To accelerate the procedure of Monte Carlo evaluation, many sample of travel times from every node to every other node are precomputed (*scenarios*). Each sample in the precomputation is a matrix with cells that represent a realization of a random variable $X_{i,j}$. Such a precomputation matrix can be seen in Fig. 1. These samples are reused for all the running time of the algorithm in our implementation. So, after the precomputation phase, we compute the objective function as described previously.

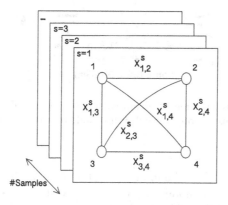

Fig. 1. Precomputed Samples. Each sample is a fully connected graph with realizations of the arrival times according to their given distribution.

MC-ANALYTICAL-MC Evaluator (M-A-M). We now consider those nodes that in a solution are visited in the temporal proximity of the deadline. We call the set of these nodes "the deadline area". When the MC evaluator is used, these nodes are visited on time in some scenarios and too late in others. Since rewards and penalties are normally not symmetric (e.g. penalty $<<$ reward), this may cause creation and propagation of errors in the objective function evaluator. If for example an evaluator considers falsely that a node is not visited on time on average then this node will contribute a penalty instead of a reward and the same is true for all the subsequent nodes until the first that is visited after the deadline on average in reality. In Fig. 2 we can see how the error propagates. In this example "MC Deadline Node" is the node where the Monte Carlo evaluator estimates the deadline will occur while it occurs on the "Deadline Node". For the nodes from "MC Deadline Node" to "Deadline Node", the evaluator wrongly assigns a penalty, resulting in computing an objective value of 0 in the end instead of 16.

In order to avoid these errors that can be big, we evaluate these nodes using the ANALYTICAL method. To define the deadline area we select a factor $\alpha (0 < \alpha < 1)$ and then we include all the nodes with deterministic travel times betweeen $[(1-\alpha)D, (1+\alpha)D]$. The other nodes (non critical) are evaluated using Monte Carlo Sampling. we refer to such an hybrid evaluator as MC-ANALYTICAL-MC (M-A-M).

REWARD-MC-ANALYTICAL-MC-PENALTY Evaluator (R-M-A-M-P). R-M-A-M-P further enhances the speed of M-A-M previously introduced by assuming that nodes very far from the deadline area with very high probability will gain reward or induce penalty. Therefore, in a similar manner with the deadline area, it defines the reward area and the penalty area where the nodes get reward and penalty respectively without any computation. To define the R-M-A-M-P areas we need as in M-A-M the factor α and also the factor

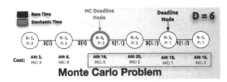

Fig. 2. Example of propagation of errors when using Monte Carlo Sampling. Monte Carlo evaluator estimates wrongly the deadline node resulting in wrong objective value estimation.

$\rho(\alpha \leq \rho \leq 1)$. The nodes in the interval $[0, (1 - \rho)D)$ are in the REWARD area and get a reward and the nodes in $[(1 + \rho)D, +\infty]$ (where $+\infty$ is the last node of the solution) are in the PENALTY area and get a penalty. As in M-A-M the nodes in $[(1 - \alpha)D, (1 + \alpha)D]$ are evaluated using the ANALYTICAL method and the rest of the nodes are evaluated using Monte Carlo sampling. R-M-A-M-P provides us with fine-grained control and it normally outperforms M-A-M (at the price of an extra parameter to be tuned).

REWARD-Analytical-PENALTY Evaluator (R-A-P). This evaluator is a simplification of R-M-A-M-P and can act as a baseline evaluator as no stochasticity is involved. Similarly to M-A-M we define a factor $\alpha(0 < \eta < 1)$ and the nodes in $[(1 - \eta)D, (1 + \eta)D]$ are evaluated using the ANALYTICAL method. The ones before the deadline area are in the REWARD area and the ones after are in the penalty area. Although this evaluator was defined as a baseline evaluator for experimental reasons, it was found that it performs really well in the cases where the deadline occurs rarely and a small analytical part is enough to keep the error low.

5   A Variable Neighborhood Search Metaheuristic

We use Variable Neighborhood Search as a metaheuristic to compare it with the seminal paper of OPSTS [3], where the VNS metaheuristic used only the ANALYTICAL evaluator and here for the first time, we present its performance when we incorporate other evaluators. VNS was first proposed by [8] and an application to the orienteering problem can be found here [17]. The basic idea is to try to escape local minima by changing search neighborhoods. The algorithm has two phases the shaking phase and the local search phase. When it is in the shaking phase, a given solution is perturbed and it is used for exploration and in the local search phase, the solution from the shaking phase is improved contributing to the exploitation of the search space. As a local search phase a variable neighborhood descent (VND) is used. In the VND, a specific neighborhood is searched until no improving solution can be found and then it proceeds to do the same thing with every avilable neighborhood. The neighborhoods used are the ones used in [3], first suggested by [4] and namely resequencing the route using 1-shift, replacing a customer on the route with one not on the route, adding a customer on the route, deleting a customer from the route and the ruin and recreate neighborhood from [16]. More specifically, the ruin and recreate heuristic, removes $\lfloor \frac{nk}{10} \rfloor$ nodes where n is the number of nodes of the current tour and k is the current iteration of VNS. We then add random nodes not previously on the tour. For full implementation details one should consult [3].

6   Experimental Results

In this section, we study the performance of metaheuristics when they incorporate the proposed evaluators. The evaluators are tuned and then we observe their effect on the metaheuristics and we compare the metaheuristics.

6.1   Dataset Generation

The Orienteering Problem with Stochastic Travel and Service Times occasionally needs to be applied in problems that have potentially thousands of nodes, like the selection of tourist destinations to visit in a Country over a long horizon [14] or the production scheduling applications in manufacturing (for example the steel rolling mill problem described in [1]). To test our methodology, we generated four datasets with thousands of nodes. This also benefits our experimental conclusions since smaller datasets tend to be trivial to solve, and the benefits of faster evaluators are therefore less appreciable. We generated datasets of 1000, 1800, 2500 nodes as follows: we assume a square with a diagonal of 1000, 1800, 2500 units respectively, and nodes are placed uniformly in both coordinates. Hamming distance is considered for baseline traveltimes, and random rewards from 1 to 100 are considered., penalties being 0.1 of the reward of each node. Given the instance, different deadlines will be set for the experiments. The datasets are made available to other interested researcher in the online addendum [10].

6.2   Experimental Design

In our previous work [11], we have presented ways to tune the evaluators in isolation so that they have a small average error. In most datasets R-M-A-M-P was able to perform the best under the error constraint, while in one dataset where the deadline was not reached often, R-A-P performed the best. Additionally, in an earlier paper [12] we had shown some evidence embedding the hybrid evaluator MC-ANALYTICAL-MC in a metaheuristic approach could yield better results than state-of-the-art evaluation approaches. In all our previous work, the original datasets of 21, 32, 33, 64, 66 customers were used as presented in the original OPSTS paper [3]. However, as discussed in Sect. 6.1, these small datasets tend to hide the advantages of our methods, so in this paper, motivated by real applications [1,14], we here extend the study to new larger datasets.

In these experiments, we try to answer several questions so that we investigate further the usefulness of the proposed objective function evaluators. The

Table 1. Final parameter tunings - VNS metaheuristic.

Instance	1000	1000	1000	1000	1800	1800	1800	1800	2500	2500	2500	2500
Deadline	500	1000	1500	2000	500	1000	1500	2000	500	1000	1500	2000
Area Ratio	0.8	0.1	0.1	0.1	0.8	0.1	0.1	0.1	0.8	0.1	0.1	0.1
RP Ratio	0.9	0.2	0.2	0.2	0.9	0.2	0.2	0.2	0.9	0.2	0.2	0.2

main investigation is about the evaluators performance and how different evaluators with different configurations (area ratio and reward-penalty ratio) affect the final metaheuristics solution found, as time progresses. To answer these questions with a limited number of experiments we conducted full factorial experiments with area ratio taking values of 0.1, 0.8, reward-penalty ratio values 0.2, 0.9 (where applicable), the objective function evaluator being one of ANALYTICAL, MC, M-A-M, R-M-A-M-P, R-A-P, metaheuristics being one the Variable Neighbourhood Search.

We executed the metaheuristic for 10 min and sample the value found every 10 s. We run the different methods for the datasets with 1000, 1800, 2500, 4000 customers with deadlines set at 500, 1000, 1500 and 2000. For each run we recorded the instance, the metaheuristic used, the objective function evaluator used, the deadline, the area ratio used, the reward penalty ratio used, the runtime, the number of evaluations and the best solution found. We also recorded information specific to each metaheuristic such as which heuristics ran and which one found better solutions. From this information we were able to analyze several characteristics of the methods and answer several research questions.

All experiments have been carried out on a Quad-Core AMD Opteron 2350 processor running at 2.0 GHz with 32 GB of RAM. Only one core was used in each run. The algorithms were coded in C++.

6.3   Parameters Tuning

The performance of the evaluators in the metaheuristics depends on the tuning of their parameters. The effects of the parameters when the evaluators are tested in isolation have been studied before in [11]. In this work we used a slightly different method to tune the parameters. In order to see the effects of Area Ratio and Reward-Penalty area ratio (RP ratio) and select the values for our application, we embedded the evaluators in the metaheuristic and we run it for 30 times for each evaluator, deadline and each area ratio and RP ratio considered. The full results for this can be seen in the online addendum [10]. We used the values emerging from this tuning campaign in the rest of the experiments presented in this paper. The final tuning results are here summarized in Table 1 for ease of consultation.

6.4   Speed of the Evaluators Inside VNS

One of the important factors for finding good solutions is to be able to examine more solutions in a fixed runtime. Notice that in this section we deliberately neglige approximation quality and we only concentrate on pure speed. A complementary analysis, focusing on approximation quality will be presented in Sect. 6.5.

In Tables 2 and 3 we can see pairwise t-tests for the number of evaluations for runtimes of 10, 20, 30, 40 seconds for all evaluators for the VNS metaheuristic for 1000 and 2500 nodes. The values in bold are $p < 0.05$ and it means that the method in the row is statistically significantly faster (achieves more evaluations at the same time).

We can observe that in all cases the proposed evaluators are faster than the conventional ANALYTICAL evaluator and in most of them they are also *significantly* faster. Also, R-M-A-M-P is very competitive in speed, being significantly faster than the others in most cases, being outperformed (in terms of pure speed) only to R-A-P in some cases. However, speed is not the definitive factor, since accuracy is also very important. As we will see, R-M-A-M-P tends to outperform the other evaluators in most cases, despite not being always the fastest one, due to its low error.

Table 2. Pairwise one-tailed t-tests p-values for all deadlines. The highlighted ones mean that the method in the row achieves statistically significantly more evaluations than the one in the column - 1000 nodes, VNS metaheuristic.

	ANALYTICAL	MAM	MC	RAP
MAM	**3.25E-62**			
MC	**5.79E-03**	1.00E+00		
RAP	**1.26E-128**	**6.28E-22**	**2.34E-110**	
RMAMP	**0.00E+00**	**0.00E+00**	**0.00E+00**	**3.03E-264**

Table 3. Pairwise one-tailed t-tests p-values for all deadlines. The highlighted ones mean that the method in the row achieves statistically significantly more evaluations than the one in the column - 2500 nodes, VNS metaheuristic.

	ANALYTICAL	MAM	MC	RAP
MAM	**6.64E-05**			
MC	3.31E-01	1.00E+00		
RAP	**2.00E-176**	**1.06E-171**	**6.63E-176**	
RMAMP	**4.77E-62**	**1.06E-49**	**1.07E-60**	1.00E+00

6.5   Quality of the Solutions Retrieved by the Evaluators Inside VNS

In Fig. 3 we can see the evolution of the objective function values of the best solutions retrieved by the VNS metaheuristic for the dataset with 1000 nodes over the course of 10 min (deadline 2000). We can observe that the solution quality when R-M-A-M-P is in use, is consistently better than that of any other evaluator. The second better evaluator is M-A-M and the third better R-A-P. We also observe that R-M-A-M-P, M-A-M and R-A-P continue to improve while ANALYTICAL and MC soon reach a plateau (stagnation).

When VNS uses R-M-A-M-P, R-A-P and M-A-M, the quality of the best solutions is not monotonically increasing. This is due to approximation errors: in the charts we report the objective value of each solution evaluated with the ANALYTICAL evaluator. Therefore, when an objective value appears to get worse then a previous one, this indicates that the respective evaluator made an approximation error of such a solution and (erroneously) accepted it as a better solution. It is interesting to notice how such a phenomenon seems to improve the performance of the VNS, introducing a behavior apparently useful to exit local minima. For further results one can consult the online addendum [10]. The results are however aligned with those presented.

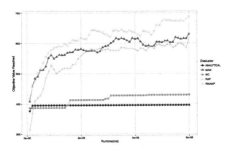

Fig. 3. Best objective function value vs Runtime, Deadline: 2000–1000 nodes, VNS metaheuristic.

In Table 4 we can see a pairwise one-sided t-test (the p-values) for the final objective values for deadline 2000, reached by VNS for the datasets of 1800 nodes when using the respective evaluators. We consider something statistically significantly better if $p < 0.05$. The values in bold mean that if we incorporate in VNS the evaluator in the row we will get a significantly better objective value than if we incorporate the evaluator in the column. Evaluators M-A-M and R-M-A-M-P are significantly better than ANALYTICAL, and all evaluators are significantly better than MC. Finally, R-M-A-M-P appears better than M-A-M, although the significance threshold is not reached. Similar patterns – sometimes showing an even stronger dominance by R-M-A-M-P – can be seen for all other deadlines and datasets in the online addendum [10].

To conclude, it appears that the proposed objective function evaluators have great impact on non-trivial metaheuristics such as the VNS we consider, since their characteristics and most notably speed and accuracy are useful to drive the metaheuristic in different neighbourhoods, leading to an overall better exploration of the search space.

Table 4. Pairwise one-tailed t-test for final objective value reached by each evaluator for deadline 2000. Values $p < 0.05$ mean that a statistically significantly better objective value is reached - 1800 nodes, VNS metaheuristic.

	ANALYTICAL	MAM	MC	RAP
MAM	**4.14E-04**			
MC	1.00E+00	1.00E+00		
RAP	1.62E-01	9.93E-01	**1.26E-09**	
RMAMP	**3.91E-04**	4.93E-01	**9.25E-14**	**6.62E-03**

7   Conclusions

In this paper, we investigated sampling-based metaheuristics with hybrid objective function evaluators for the Orienteering Problem with Stochastic Travel and Service Times. We saw that by using hybrid objective function evaluators inside a Variable Neighbourhood Search metaheuristic, better solutions can be obtained in a given amount of time. This is due mainly to two factors, namely the dramatic increase of speed guaranteed by sampling-based objective function evaluators, and a higher capability of the metaheuristic to explore the search space, the latter factor being a side-effect of the use of approximated evaluators. As a future work, it remains to show that similar results are achieved by the proposed evaluators inside other metaheuristics.

References

1. Balas, E.: The prize collecting traveling salesman problem: Ii. polyhedral results. Networks **25**(4), 199–216 (1995). http://dx.doi.org/10.1002/net.3230250406
2. Birattari, M., Balaprakash, P., Dorigo, M.: The ACO/F-race algorithm for combinatorial optimization under uncertainty. In: Doerner, K.F., Gendreau, M., Greistorfer, P., Gutjahr, W., Hartl, R.F., Reimann, M. (eds.) Metaheuristics. Operations Research/Computer Science Interfaces Series, vol. 39, pp. 189–203. Springer, Heidelberg (2007)
3. Campbell, A., Gendreau, M., Thomas, B.: The orienteering problem with stochastic travel and service times. Ann. Oper. Res. **186**, 61–81 (2011)

4. Feillet, D., Dejax, P., Gendreau, M.: Traveling salesman problems with profits. Transp. Sci. **39**(2), 188–205 (2005)
5. Gutjahr, W.J.: S-ACO: an ant-based approach to combinatorial optimization under uncertainty. In: Dorigo, M., Birattari, M., Blum, C., Gambardella, L.M., Mondada, F., Stützle, T. (eds.) ANTS 2004. LNCS, vol. 3172, pp. 238–249. Springer, Heidelberg (2004). doi:10.1007/978-3-540-28646-2_21
6. Johnson, N.L., Kotz, S., Balakrishnan, N.: Continuous Multivariate Distributions, vol. 1, Models and Applications, vol. 59. New York: John Wiley & Sons (2002)
7. Lei, C., Lin, W., Miao, L.: A multicut l-shaped based algorithm to solve a stochastic programming model for the mobile facility routing and scheduling problem. Eur. J. Oper. Res. **238**(3), 699–710 (2014)
8. Mladenović, N., Hansen, P.: Variable neighborhood search. Comput. Oper. Res. **24**(11), 1097–1100 (1997)
9. Papapanagiotou, V., Montemanni, R., Gambardella, L.: Objective function evaluation methods for the orienteering problem with stochastic travel and service times. J. Appl. Oper. Res. **6**(1), 16–29 (2014)
10. Papapanagiotou, V., Montemanni, R., Gambardella, L.: Further results for opsts, caor (2015). http://people.idsia.ch/~papapanagio/
11. Papapanagiotou, V., Montemanni, R., Gambardella, L.: Hybrid sampling-based evaluators for the orienteering problem with stochastic travel and service times. J. Traffic Logistics Eng. **3**(2), 1–25 (2015)
12. Papapanagiotou, V., Montemanni, R., Gambardella, L.: Sampling-based objective function evaluation techniques for the orienteering problem with stochastic travel and service times. German Oper. Res. Soc. (GOR) (to appear)
13. Papapanagiotou, V., Weyland, D., Montemanni, R., Gambardella, L.: A sampling-based approximation of the objective function of the orienteering problem with stochastic travel and service times. In: 5th International Conference on Applied Operational Research, Proceedings, Lecture Notes in Management Science, pp. 143–152 (2013)
14. Vansteenwegen, P., Souffriau, W., Oudheusden, D.: The orienteering problem: A survey. Eur. J. Oper. Res. **209**(1), 1–10 (2011). http://www.sciencedirect.com/science/article/pii/S0377221710002973
15. Rauner, M., Gutjahr, W., Brailsford, S., Zeppelzauer, W.: Optimal screening policies for diabetic retinopathy using a combined discrete-event simulation and ant colony optimization approach (2005)
16. Schrimpf, G., Schneider, J., Stamm-Wilbrandt, H., Dueck, G.: Record breaking optimization results using the ruin and recreate principle. J. Comput. Phys. **159**(2), 139–171 (2000)
17. Sevkli, Z., Sevilgen, F.E.: Variable neighborhood search for the orienteering problem. In: Levi, A., Savaş, E., Yenigün, H., Balcısoy, S., Saygın, Y. (eds.) ISCIS 2006. LNCS, vol. 4263, pp. 134–143. Springer, Heidelberg (2006). doi:10.1007/11902140_16
18. Spall, J.: Introduction to stochastic search and optimization: estimation, simulation, and control, vol. 65. John Wiley & Sons (2005)
19. Weyland, D., Bianchi, L., Gambardella, L.: New heuristics for the probabilistic traveling salesman problem. In: Proceedings of the VIII Metaheuristic International Conference (MIC 2009) (2009)

20. Weyland, D., Montemanni, R., Gambardella, L.: Heuristics for the probabilistic traveling salesman problem with deadlines based on quasi-parallel monte carlo sampling, submitted for publication (2011)
21. Weyland, D., Montemanni, R., Gambardella, L.M.: Hardness results for the probabilistic traveling salesman problem with deadlines. In: Mahjoub, A.R., Markakis, V., Milis, I., Paschos, V.T. (eds.) ISCO 2012. LNCS, vol. 7422, pp. 392–403. Springer, Heidelberg (2012). doi:10.1007/978-3-642-32147-4_35
22. Yoshitomi, Y., Yamaguchi, R.: A genetic algorithm and the monte carlo method for stochastic job-shop scheduling. Int. Trans. Oper. Res. 10(6), 577–596 (2003)

Real Time Traffic Intersection Management Using Multi-objective Evolutionary Algorithm

Kazi Shah Nawaz Ripon[(⊠)], Håkon Dissen, and Jostein Solaas

Department of Computer and Information Science,
Norwegian University of Science and Technology, Trondheim, Norway
ksripon@idi.ntnu.no, hakon.dissen@gmail.com, josteinsolaas@gmail.com

Abstract. With the advent of autonomous vehicles, the field of traffic intersection management has changed. Most of the current methods for intersection management use either stochastic methods for optimizing single scheduling scenarios or deterministic algorithms to optimize parameters for intersection traffic lights. This paper proposes and explores the application of multi-objective evolutionary algorithm (MOEA) to manage a traffic intersection in real time. To achieve this goal, this work implements an intersection manager (IM) that divides the continuous problem into smaller discrete time steps. The vehicular behaviour in single time steps is then optimized, considering several optimization objectives with different goals in terms of overall performance.

Keywords: Evolutionary computation · Real time traffic management · Multi-objective optimization · Intersection manager · Discrete time steps

1 Introduction

In 2008, citizens of the USA spent an average of 46 h a year per capita in congested traffic, up from 16 h in 1982 [5]. In the EU, the total cost of traffic congestion was estimated at 1 % of the total GDP in 2010 [6]. Considering such scenarios, the main motivation behind intersection management is to reduce the amount of time vehicles spent in traffic intersections as a way to ease traffic congestion, mostly in urban areas. In addition, intersection management reduces the total emissions of vehicles idling by or traversing an intersection.

Most of the current literature on intersection management are focused on using either deterministic algorithms or stochastic algorithms. Intersection managers (IMs) using deterministic methods for real time intersection management of autonomous vehicles have shown to drastically improve traffic flow and congestion over conventional traffic lights [2,11]. On the other side, evolutionary and stochastic methods have shown promising results for optimal sequencing of vehicles in single states [7,9]. This work proposes and investigates an IM based on a hybrid of these two concepts.

This work also investigates the real time use of a multi-objective evolutionary algorithm (MOEA) to manage traffic in an intersection. It looks at splitting

© Springer International Publishing AG 2016
C. Martín-Vide et al. (Eds.): TPNC 2016, LNCS 10071, pp. 110–121, 2016.
DOI: 10.1007/978-3-319-49001-4_9

the continuous problem of intersection management into smaller independent scenarios which has never been attempted to date for real time intersection management. Then it explores the application of MOEA to find solutions for each scenario, optimizing several objectives. This paper also provides an insight into whether or not splitting the continuous problem of intersection management into smaller independent scenarios is a good approach to intersection management.

As mentioned earlier, one of the main goals of this paper is to look at the effectiveness of real time usage of an MOEA given full control of the speeds of all incoming vehicles. In order to fulfill the goals of this work, it is necessary to implement an IM that will use an MOEA to measure vehicle speeds in accordance with the given objectives. No simulator has been found that meets all requirements of this work. Thus, we have implemented a modified version of the AIM4 simulator [1].

To study the effect of splitting the large problem of organizing the vehicles over time into smaller discrete time steps, we have introduced two time step parameters: (i) t_{main} that determines for how long each solution is deployed, and (ii) t_{sim} that specifies how much extra time beyond t_{main} each solution is evaluated for. To ensure a fair evaluation of the IM and to study the effects of different time steps, the IM is tested with different values for those parameters. The IM is also tested for specific scenarios, and for continuous operation with different amounts of traffic. To compare the *effectiveness* of the IM in different settings, four performance metrics are used: (i) throughput, (ii) mean evacuation time (MET), (iii) total loss of kinetic energy, and (iv) the amount of collisions.

The goal of the IM itself is to optimize its performance in terms of the performance metrics. There is no direct relation between the performance metrics and what is being optimized for. Hence, we have optimized several distinct objectives. Each objective contributes to improve the behaviour of the IM at a single independent time step. This work does not target a complete replication of the real world scenarios. Therefore, the simulator used to evaluate solutions will also be used to simulate the real world. The vehicles are modelled as single entities travelling along predefined paths, where the only variable parameter is a target speed that the vehicle should accelerate/decelerate to. Vehicle collision and control after traversing through the intersection is beyond the scope of this work. So are the interactions between multiple intersections.

The experimental results suggest that the proposed IM is able to efficiently route vehicles through the intersection with an MET close to the measured optimal value for low to medium amount of traffic. However, the proposed IM is found to be sensitive to both its own internal parameters and the complexity of the intersection states it has to solve. This paper also suggests the effects of the most important parameters, and identifies the primary reasons for the occurrence of collisions at higher levels of traffic. The rest of this paper is organized as follows. Section 2 explains the background and related works in intersection management. Section 3 outlines the functionality of the system. It also presents the implementation details for the experiments. Section 4 provides the experimental results and discusses the findings. Section 5 concludes the paper with suggestions for future research.

2   Background

The most common way of managing busy intersections, aside from explicit right of way rules or roundabouts, is by traffic lights. Fixed time cycles are the simplest method for traffic light operation. In 1981, a system called split cycle offset optimization technique (SCOOT) [8] was introduced. SCOOT allows regular traffic lights to adapt to incoming traffic with sensors along the road. While SCOOT is an improvement over the normal timed cycles approach, it does not take advantage of modern vehicle to vehicle (V2V) communications. It also relies on intersection infrastructure to sense the locations of vehicles, even though new vehicles may know their own location.

Autonomous vehicles introduce capabilities far beyond the capabilities of human drivers. A very important feature of these new vehicles, in regards to the problem of intersection management, is the capabilities of cars to sense their location in the world and use sophisticated measures to plan their travel paths [5]. This allows the intersection controller much finer control over the specific vehicles, opening up for more advanced methods of IM. Because autonomous vehicles have such fine control over their own movements, newer autonomous intersection management (AIM) research [5,11,12] use an intersection organizing system where cars have to travel along predefined trajectories. These trajectories traverse the intersection from one source lane to the destination lane. Trajectories may cross each others paths, which are referred as *conflicting* trajectories.

FCFS (based on the first-come first-served principle of the same name) is an intersection control mechanism developed by the *AIM* project at the University of Texas at Austin [5]. FCFS has been shown to significantly outperform traffic lights, stop signs, and overpass – regulated intersections in terms of vehicle delay [4,5]. The method proposed in this work is based on some of the ideas introduced in AIM, most importantly the idea that the vehicles can simulate their own behaviour based on parameters related to each vehicle, and having vehicles travel along predefined paths.

Intersection management problem has been tackled in many different ways. Recent methods often assume the driver to be autonomous [5,11,12], and allow new and creative approaches that are otherwise impossible when the vehicles are under human control. However, all the autonomous approaches are built on ideas and results from research on human drivers, and therefore have to be understood in that context. Wu et al. showed that vehicles passing an intersection can be modelled as an ordering problem, and proposed a searching algorithm to find the optimal order for vehicles approaching an intersection [10]. While this approach can find the optimal ordering, the computational expense is too high. Therefore, this approach is not suitable in a real-world scenario. Based on [10], Yan et al. proposed a genetic searching approach to reduce the complexity of the problem [12]. It is important to note that these approaches use only single objective function, namely overall evacuation time. There is no consideration of other important objectives. In this work, different optimization objectives, with different goals in terms of overall performance, have been used at the same time.

3   Methodology

3.1   System Overview

The goal of the work is to control the behaviour of autonomous vehicles in an intersection by controlling the speed of each vehicle. In order to achieve this, we have implemented a system with a central IM that communicates with each vehicle. The speed of each vehicle is optimized based on the objectives specified in Sect. 3.2. The system can be split into three main parts (Fig. 1): (*i*) the *IM*, (*ii*) the *Evolutionary Processor* (EP), and (*iii*) the *simulator*. In Fig. 1, grey rounded squares signify entities, and yellow slanted rectangles are the information shared among them.

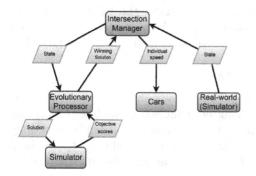

Fig. 1. A complete overview of the system (Color figure online)

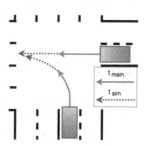

Fig. 2. A visual representation of t_{sim}, t_{main}, and $t_{evaluate}$ (Color figure online)

The IM reads the current *state* of the physical intersection and passes that to the EP, so this it can develop a *speed vector* **v**. In the context of the EP, each **v** is an individual – a solution to the problem that it is trying to solve. It is important to note that **v** is not a multi-dimensional vector specifying the speed of a single vehicle, but rather an n-dimensional vector describing the target speed of n vehicles. Since the vehicles travel along predefined trajectories, their speeds can be described with one variable. A *state* consists of every piece of information that is needed to recreate the current physical world, including vehicles and their current speeds, in the simulator.

Using the MOEA, the EP evaluates the individuals by emulating them in multiple instances of the simulator. Once the stopping condition of the MOEA is met, a decision maker (DM) selects one of the available Pareto-optimal solutions, before a speed vector is returned to the IM. The IM then sets the target speed of each vehicle in the intersection in accordance with the solution. This determines how fast vehicles should travel for the next time step.

We assume that the vehicles report perfect positions and speeds to the IM. In other words, the IM's internal representation of the intersection is a perfect representation of the real world. Thus, as long as the simulator used by the EP perfectly simulates the real world, the resulting speed vector produces a result identical to the one that is simulated in the EP. Since we have used the same deterministic simulator for representing the real world and evaluating the solutions, perfect reproduction between the modelled world and the real world is guaranteed.

For managing the intersection, the IM is concerned with two time step sizes: t_{main} and t_{sim}. As mentioned earlier, t_{main} is the lifetime of one solution in the real world. Once the EP has decided on a solution, that solution is used for the next t_{main} seconds before the EP is ordered to come up with a new solution. However, if the EP only validates the solution for t (current time) $+ t_{main}$, there is no guarantee that the intersection will not end up in an *unsolvable state* (a state where a collision is unavoidable for the next t_{main}). In order to guarantee that the IM never approves such an unsolvable state, the EP is designed to evaluate the solutions for an extra amount of time. We term it as t_{sim}. The total amount of time that the EP evaluates each solution, $t_{evaluate}$, is then given by:

$$t_{evaluate} = t_{main} + t_{sim} \tag{1}$$

Figure 2 shows these time steps visually. As shown in this figure, $t_{evaluate}$ is the time taken by the cars to travel along both the solid blue line (t_{main}) and the dotted red line (t_{sim}). Because the state of an intersection can be incredibly complex, there is no simple way to calculate the minimum value for t_{sim} to keep the system safe. Therefore, we explored different values for these time parameters in the experiments.

3.2   MOEA Details

We used NSGA-II [3] as the MOEA. The genotype is an array of the speed of each vehicle (s_i) in the intersection. It is equivalent to the speed vector $\mathbf{v}$, and can be represented as:

$$\mathbf{v} = [s_1, s_2, \ldots, s_n]; \quad s_i \in [0, speedlimit] \tag{2}$$

The genotype is ordered so that new vehicles are appended on the right side; vehicle $i + 1$ spawned right after vehicle i. The MOEA tries to optimize the speed of each vehicle based on a given set of objective functions. The optimization functions are (i) to maximize throughput in the inner intersection, (i) to maximize the distance traveled for each vehicle, (iii) to minimize total stoppage time, and (iv) to minimize total kinetic energy lost. It is important to mention that while these objectives are important in terms of performance, they are not the final performance metrics by which the system is measured. The performance metrics are discussed in Sect. 1.

During crossover, the tails of the parent genomes are switched from a random index. This results in two new individuals based on both parents. For mutation, each s_i in the new individual ($\mathbf{v}$) has a certain probability of mutating. If a mutation occurs, a new speed is picked based on a random draw. For a random draw, a random number between -1 and speed limit $+1$ is generated and used as the new speed. However, if the number is below 0, the new speed is set to 0. If the number is above the speed limit, it is set to the speed limit.

3.3 Parameters

The system was tested multiple times with the spawn rate set to 0.5, t_{main} and t_{sim} to 1.5 s and given 25000 evaluations, with different values for $P_{mutation}$, $P_{crossover}$, population size and the objective weightings (α) in order to find the appropriate values for these parameters. The values mentioned below were selected as they were found not to cause collisions, and produced acceptable values for MET and total kinetic energy lost.

For our experiments, the parameter values were set as follows. Population size $= 100$, crossover probability $= 0.9$, mutation probability $= 0.1$, $t_{main} = 1.5$ s, $t_{sim} = 1.5$ s, speed limit $= 25\,\mathrm{m\,s^{-1}}$, vehicle mass $= 1000\,\mathrm{kg}$, $\frac{evaluations}{second}$ (the amount of evaluations available per second of t_{main}) $= 50,000$, and $\alpha = 0.25$ (same weight for all objectives).

3.4 Decision Maker (DM)

In order to automate the system, we have applied a simple decision maker (DM) that picks up a preferable solution from the *Pareto-set* returned by the MOEA. For this, the Pareto-set is first sorted based on the number of collisions. If the number of collisions are equal, a secondary sorting is applied. For this, each remaining objective score is multiplied by their corresponding weighting factor (α) and summed up. In a run where there is no collision, this function priorities the objectives based on the weights provided to the IM.

4 Results and Discussion

Figure 3 presents the effects of the independent time segments on the overall behaviour of the system. The goal of these experiments is to find the range for t_{main} that gives the best performance with regards to the performance metrics, focusing mainly on minimizing collisions in an intersection. These experiments also suggest a reasonable t_{main} value for the later experiments. Finding a reasonable t_{main} is important, because it allows less uncertainty when determining reasons for different observed behaviours. The specific time steps values for the experiments are shown in Table 1. The results are generated by running the IM 5 times for each scenario (a total of 75 runs per t_{main}), and computing an average.

Figure 3a displays the average number of collisions per time step in the intersection. As can be seen in the figure, the average amount of collisions drops around 0.5s, stays low until 2.0 s and then rises slightly. When $t_{main} > 2.0$ s, the difference between averages is not significant. However, there is a clear trend of collisions for small values of t_{main}. Figure 3b shows that MET is at its lowest when $t_{main} = 2.0$ s. However, the difference is negligible from that of 1.5 s

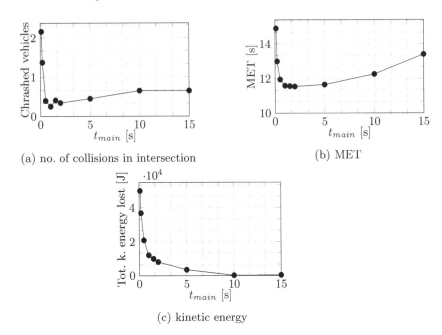

(a) no. of collisions in intersection

(b) MET

(c) kinetic energy

Fig. 3. Effects of the independent time segments

Table 1. Time step values in seconds (each column represents the values used for one configuration)

t_{main}	0.1	0.2	0.5	1.0	1.5	2.0	5.0	10.0	15.0
t_{sim}	2.0	2.0	2.0	2.0	2.0	2.0	2.0	2.0	2.0
$t_{evaluate}$	2.1	2.2	2.5	3.0	3.5	4.0	7.0	12.0	17.0

and 1.0 s. The MET increases as t_{main} increases past 5.0 s. Figure 3c shows how varying t_{main} affects the total kinetic energy lost. The total kinetic energy lost increases when the time step size decreases. This is again because the IM has more control in lower time steps. The more often the IM can update the speed for each vehicle, the higher the chance of applying breaks becomes.

To find the best combinations of t_{main} and $t_{evaluate}$ for an appropriate behaviour in the IM, we tested different values of t_{sim} coupled with the most promising values for t_{main}. The values for t_{sim} are the same as mentioned in Table 1. The values for $t_{evaluate}$ are calculated using Eq. (1) by inserting the values of 0.2 s, 0.5 s, 1.0 s and 1.5 s for t_{main}. Each scenario was evaluated once for every configuration of t_{sim} and t_{main}. Figure 4 presents the results, where each sub-figure contains one of the performance metrics for four different t_{main} values.

From Fig. 4a, it is clear that when t_{sim} remains low, the vehicles collide. This is as expected, because the evaluation of the speed vector does not consider what happens after t_{main} has passed. As such the solutions chosen in each step create

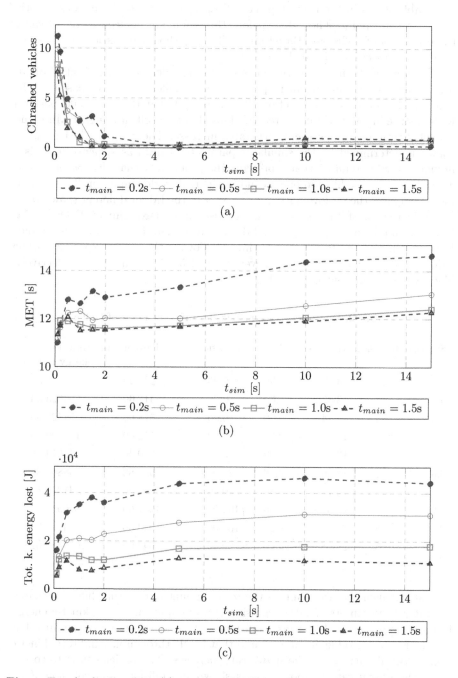

Fig. 4. Trends showing how (a) number of collisions in intersection, (b) MET, and (c) total kinetic energy lost is changed based on different values of t_{sim}

unsolvable states in the next step. For all t_{main} values, MET increases slightly after a certain point. The values before this point are not considered because there is a lot of collisions. Based on MET, t_{sim} should be as low as possible, until collisions can be avoided.

The goal of the next experiment is to better understand the effect of dividing the intersection management problem into smaller time steps based on the amount of cars in the intersection. It is expected that the IM would perform worse as the amount of cars increased. This should result in a higher MET and loss of kinetic energy as the spawn rates increase. The rate at which vehicles spawn is determined by the simulator parameter known as *spawn rate*. It is a number between 0 and 1 that represents the probability that the *spawn zone* is going to spawn a vehicle in one second in the real world simulator. This experiment compares the performance metric scores of the IM for different spawn rates (in an increment of 0.1). No scenarios are used in this experiment. Each simulation was run for a total of 300 s and did not terminate before the time ran out. Each spawn rate was tested for five times. Following the earlier experiments, the values for t_{main}, t_{sim}, and $t_{evaluate}$ were set to 1.5 s, 1.5 s, and 3.0 s, respectively. The results are presented in Table 2.

Table 2. IM performance metrics for different levels of traffic

Spawn rate	Runs	MET (s)	Collisions	Collisions (%)	Throughput	Total kinetic energy lost (J)
0.1	5	13.37	0.00	0.00	236.20	4539.93
0.2	5	13.37	0.00	0.00	417.60	16923.33
0.3	5	13.44	0.00	0.00	578.60	54323.80
0.4	5	13.46	0.00	0.00	712.60	126729.28
0.5	5	13.64	0.00	0.00	820.40	343614.86
0.6	5	13.89	0.40	20.00	926.80	768865.80
0.7	5	14.17	0.80	20.00	1025.80	1641376.12
0.8	5	17.59	68.80	100.00	1042.60	4810951.97
0.9	5	25.08	189.20	100.00	943.00	9604215.88
1.0	5	28.08	204.00	100.00	943.60	11658489.02

Table 2 displays throughput – the total amount of cars that have evacuated the intersection in 300 s. MET, collisions, throughput, and total kinetic energy lost are averages over the 5 runs. Collisions (%) is the percentage of the runs that collide. From this table, it can be found that MET, throughput, and total kinetic energy lost all increase as the spawn rate increases. The vehicles start to collide when the spawn rate is above 0.6, as shown by collisions and collisions (%). This is in line with the observations from earlier experiments where collisions could only be observed in scenarios with high amounts of traffic. The measured throughput for lower spawn rates is not very interesting, but simply shows that increasing the spawn rate does, in fact, increase the amount of vehicles that has to be routed through the intersection in the given time. For higher spawn rates, throughput stops increasing and goes slightly down. This occurs at the same spawn rates that produces queuing and congestion in the inner intersection.

Next, we investigate effects of each objective on the overall performance of the system. This is done by removing each objective from the evaluation in four separate runs. For this experiment, the investigation in regards to MET and total kinetic energy lost is constrained to spawn rates below 0.7, as they include collisions. The results are presented based on performance metrics. Figure 5a shows the relationship between the different objective configurations and MET. In fact, it shows how MET is affected by removing each of the objectives in the MOEA at different spawn rates. This figure has five trends. Among them, the first four present the MET values when one of the objectives is not evaluated. Similarly, Fig. 5b shows the effect on total kinetic energy lost by removing each of the objectives in the MOEA at different spawn rates. This figure also has five trends. Similarly, the first four show the total kinetic energy lost values when one of the objectives is not evaluated. For both figures, the last trend shows the default behaviour when all objectives are evaluated.

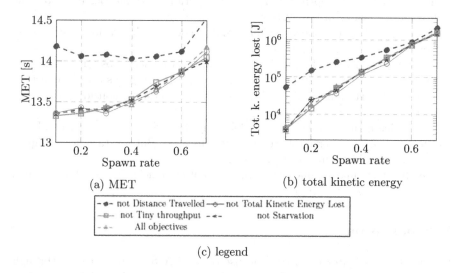

(a) MET

(b) total kinetic energy

(c) legend

Fig. 5. Relationship between different objective configurations and (a) MET, (b) total kinetic energy

Figure 5a shows a clear trend: not optimizing for distance traveled produces a significantly higher MET. Interestingly, ignoring distance traveled is also the one that stands out when measuring the total kinetic energy lost (Fig. 5b). However, removing the objective for minimizing this loss has an almost negligible effect, even scoring slightly better for values above 0.3. From Fig. 5a and b, it is apparent that maximizing the distance travelled in each time step strongly affects the overall performance of the IM. In fact, the IM performs considerably worse when this objective is ignored. This effect is most noticeable at lower spawn rates. No statistically significant results are found when comparing for collisions, nor does the results show any deviation from the baseline when removing the tiny throughput or starvation. Some small trends can be observed for the amount of collisions and how often collisions occur, but no statistically significant relationship can be established. This could be because no such relationship exists, or because the results were counted over longer periods of continuous simulation.

In short, we can summarize the following observations from the experimental results:

- t_{main} and t_{sim} have strong influence on the performance of the IM. Small values for both variables cause a large amount of collisions. In particular, a small t_{sim} has the obvious drawback that the IM does not evaluate far enough into the future to avoid collisions in the next time step.
- Experiments with different time step values suggest that there is no set of values that performs best in all scenarios. Therefore, for the later usage of the IM, one must find a compromise between the available objective scores.
- While solving one state at a time, we did not find any direct relation between the objectives being optimized for and the performance metrics used to measure the behaviour of the system.
- The proposed system never suffers from single lane starvation which is an usual problem of existing systems.
- Experiments with MET (Fig. 5a) and total kinetic energy lost (Fig. 5b) show that maximizing the distance traveled in each time step has a large effect on the overall performance of the IM, and the IM performs considerably worse when this objective is ignored.
- No significant changes were observed for tiny throughput and starvation. However, for collisions, negligible trends were observed. But no statistically significant relationship could be established.
- The objectives may conflict when the amount of vehicles in the intersection is high, or the state is complex.

5   Conclusion

This work investigates the real time use of MOEA to manage traffic through an intersection. For this, an IM has been implemented which is divided into two logical parts. The first part controls the vehicles in the intersection by modulating their speed. The other part analyzes a state of the intersection, and finds a speed for each vehicle in the given state by using MOEA. The results show that MOEA can be used in real time to control the intersection. It is also found that the proposed IM is able to efficiently and safely route vehicles through the intersection, with only small deviations from the measured optimal MET for small to medium amounts of vehicles. However, when splitting the large and continuous problem of intersection management into smaller time steps, the two time variables (t_{main} and t_{sim}) have considerable impact on the performance of the IM. The experimental results also suggest that the complexity of each state is one of the reasons why collisions occur in the current system. It would be interesting to see how it behaves when efforts are made to reduce this complexity. Reducing the amount of vehicles in the intersection by some external mechanism could also be explored. Another possible exploratory point for future work would be to implement other optimization objectives to avoid congestion by limiting the amount of vehicles present in the inner intersection.

References

1. AIM: The aim4 simulator v1.0.3 (2016). http://www.cs.utexas.edu/aim/. Accessed 20 Jan 2016
2. Chen, L., Englund, C.: Cooperative intersection management: a survey. IEEE Trans. Intell. Transp. Syst. **17**(2), 570–586 (2016)
3. Deb, K., Pratap, A., Agarwal, S., Meyarivan, T.: A fast and elitist multiobjective genetic algorithm: NSGA-II. IEEE Trans. Evol. Comput. **6**(2), 182–197 (2002)
4. Dresner, K., Stone, P.: Multiagent traffic management: a reservation-based intersection control mechanism. In: Proceedings of the Third International Joint Conference on Autonomous Agents and Multiagent Systems, vol. 2, pp. 530–537. IEEE Computer Society (2004)
5. Dresner, K., Stone, P.: A multiagent approach to autonomous intersection management. J. Artif. Intell. Res. **31**, 591–656 (2008)
6. Gemeinschaften, K.E.: White paper-European transport policy for 2010: time to decide. Office for Official Publications of the European Communities (2001)
7. Hausknecht, M., Au, T.C., Stone, P.: Autonomous intersection management: multi-intersection optimization. In: 2011 IEEE/RSJ International Conference on Intelligent Robots and Systems, pp. 4581–4586. IEEE (2011)
8. Hunt, P., Transport and Road Research Laboratory: SCOOT: A Traffic Responsive Method of Coordinating Signals. Leaflet/Transport and Road Research Laboratory, Transport and Road Research Laboratory (1981)
9. Kwatirayo, S., Almhana, J., Liu, Z., Siblini, J.: Optimizing road intersection traffic flow using stochastic and heuristic algorithms. In: 2014 IEEE International Conference on Communications (ICC), pp. 586–591. IEEE (2014)
10. Wu, J., Abbas-Turki, A., El Moudni, A.: Discrete methods for urban intersection traffic controlling. In: IEEE 69th Vehicular Technology Conference, VTC Spring 2009, pp. 1–5. IEEE (2009)
11. Wuthishuwong, C., Traechtler, A., Bruns, T.: Safe trajectory planning for autonomous intersection management by using vehicle to infrastructure communication. EURASIP J. Wirel. Commun. Netw. **2015**(1), 1–12 (2015)
12. Yan, F., Dridi, M., El Moudni, A.: An autonomous vehicle sequencing problem at intersections: a genetic algorithm approach. Int. J. Appl. Math. Comput. Sci. **23**(1), 183–200 (2013)

Formal Models

Natural and Efficient Subtraction Operation in Carry Value Transformation (CVT)-Exclusive OR (XOR) Paradigm

Jayanta Kumar Das[1]([✉]), Pabitra Pal Choudhury[1]([✉]), and Ayesha Arora[2]

[1] Applied Statistics Unit, Indian Statistical Institute,
203 B. T. Road, Kolkata 700108, India
dasjayantakumar89@gmail.com, pabitrapalchoudhury@gmail.com
[2] Mathematics and Computing Department, Birla Institute of Technology, Mesra,
Ranchi 835215, Jharkhand, India
ayeshaarora012@gmail.com

Abstract. Carry value transformation (CVT) and Exclusive OR (XOR) operations on two non-negative integers have been defined previously in several articles. In this paper, the definition of CVT and XOR operations are extended from non-negative integer to integer domain. Thereafter various cases of integer pairs towards their convergence behaviour are thoroughly discussed. Our analyses through the convergence behavior of integer pairs are easily directed to capture the natural subtraction operation in this paradigm by representing negative integer in 2's complement form. The average time complexity of the addition/subtraction operation is seen to be highly competitive in any bulk computation in real life scenario. In other words, in the event of bulk addition/subtraction operation to be performed, the average time complexity is seen to be highly efficient.

Keywords: CVT-XOR operations · Subtraction · Convergence behaviour · Complexity

1 Introduction

For modern digital computer, faster Arithmetic Logic Unit (ALU) circuit design is essential where portable computers have become as small as the size of palm limitation. This had been possible over the decades due to the revolution that took place in the area of Very Large Scale Integration (VLSI) design.

Various circuits are designed for the purpose of arithmetic computation towards some specific directions such as fast binary adder with conditional carry generator [1], carry save adder [2], self-time carry look ahead adder [3], a spanning tree carry look-ahead adder [4], low voltage full adder [5], recursive mechanism on a parallel self-time adder [6], fast two's complement VLSI adder [7] etc. Further, Quantum dot Cellular Automata (QCA) which is the transistor

© Springer International Publishing AG 2016
C. Martín-Vide et al. (Eds.): TPNC 2016, LNCS 10071, pp. 125–136, 2016.
DOI: 10.1007/978-3-319-49001-4_10

less computational model and is expected to provide high density nanotechnology implementations of various Complementary Metal Oxide Semiconductor (CMOS) circuits are found in [8]. Also some theoretical studies are done in [9] for the arithmetic addition and subtraction functions of logarithmic number system. But all the designed circuits are combinational in nature and complexity is dependent on the use of number of logic gates and associated delays. Integral Value Transformation (IVT) is designed in 2009 [10] in discrete field of mathematics which operates on strings of any base. Also, Carry Value Transformation (CVT) which is a special case of IVT and Exclusive OR (XOR) are the two most important transformations operating on bits of strings, recently found many of their applications [11–15]. CVT and XOR transformations have been observed to provide addition of two positive integers for any base of number system [12,13].

For the large scale cellular automata (CA) experiments, Cellular Automata Machines (CAMs) become very special compared to any kind of computing machine [16]. The first version of CAM machine is CAM-6 which is produced commercially 20 years back and various CAMs are now available for all the research communities. In CVT-XOR paradigm, CAM is used for the addition of two non-negative integers where internal circuit is designed using AND and XOR gates with carry bit shifting logic. It has been easily seen from the theory of CVT-XOR convergence behavior that CVT-XOR using CAMs can perform better than any other circuit. This is because the CAM used here operates on clock cycle only (without any gate delays) [14]. Along with this multi number CVT-XOR theory is developed and proposed to offer a parallel model for multi number addition using CAM which can be implemented for VLSI design [13]. As hardware complexity for addition or subtraction is same, it is highly needed for the extension of CVT-XOR operations over the integer domain including both positive and negative integers. This is the main agenda of this paper.

The addition of two non-negative integers (Say X and Y) is exactly equal to their CVT and XOR operations sum i.e. $X + Y = CVT (X, Y) + XOR (X, Y)$. And using CVT and XOR operations in recursive manner the maximum number of steps to get CVT = 0 is n+1 where n = MAX (X, Y) number of bits in binary [12]. So in CVT-XOR paradigm, we have to check/concentrate on CVT part which is to be zero to get for both the addition or subtraction result on XOR part. Therefore understanding the dynamics of integer pair with regards to convergence behaviour is an important task in this regard. And the convergence behavior of integer pair is interdependent on bits representing the integer pair.

For example (Fig. 1), let there be a positive integer N = 14. There are 15 integer pairs as (X, Y) whose pair sum is 14 = (X + Y). Now in this paradigm we can easily visualize the nature-inspired tree data structure. If we draw the CVT-XOR convergence tree [17] whose nodes are represented by integer pairs where first part is CVT value and second part is XOR value and root is with CVT = 0 and XOR = X + Y. As can be seen from the following figure, among the 15 integer pairs, seven integer pairs are ((10, 4), (12, 2), (4, 10), (8, 6), (14, 0), (6, 8), (2, 12)) which take one iteration to get CVT = 0 and similarly seven integer pairs are ((7, 7)..., (1, 13)) which take two iterations to get CVT=0 and

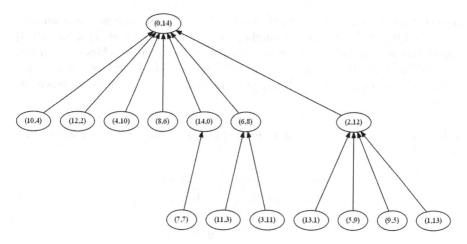

Fig. 1. Nature inspired tree data structure for the non-negative integer 14 and pairs (whose sum is 14) are converging towards (0, 14).

for one integer pair (0, 14) is taking zero iteration. Clearly, it can be seen that the integer 14 is with binary 4 bits and all the integer pairs involving 14 get at least one 4 bits number except the pair (7, 7) which needs 3 bits. So we are able to get sum on XOR part most of the cases in lesser number of iterations.

The paper is organized as follows: Sect. 2 discusses the modified definition of CVT and XOR operations. In Sect. 3, various cases of CVT-XOR properties towards their convergence behaviour to capture the subtraction operation are proposed. Section 4 deals with the complexity and performance analysis of subtraction operation. Lastly, Sect. 5 concludes the paper.

2   Modified Definition of CVT and XOR Operations for Integer Domain

Let A and B are two integers and their signed binary representation be $A = a_s a_n...a_1$ and $B = b_s b_n...b_1$ respectively where a_s and b_s are the two sign bits in Most Significant Bit (MSB) position. The CVT of A and B is $a_s \wedge b_s a_n \wedge b_n...a_1 \wedge b_1 0$ and XOR of A and B is $a_s \oplus b_s a_n \oplus b_n...a_1 \oplus b_1$. It is to be noted that ith column bits of two integers with ANDing operation is saved in $(i+1)$th column for CVT calculation with 0 padded in Least Significant Bit (LSB) position. In this binary notation the negative integer is always represented in 2's complement form. Now three cases can happen for sign bits of two integers: (i) if $a_s = b_s = 1$, then CVT is negative and obviously XOR is positive, (ii) if sign bits are complement to each other i.e. $a_s = 1$ and $b_s = 0$ or $a_s = 0$ and $b_s = 1$, then CVT is positive and XOR is negative and (iii) if $a_s = b_s = 0$, then both the CVT and XOR are positive.

Illustration 1: An example is shown in Table 1 taking one negative number A = −6 (1010) and one positive number B = 12 (1100) and one extra bit (MSB) considering for sign bit. All the most significant bits are the sign bits respectively. The CVT of above two numbers is +16 and XOR is −10. Therefore, with regards to the additive property of CVT and XOR operations [12], here 12 − 6 = 6 is equal to 16 − 10 = 6.

Table 1. CVT and XOR operations for one negative integer (−6) and one positive integer (12).

Operation	Binary						Decimal
CVT	0	1	0	0	0	0	16
		1	1	0	1	0	−6
		0	1	1	0	0	12
XOR		1	0	1	1	0	−10

3   Convergence Behaviour of CVT and XOR Operations for Various Cases of Integer Pairs

Previously in [12] for any two non-negative integers A and B, $A + B = CVT(A, B) + XOR(A, B)$ and maximum number of iterations leading to CVT = 0 or XOR = 0 is $n + 1$ are proved where n is the number of significant bits of bigger number. Here we are dealing with integer domain and observe different cases of CVT and XOR operations targeted mainly for capturing subtraction operation. The convergence behavior of different cases of integer pairs are shown in different figures where CVT and XOR values are considered as x and y coordinates respectively. We start with any (CVT, XOR) integer pair as initial quadrant in the figure and traversing into the next (CVT, XOR) integer pair after calculating and so on serially one after another until CVT value becomes 0. Thus the final result of addition/subtraction can be found on the y axis except the non-converging case of CVT-XOR operations.

3.1   Both the Integers A and B Are Positive

Various properties are already discussed and some of them are in the form of important theorems [11–13].

3.2   Both the Integers A and B Are Negative

Lemma 1. *CVT and XOR will be negative and positive respectively after the first iteration, but from the second iteration onwards, CVT will always be positive and XOR will always be negative.*

Proof: Let $A = a_s a_n...a_1$ and $B = b_s b_n...b_1$ be the signed binary representation where the MSB are a_s and b_s. As A and B are negative integers therefore $a_s = b_s = 1$. So CVT of two negative integers is negative and XOR is positive after the first iteration. But from the second iteration onwards MSB is always 0 for CVT and 1 for XOR operation, so XOR will always be negative and CVT will always be positive and this would continue.

Illustration 2: Convergence behavior of three (negative, negative) integer pairs are shown in Fig. 2 using state transition diagram: $(a)(-14, -14) \rightarrow (-28, 0) \rightarrow (0, -28)$, $(b)(-1, -6) \rightarrow (-12, 5) \rightarrow (8, -15) \rightarrow (0, -7)$, and $(c)(-3, -11) \rightarrow (-22, 8) \rightarrow (16, -30) \rightarrow (0, -14)$. CVT patterns for all negative-negative integer pairs $(0, 0)$, $(0, -1)...(-16, -16)$ are shown in Table 2 where from -1 to -16 with regards to rows and columns, a beautiful pattern is conserved having exactly same 1st, 3rd and 4th quadrants.

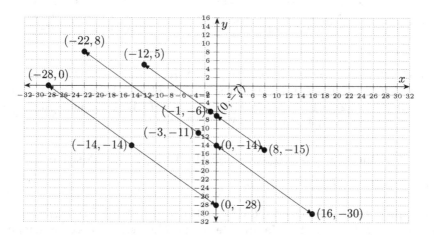

Fig. 2. State transition diagram of three integer pairs: (a) $(-14, -14)$, (b) $(-1, -6)$, and (c) $(-3, -11)$.

Lemma 2. *For any two negative integers A and B, $|CVT(A, B)| \geq |CVT(A, A)|$ where $|A| \geq |B|$.*

Proof: Let $A = a_s a_n...a_1$ and $B = b_s b_n...b_1$ be the signed binary representation where $|A| \geq |B|$. As MSB is 1 for both the integers, therefore MSB of both CVT (A, B) and CVT (A, A) are 1. Hence the result can be seen very easily.

Illustration 3: $CVT(-3, -2) = CVT(101, 110) = 1000$ which is -8 and $CVT(-3, -3) = CVT(101, 101) = 1010$ which is -6.

Lemma 3. $|CVT(A, B)| \geq [MAX(|A|, |B|) \times 2]$.

Table 2. CVT pattern for negative-negative integer pairs.

	0	−1	−2	−3	−4	−5	−6	−7	−8	−9	−10	−11	−12	−13	−14	−15	−16
0	0	0	0	0	0	0	0	0	0	0	0	0	0	0	0	0	0
−1	0	−2	−4	−6	−8	−10	−12	−14	−16	−18	−20	−22	−24	−26	−28	−30	−32
−2	0	−4	−4	−8	−8	−12	−12	−16	−16	−20	−20	−24	−24	−28	−28	−32	−32
−3	0	−6	−8	−6	−8	−14	−16	−14	−16	−22	−24	−22	−24	−30	−32	−30	−32
−4	0	−8	−8	−8	−8	−16	−16	−16	−16	−24	−24	−24	−24	−32	−32	−32	−32
−5	0	−10	−12	−14	−16	−10	−12	−14	−16	−26	−28	−30	−32	−26	−28	−30	−32
−6	0	−12	−12	−16	−16	−12	−12	−16	−16	−28	−28	−32	−32	−28	−28	−32	−32
−7	0	−14	−16	−14	−16	−14	−16	−14	−16	−30	−32	−30	−32	−30	−32	−30	−32
−8	0	−16	−16	−16	−16	−16	−16	−16	−16	−32	−32	−32	−32	−32	−32	−32	−32
−9	0	−18	−20	−22	−24	−26	−28	−30	−32	−18	−20	−22	−24	−26	−28	−30	−32
−10	0	−20	−20	−24	−24	−28	−28	−32	−32	−20	−20	−24	−24	−28	−28	−32	−32
−11	0	−22	−24	−22	−24	−30	−32	−30	−32	−22	−24	−22	−24	−30	−32	−30	−32
−12	0	−24	−24	−24	−24	−32	−32	−32	−32	−24	−24	−24	−24	−32	−32	−32	−32
−13	0	−26	−28	−30	−32	−26	−28	−30	−32	−26	−28	−30	−32	−26	−28	−30	−32
−14	0	−28	−28	−32	−32	−28	−28	−32	−32	−28	−28	−32	−32	−28	−28	−32	−32
−15	0	−30	−32	−30	−32	−30	−32	−30	−32	−30	−32	−30	−32	−30	−32	−30	−32
−16	0	−32	−32	−32	−32	−32	−32	−32	−32	−32	−32	−32	−32	−32	−32	−32	−32

Proof: $CVT(A, A) = a_s \wedge a_s a_n \wedge a_n ... a_1 \wedge a_1 = a_s a_n ... a_1 0$. The place values of $CVT(a_i, a_i)$ is 2 times the place values of sign binary bits of A i.e. $CVT(A, A) = |2 \times A|$. Now $CVT(A, B) \geq CVT(A, A)$ for any $|A| \geq |B|$ (Lemma 2). So $|CVT(A, B)| \geq [MAX(|A|, |B|) \times 2]$.

3.3   The Integer A is Negative and the Integer B is Positive

Property 1. $CVT(A, B) \leq 2 \times B$.

Examples: $CVT(-1, 11) = 22$, $CVT(-4, 11) = 16 < 22$, $CVT(-7, 2) = 0 < 4$. **When $|A| > |B|$ i.e. the Magnitude of the Negative Integer is Bigger.**
In this case CVT will always converge. For the proof, similar arguments can be seen from [12].

Illustration 4: Convergence behavior of two integer pairs (one negative and another positive) are shown in Fig. 3 using state transition diagram: $(a)(-17, 11) \rightarrow (22, -28) \rightarrow (8, -14) \rightarrow (0, -6)$, $(b)(-1, -6) \rightarrow (-12, 5) \rightarrow (8, -15) \rightarrow (0, -7)$ and $(c)(-9, 1) \rightarrow (2, -10) \rightarrow (4, -12) \rightarrow (8, -16) \rightarrow (0, -8)$. CVT patterns for all negative-positive integer pairs $(0, 0), (-1, 0)...(-16, 16)$ are shown in Table 3. Here $2nd$, $3rd$ and $4th$ quadrants are exactly same.

Lemma 4. If $B = |A| - 1$, then their $CVT = 0$ and $XOR = -1$.

Proof: The binary representation of A and B are complement to each other when A is negative and $B = |A| - 1$. So their CVT becomes 0. As $A + B = CVT(A, B) + XOR(A, B)$ and their CVT is 0, $XOR = -1$.
For e.g. Let $A = -3$ (1 0 1) and $B = 2$ (0 1 0). We can observe that signed binary representation of A and B are complement to each other. So clearly their CVT will be 0 (0000) and XOR will be −1 (111).

Table 3. CVT pattern for negative-positive integer pairs.

	0	1	2	3	4	5	6	7	8	9	10	11	12	13	14	15	16
0	0	0	0	0	0	0	0	0	0	0	0	0	0	0	0	0	0
−1	0	2	4	6	8	10	12	14	16	18	20	22	24	26	28	30	32
−2	0	0	4	4	8	8	12	12	16	16	20	20	24	24	28	28	32
−3	0	2	0	2	8	10	8	10	16	18	16	18	24	26	24	26	32
−4	0	0	0	0	8	8	8	8	16	16	16	16	24	24	24	24	32
−5	0	2	4	6	0	2	4	6	16	18	20	22	16	18	20	22	32
−6	0	0	4	4	0	0	4	4	16	16	20	20	16	16	20	20	32
−7	0	2	0	2	0	2	0	2	16	18	16	18	16	18	16	18	32
−8	0	0	0	0	0	0	0	0	16	16	16	16	16	16	16	16	32
−9	0	2	4	6	8	10	12	14	0	2	4	6	8	10	12	14	32
−10	0	0	4	4	8	8	12	12	0	0	4	4	8	8	12	12	32
−11	0	2	0	2	8	10	8	10	0	2	0	2	8	10	8	10	32
−12	0	0	0	0	8	8	8	8	0	0	0	0	8	8	8	8	32
−13	0	2	4	6	0	2	4	6	0	2	4	6	0	2	4	6	32
−14	0	0	4	4	0	0	4	4	0	0	4	4	0	0	4	4	32
−15	0	2	0	2	0	2	0	2	0	2	0	2	0	2	0	2	32
−16	0	0	0	0	0	0	0	0	0	0	0	0	0	0	0	0	32

Lemma 5. *XOR will never be 0.*

Proof: Here A is negative and B is positive so their sign bits are 1 and 0 respectively and hence XOR $(1, 0) = 1$. Therefore, XOR will never be 0.

When $|A| < |B|$ i.e. the Magnitude of the Negative Integer is Smaller.

Lemma 6. *CVT will always increase and never converge to 0.*

Proof: Let the signed binary representation of $A = a_s a_n ... a_1$ and $B = b_s b_n ... b_1$. As A is negative and B is positive, $a_s = 1$ and $b_s = 0$. So $XOR(a_s, b_s) = 1$. Here we are considering that $|A| < |B|$, so $A + B > 0 \implies CVT + XOR > 0$ ($A + B = CVT(A, B) + XOR(A, B)$). But XOR is negative, so CVT will be positive which is greater than the XOR value. Therefore, CVT can never converge to 0.

Illustration 5: Convergence behavior of two integer pairs (positive integer magnitude is bigger) are shown in Fig. 4 using state transition diagram: $(a)(17, -11) \rightarrow (34, -28) \rightarrow (64, -58)...$ $(b)(2, -1) \rightarrow (4, -3) \rightarrow (8, -7) \rightarrow (16, -15) \rightarrow (32, -31) \rightarrow (64, -58)....$

Lemma 7. *XOR will never be 0.*

Proof: Same as Lemma 5.

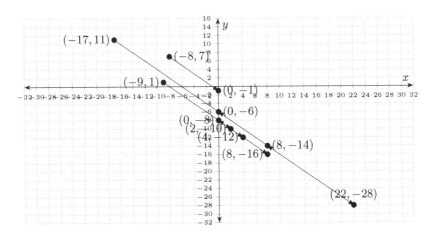

Fig. 3. State transition diagram of three integer pairs: (a) $(-17, 11)$, (b) $(-8, 7)$, and (c) $(-9, 1)$.

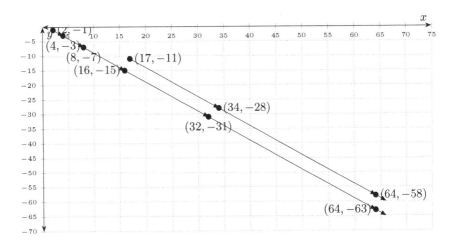

Fig. 4. State transition diagram of two integer pairs: (a) $(17, -11)$ and (b) $(2, -1)$.

When $|A| = |B|$ i.e. the Magnitude of the Negative and Positive Integer is equal.

Lemma 8. *CVT will never converge to 0.*

Proof: We know that XOR is negative. Here $|A| = |B|$, so $A + B = 0 \implies CVT + XOR = 0$, but XOR is a negative integer, so CVT must be a positive integer with magnitude $= |XOR|$. Therefore CVT will never converge to 0.

Lemma 9. *In the first iteration (A, B) will be $(2, -2)$ when $|A| = |B|$ is an odd integer.*

Proof: For equal odd integers with opposite sign, their signed binary representation is complement to each other except their LSB. So their CVT is of the form in binary 00...10 which is decimal 2 and XOR is of the form in binary 11...10 which is decimal -2.

It is to be noted that the convergence behaviour for $|A| = |B|$ is same as the previous case (Fig. 4). In all the cases it may be noted that a straight line is found starting with any random integer pair that signifies the same addition/subtraction result happening on the same straight line and having the final destination on the y axis.

4   Performance Analysis and General Circuit Diagram for CVT-XOR Operations

We have seen that the negative-negative integer pair on successive CVT-XOR operations is converging to CVT = 0. Therefore, result of addition/subtraction is stored in XOR part as in [14]. Similar is the case for negative-positive integer pair where magnitude of negative integer is bigger (Sect. 3.3, when the magnitude of negative integer is bigger), therefore expected result of addition/subtraction is negative and is also converging; we are able to get the result from XOR part. On the other hand, positive-negative integer pair where negative integer is smaller, result of addition is positive (Sect. 3.3, when the magnitude of negative integer is smaller). This is a case which is non-converging. The CVT part is increasing infinitely keeping addition/subtraction result same, thereby increasing the number of bits in binary to represent them. But in practical scenario, hardware register slots (say width w) are fixed which can store finite number of bits for each integer including the sign bit. Therefore, when CVT-XOR operations are performing we have to concentrate only for fixed number of bits. Doing so we can ultimately find that for both the cases CVT is converging and subtraction/addition result can be found in XOR part. It has been seen that given an n bit integer, we have to consider $n + 1$ bits by padding zeros in MSB position for the positive integer. Here we are dealing with general form for all integers and negative integer is represented in 2's complement form, we have to deal with $n + 2$ bits including sign bit for maximum of n bit integer in our paradigm. We have to pad at least two extra bits 0's in MSB for positive integer and 1's in MSB for negative integer. Below Table 4 shows two examples when $|A| \leq |B|$ (Sect. 3.3, when the magnitude of negative integer is smaller or equal to positive integer) for (14, -11) and (2, -2) as initial pairs where CVT is not converging theoretically, but in practical scenario by fixing the bit numbers it can be seen that CVT is converging and XOR part is giving the expected result after maximum of $n + 1$ iterations. Here we obtained the result for (14, -11) pair in $4th$ iteration and for (2,-2) pair in $3rd$ iteration. Iteration numbers can vary depending on the integer pairs and their binary representation.

Therefore, the time complexity in general for getting the CVT part having all zeros and XOR part holding expected result is of the order of n i.e. O (n) where maximum is n+1 and minimum is 1 is same as [14]. Figure 5 shows the

Table 4. Repetitive CVT and XOR operations for one 4 bits $(14, -11)$ and one 2 bits $(2,-2)$ integer pairs to get their subtraction result.

Iteration	Operation	Bit position 654321	Decimal	Bit position 4321	Decimal
Iteration-0	CVT	001110	14	0010	2
	XOR	110101	-11	1110	-2
Iteration-1	CVT	001000	8	0100	4
	XOR	111011	-5	1100	-4
Iteration-2	CVT	010000	16	1000	8
	XOR	110011	-13	1000	-8
Iteration-3	CVT	100000	32	0000	0
	XOR	100011	-29	0000	0
Iteration-4	CVT	000000	0		
	XOR	000011	3		

previous CAM circuit from [14], with redrawing to get easy understanding how CVT-XOR operation is performing in parallel and recursive manner. We have seen that we have to consider extra two bits in general. So with 5 slots circuit (Fig. 5) which can performed the addition/subtraction result for 3 bit integer pairs. Given any two integers, binary representation of one integer is stored in CVT part right (LSB) to left (MSB) X1...X5 and another integer is stored in XOR part right (LSB) to left (MSB) Y1...Y5. X1 is connected to voltage ground zero. Therefore, once the operation is started from the second iteration onwards X1 is always holding binary zero. Once all the positions of CVT part become zeros, XOR part gives the expected result. If MSB of XOR part is binary 0

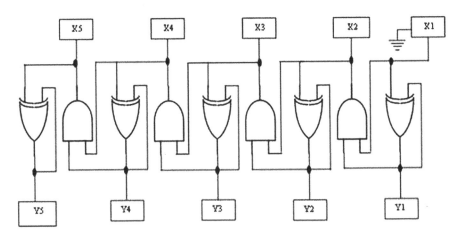

Fig. 5. Proposed CAM circuit diagram in simplified form for CVT-XOR operations in general as discussed in [14]

number is positive, and if MSB of XOR part is binary 1 number is negative, in this case we have to take 2's complement of the number.

Looking back the descriptions of CVT-XOR tree in the introduction, we do the experiment from positive integer 8 to 14 and results of average height can be seen from 2.7, 1.9, 1.72, 1.25, 2.07, 1.05, and 1.4 respectively. It may be remarked that when the number of bits are increasing signifying the larger pairs the average heights are significantly less. On repeating the experiments with random selection up-to 10 bit integer pairs, we find that average iterations is under 3.5 to reach the root of the CVT-XOR tree.

5   Conclusion

In this paper, we have proved that CVT-XOR paradigm is valid for all integers. It has been seen that main property $A + B = CVT(A, B) + XOR(A, B)$ is also valid for all integers i.e. both for the negative and positive. We thoroughly discussed the convergence behaviour of all types of integer pairs. Some of the related important theorems are proved and shown for the integer pairs in different cases. When initial integer pairs are taken from $1st$ and $3rd$ quadrant, CVT of the pair converge to 0 after maximum of $n + 1$ steps; where n is the number of significant bits required for representing bigger integer including sign bit. On the other hand, when initial integer pairs are taken from $2nd$ and $4th$ quadrant, their CVT converges to 0 as usual when final result becomes negative. But if the final result becomes zero or positive, CVT goes on increasing keeping their sum result invariant. But under practical scenario, it has been seen that their summation result can be observed in the XOR register after $w = n + 1$ steps. Thus this CVT-XOR paradigm is naturally amenable to VLSI circuit design for faster arithmetic computation.

Acknowledgments. Authors would like to thank Dr. Sudhakar Sahoo (Institute of Mathematics and Applications, Bhubaneswar-751029, India) for his valuable suggestion.

References

1. Lo, J.C.: A fast binary adder with conditional carry generation. IEEE Trans. Comput. **46**(2), 248–253 (1997)
2. Ercegovac, M., Lang, T.: Digital Arithmetic. Morgan Kaufmann, San Francisco (2004)
3. Cheng, F.-C., Unger, S.H., Theobald, M.: Self-timed carrylookahead adders. IEEE Trans. Comput. **49**(7), 659–672 (2000)
4. Lynch, T., Swartzlander, E.E.: A spanning tree carry lookahead adder. IEEE Trans. Comput. **41**(8), 931–939 (1992)
5. Lee, H., Sobelman, G.E.: A new low-voltage full adder circuit. In: Proceedings of IEEE Great Lakes Symposium on VLSI, pp. 88–92 (1997)
6. Rahman, M.Z., Kleeman, L., Habib, M.A.: Recursive approach to the design of a parallel self-timed adder. IEEE Trans. Very Large Scale Integr. (VLSI) Syst. **23**(1), 213–217 (2015)

7. Dobson, J.M., Blair, G.M.: Fast two's complement VLSI adder design. Electron. Lett. **31**(20), 1721–1722 (1995)

8. Chawla, R., Kumar, P., Yadav, P.: Adder circuit design using advanced quantum dot cellular automata (AQCA). In: National Conference on Recent Advances in Electronics and Computer Engineering (RAECE 2015) (2015)

9. Naziri1, S.Z.M., Ismail1, R.C., Shakaff, A.Y.M.: Arithmetic addition and subtraction function of logarithmic number system in positive region: an investigation. In: 2015 IEEE Student Conference on Research and Development (SCOReD) (2015). 978-1-4673-9572-4/15/$31.00

10. Hassan, Sk.S., Pal Choudhury, P., Nayak, B.K., Ghosh, A., Banerjee, J.: Integral value transformations: a class of affine discrete dynamical systems and an application. J. Adv. Res. Appl. Math. **7**(7), 62–73 (2015)

11. Pal Choudhury, P., Sahoo, S., Nayak, B.K.: Theory of carry value transformation and its application in fractal formation. In: IEEE International Advance Computing Conference (2009). doi:10.1109/IADCC.2009.4809146

12. Pal, S., Sahoo, S., Nayak, B.K.: Properties of carry value transformation. Int. J. Math. Math. Sci. **2012**, 10 pages (2012). doi:10.1155/2012/174372. Article ID 174372

13. Das, J.K., Pal Choudhury, P., Sahoo, S.: Multi-number CVT-XOR arithmetic operations in any base system and its significant properties. In: 2016 IEEE 6th International Conference on Advanced Computing (2016). doi:10.1109/IACC.2016.147

14. Pal Choudhury, P., Sahoo, S., Chakraborty, M.: Implementation of basic arithmetic operations using cellular automata, pp. 79–80. IEEE Computer Society (2008). http://doi.ieeecomputersociety.org/10.1109/ICIT.2008.18

15. Pal Choudhury, P., Hassan, Sk.S., Sahoo, S., Nayak, B.K.: Act of CVT and EVT in the formation of number theoretic fractals. Int. J. Comput. Cognit. **9**(1), 18 (2011). http://www.ijcc.us

16. Toffoli, T., Margolis, N.: Cellular Automata Machines. MIT Press, Cambridge. MA (1987)

17. Das, J.K., Pal Choudhury, P., Sahoo, S.: Carry Value Transformation (CVT) - Exclusive OR (XOR) Tree and Its Significant Properties. https://arxiv.org/pdf/1506.01544v1.pdf

Decreasing Entropy: How Wide to Open the Window?

Balázs Indig[1,2(✉)], Noémi Vadász[1,3], and Ágnes Kalivoda[3]

[1] MTA–PPKE Hungarian Language Technology Research Group, Budapest, Hungary
indig.balazs@itk.ppke.hu
[2] Pázmány Péter Catholic University, Faculty of Information Technology
and Bionics, Budapest, Hungary
[3] Pázmány Péter Catholic University, Faculty of Humanities and Social Sciences,
Piliscsaba, Hungary
{vadasz.noemi,kalivoda.agnes}@itk.ppke.hu

Abstract. On the basis of the literature about human sentence processing we examined the parsing process from two aspects. With the help of
a sentence-completion experiment we show that there is a strong relationship between the entropy of the words in the sentence and the look-
ahead window of a two-phase sentence processing model. The result of
our experiment showed that people intend to close the verbal complex
and the noun phrase as soon as possible and our corpus-measurements
support that it happens in a trigram window.

Keywords: Natural language processing · Psycholinguistics · Entropy

1 Introduction

Natural language processing (NLP) is the task of handling human languages
with the aid of computers. Unfortunately, in complex tasks, such as machine
translation, computers are far behind the human alternative even though to
train a system, scientists use more text than one would see in a life. We think
that the difference in performance is based on the main principles of how the
two parsers or translators (machine and human) work.

Our parsing model, ANAGRAMMA [1,5] is a performance-based, psycholin-
guistically motivated system following the patterns of human language processing as much as possible. The model utilizes a strictly left-to-right approach for
processing the input word by word imitating the language input.

In this paper we examine human sentence processing. We explore the first
phase of a two-phase sentence processing model, on one hand in production –
with a sentence-completion experiment based on entropy –, and on the other
hand in perception – with measurements on multiple corpora using a look-ahead
window.

As the theory of entropy is widely-used in other disciplines, its application
introduced in the paper in conjunction with the look-ahead window can be

© Springer International Publishing AG 2016
C. Martín-Vide et al. (Eds.): TPNC 2016, LNCS 10071, pp. 137–148, 2016.
DOI: 10.1007/978-3-319-49001-4_11

directly applied in other fields as well[1]. After a short theoretical background we present our results from the experiment and the corpus measurements.

2   Background

2.1   Sausage Machine

The ANAGRAMMA system aims to model the human language processing based on the *Sausage Machine* where the parsing process consists of two main phases. The first phase is – as Frazier and Fodor [4] calls it – the *Preliminary Phrase Packager* which assigns the lexical and phrasal nodes to groups of words within the string input. In the second phase, these packaged phrases get their roles in the sentence by adding non-terminal nodes, this phase is called the *Sentence Structure Supervisor*.

Frazier and Fodor [4] set a window of roughly six words which is used in the first phase of the sentence processing for preparing the packages for the second phase. In Sect. 4 we prove that for Hungarian a trigram window is enough due to its agglutinative nature. As human parsers try to bind the arguments of the verb as soon as possible [7], they sometimes fail and therefore need to backtrack. The most extreme manifestations of reanalysis are garden path sentences as in Example 1.

(1)   The horse raced past the barn fell.

During the reading of these garden path sentences word by word we need to backtrack which increases the time required to understand them. It is related to Kimball's *principle of Fixed Structure* [7], which claims that *'recalling a shunted phrase out of memory to restructure it is costly'*.

2.2   Entropy

Traditionally, entropy is a quantitative measure of the *randomness* of a system. For example a brand new deck of cards has low entropy since it is ordered, and a shuffled one has high entropy. Shannon and Weaver introduced entropy into information theory [13,14]. Miller was trying to show that statistical approximations to English have a predictive value for sentence recognition [12].

According to Shannon and Weaver *information* is the measure of one's freedom of choice when one selects a message [14]. Natural language that produces a sequence of symbols (letters and phonemes) according to certain probabilities is a *stochastic* process, and when the probabilities depend on the previous events it is called a *Markov chain*.

---

[1] For example in music, because it has essential relationship with natural language. Similarly to language, in music perceptually discrete events are structured into hierarchical sequences according to syntactic principles [9]. According to this, music can also be observed from this aspect.

On the level of words this probabilistic behaviour of natural language works as well: *'...If we are concerned with English speech, and if the last symbol chosen is 'the', then the probability that the next word be an article, or a verb form other than a verbal, is very small. This probabilistic influence stretches over more than two words, in fact. After the three words 'in the event' the probability for 'that' as the next word is fairly high, and for 'elephant' as the next word is very low.'* [14].

Pléh et al. attempted to demonstrate the relevance of information theoretical accounts to understanding word recognition and morphological processing in Hungarian [2]. Their work is based on that of Antal [10,11] who used the entropy notion developed by Shannon and Weaver [14] for equal probability outcomes where entropy is a function of the number of possible outcomes. See these papers for details on statistical complexity and entropy of language.

Morphological boundaries influence the degree of this monotonous decrease and intuitively correspond to slowing declining (locally increasing entropy values). Figure 1 shows the entropy values over the graphemes of a morphologically complex word[2], the entropy value gradually decreases over the stem, and then a suddenly increasing entropy indicates a morpheme boundary.

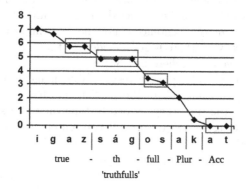

Fig. 1. Entropy value changes over a multiple suffixed Hungarian noun

Entropy can be captured between not only morpheme boundaries but bigger units like words as well. In the following section we show an experiment in which the effect of entropy fluctuation is measured on subsequent words in order to show empirically the inner-workings of the first phase of the Sausage Machine [4] for Hungarian to shed light on this detail of human parsing.

2.3 Corpora

We have made our measurements in two corpora:

The InfoRádió Corpus contains short Hungarian political and economical news. Each utterance here consists of a title and a body containing 2–3 sentences

---

[2] The example and the figure is from Pléh et al. [2].

that describe a single political or economic event. The corpus of 54.996 leads containing 135.587 sentences and 2 million tokens taken from a news portal's RSS feed (www.inforadio.hu).

The *Pázmány Corpus* [6] consists of Hungarian texts collected from the internet. The downloaded texts form the basis of the Pázmány Corpus with 1.2 billion tokens from more than 30 000 domains.

3 An Entropy Experiment

We performed an on-line test which focused on the entropy in processing a sentence word by word. We were curious to see how some words constrain the possible continuation of a sentence. In order to achieve this, the participants could see a Hungarian sentence with each successive word revealed one after another; each time they had to guess the next word in no more than 20 s. After their guess the solution has appeared and they had another 20 s to guess the next word, seeing its right context.

This test simulates how the human parser processes a sentence left to right and word by word, skipping uninformative words and making predictions to speed up reading which is to be modeled in ANAGRAMMA. Our prediction regarding to the meaning of a sentence is not the most important factor of language processing, however, 'there is good evidence[3] that expectancy generation plays a role in language comprehension' [3].

60 participants were involved in our test: 45 women and 15 men. The average age was 32 years, more than half of the participants had a university degree. Their reaction times (the time they needed to type their guess) were measured as well[4]. In the following section we present two sentences from the experiment and discuss the results.

3.1 Results

Two sentences from our test are presented below. Figures 2 and 3 show the reaction times needed to guess the next word by every segment of the sentences. The figures are followed by a detailed description of the results.

The first word (Fig. 2) was a verb in imperative, *Térjünk* 'Turn+Imp+p2'. Most of the participants thought that a detached preverb in post-position could be the next word. 40 % guessed the preverb *vissza* 'back', thus implying the meaning *visszatér* 'to return', with a reaction time of 5.3 s which is really fast. In case of *Térjünk még* (*még* 'still' is just a filler-word) the guessed word was

---

[3] EEG experiments show that the N400, a component of EEG signals is sensitive to semantic and structural priming. This amplitude is high when an already introduced fragment of a sentence is followed by a word that is not related to it [8].

[4] The test was performed under uncontrolled circumstances. Something may have diverted the participant's attention or he/she may have typed slowly. Nevertheless, thanks to a sufficient number of participants, these time frames provide valuable information regarding to the sentence processing tendencies.

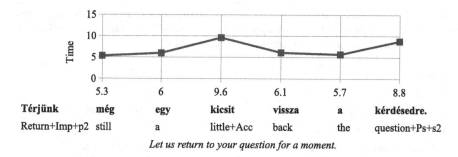

Fig. 2. Average reaction time influenced by the newly appearing word (The translated sentence and separately the translation of each individual word according to the full sentence i.e. after the part-of-speech and word-sense disambiguation are displayed.)

vissza 'back' again, now with 50 %. Other preverbs appeared as well (e.g. *ki* 'out', *be* 'in', *le* 'down').

After *egy* 'a(n)' indefinite article appeared, the reaction time increased with another 3.6 s: the participants thought of a collocation (*egy kicsit* 'a little') or wrote a noun which indicates a direction (where to turn to). After the word *kicsit*, only preverbs were guessed: *vissza* 'back' had 60 % at this point. This happened because the resulting sentence is not typical, it would be more natural if the preverb would follow the verb immediately. This tendency is quite obvious, because some participants reported that they became irritated when the newly appearing word was not a preverb, even though their guess was a preverb for the second time already, because they wanted to close the verbal complex as soon as possible.

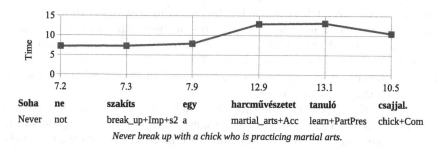

Fig. 3. Average reaction time influenced by the newly appearing word (The translated sentence and separately the translation of each individual word according to the full sentence i.e. after the part-of-speech and word-sense disambiguation are displayed.)

In step 1 of the second sentence (Fig. 3 and Table 1) the starting word was *Soha* 'Never'. Most of the participants tried to continue it by extending the negation with the following words: *nem/ne* 'not', *sem/se* 'not even', *többé/többet* 'no more', *sehol* 'nowhere', *napján* 'never ever'. They needed 7.2 s on average to

Table 1. The second sentence (Fig. 3) as the participants saw it step-by-step (first column). The words that have just appeared are in **boldface**. The second column is the translation of the last words according to their left-context.

1. **Soha**	'Never'
2. Soha **ne**	'not'
3. Soha ne **szakíts**	for the meaning see Table 2
4. Soha ne szakíts **egy**	'a'
5. Soha ne szakíts egy **harcművészetet**	'martial_arts+Acc'
6. Soha ne szakíts egy harművészetet **tanuló**	'learn+PartPres'
7. Soha ne szakíts egy harművészetet tanuló **csajjal**	'chick+Com'

make this decision and type in the answer, this could be regarded as a fast reaction. This can be explained with the frequent co-occurrence of *soha* 'never' and these words.

In step 2 the starting word was extended with the next word resulting in the sequence *Soha ne*, 'Never ever' (literally 'Never not'). Every participant thought of a verb in imperative, second person singular, mostly *mondd* 'say', *tedd* 'do', *gondold* 'think' – these tend to be frequently used warnings and requests. The average reaction time was nearly the same as before (7.3 s).

Step 3 presented the sequence *Soha ne szakíts*. The resulting sequence is quite complex, because the meaning of the verb *szakít* depends on the particle used with it, furthermore, it can stand without a particle or form collocations like *szakít időt* 'to find the time to do sth'[5] (see Table 2). Almost half of the participants (27 people) thought of *szakíts félbe* ('interrupt'+Imp+s2), 12 people gave an answer that suggests the meaning 'to break up with sb' where the Hungarian verb doesn't have a particle but an argument in instrumental case. Some of the answers imply the meaning 'to tear apart sth' (*szakíts szét, szaíts ketté*) and 'to tear off sth' (*szakíts le*). Due to this large amount of options we can see a slightly increasing reaction time (7.9 s). It is caused by the predicted – however, different – verb modifier as a consequence of the intention to close the verbal complex as soon as possible.

In step 4 the appearance of *egy* ('a', indefinite article) caused a sudden increase in reaction time (+5 s), 6 participants didn't write a new guess at all. Those who were waiting for a verb modifier are now forced to backtrack to the beginning of the sentence to correct the path of the parse which needs time. Furthermore, the indefinite article indicates the beginning of a noun phrase which can continue in many ways. This high entropy regarding to the possible continuation is the cause of increased reaction times and 43 different answers[6].

---

[5] The more common word order would be *időt sza t* or *félbeszakít* (in this case, *félbe* functions as a prefix).

[6] The most common answers were *virágot* ('flower'+Acc, resulting in 'Never tear off a flower', guessed by 7 people) and *nővel* ('woman'+Com, resulting in 'Never break up with a woman', guessed by 3 people).

Table 2. The argument structures of the Hungarian *szakít* verb and some of its possible verb modifiers

(verb modifier) + verb	meaning	arguments		
szakít$_1$	to break up with	Nom	Com	
szakít$_2$	to tear	Nom	Acc	
meg + szakít	to cut off	Nom	Acc	
félbe + szakít	to interrupt	Nom	Acc	
ketté + szakít	to tear in two	Nom	Acc	
szét + szakít	to tear apart	Nom	Acc	
le + szakít	to tear off	Nom	Acc	Del
ki + szakít	to pluck	Nom	Acc	Ela
el + szakít	to tear apart	Nom	Acc	(Abl)

In step 5 the task became even more difficult when the next word of the sentence appeared. 17 people wrote *félbe*, even if this answer doesn't have a reasonable explanation. It would indicate the meaning 'Never interrupt [a] martial arts' which has a semantic incompatibility. The explanation behind the results is that two phenomena are opposed to each other: the content does not match the semantic expectations[7] and the urge to place the verb modifier, which has been proven stronger. 11 people didn't guess. Only less than half of the participants recognized this as the beginning of a complex noun phrase. They wrote present participles, e.g. *tanuló* 'someone who studies sth', *ismerő* 'someone who knows sth', etc. The highest reaction time (13.1 s) can be seen at this point. It is caused caused both by the aforementioned opposing phenomena and the complex noun phrase containing a participle.

In step 6 (final step), participants guessed a noun in comitative or accusative case. The latter can be explained as the participant's plan to add the verb modifier *félbe* to the end of the whole sentence (as it was unclear when the sentence will come to an end)[8], thus he or she chose the meaning 'Never interrupt [someone] who is practicing martial arts!'. The former case (words in comitative case (58 %)) imply the meaning 'Never break up with a [man/girl/friend/person] who is practicing martial arts!'. Both solutions make sense, however, the decision depends on whether the participant is influenced by his or her answers in the earlier steps. The average reaction time decreased (10.5 s) due to the semantic and structural constraints of the context. Still, the time needed is high, because of the urge to complete the complex NP and identify it as an argument of main verb.

---

[7] The existence of this phenomenon has been verified using EEG experiments by [8].

[8] This form is unlikely in edited texts, and has minimal occurrences in unedited ones, however, some participants were desperately stuck at the form *félbeszakít*. This phenomena is responsible for these rare forms found in corpora.

3.2   Discussion

The diversity of the answers and the length of reaction times show how easily and accurately the next item (the word itself or at least its part of speech without its adjuncts) can be predicted based on the context already known matching the concept of entropy [14]. In the results two trends can be observed: Firstly, when the lexical elements are predominant because of the strong lexical collocations like in *Soha ne* and *Térjünk vissza/rá*. We also have found that when a collocation can not be ruled out, the participants' decision strategy was risky and fast by choosing a collocation to speed up parsing like in *Soha ne [imperative]*.

Secondly, in view of the results we can state that the participants tried (1) to choose a verb modifier for the verb as soon as possible (*Térjünk [verb modifier]*), and (2) to close the NPs quickly with a case marker corresponding to the requirements of the verb (*Soha ne szakíts [commitative/accusative]*) even though it is less constrained lexically, because the appropriate category is more important. The aforementioned intention of closing the verbal complex and the NP is related to the Preliminary Packaging Phase [4].

As a side-effect, we empirically have found a way how the rare occurrences of far-strolled verb modifiers (see Sect. 4.1) are created. This rare case happens when the intentions to close the verbal complex and not to distract the more meaningful constituents are conflicting. This problem is usually solved by putting the verb modifier right after the verb, but when this phase is missed for some reasons in production, the other constituents become more important and the verb modifier is held back till the end of the sentence. In the following section we will show how the aforementioned phenomena are manifested in real word texts. To achieve this, we use written corpora.

4   Window in Parsing

In the previous section we presented an experiment which helped us to capture the phenomena of word-level entropy. To verify Fodor and Frazier's statement [4] that the size of the window used in the first phase of the Sausage Machine is 'approximately six words' we used corpora and measured the right detached verb modifier and the nominative possessor – possessum distance for Hungarian. As Hungarian is an agglutinative language (and most of the information is stored in morpheme suffixes of the content words in contrast to the many function words and fixed word-order in English) we show that a narrower window is enough. Based on our preliminary experiments we set the size to 'three content words'. In those cases where this window is not enough we show that it is likely that another strategy is used for parsing.

4.1   The Verb and Its Preverb

Figure 4 shows the distribution of the Hungarian verbs that can bear preverb, grouped by the number of their possible preverbs. A little more than half of these

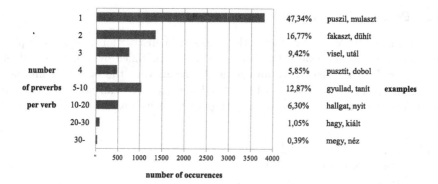

Fig. 4. Number of possible preverbs per verb. A little more than half of the Hungarian verbs that have preverbs can bear various preverbs in the sentence.

verbs can take various preverbs in the sentence, which is crucial because the verb itself can have more than one possible – but contradicting – argument structures (see Table 2 for example in the previous section) at this point of processing. The appearance of a preverb after the verb itself can filter impossible argument structures and prune false branches of the analysis resulting in faster parsing.

We measured the distances between verbs and their right detached preverbs[9] on the InfoRádió Corpus. Table 3 summarizes our findings.

Table 3. Positions of post-verbal detached preverbs – In edited texts 99 % of the detached preverbs appear immediately after the verb, even in unedited texts the maximum two tokens after the verb contain the 99 % of preverbs

FIN	+1	+2	+3	+4	+5	+6	+7
SUM	23.552	220	-	-	-	-	-
%	99.999 %	0.001 %	-	-	-	-	-

In the InfoRádió corpus there is no example of a preverb following the verb at a distance larger than two positions[10].

Our results show that a trigram window is enough for connecting the verb and its right detached preverb. It means that in the first phase of the Sausage Machine the verbal complex is completed and its argument structure is disambiguated, so the speed-up effect of the window can prevail.

---

[9] In Hungarian the preverb can take various places: (1) on the verb as a prefix, (2) detached to the left, (3) detached to the right.

[10] There is a low number of examples of more than two positions distance, but all of them are caused by tagging errors which were not counted.

4.2 Possessive Structure

In Hungarian there are two syntactic possessive constructions. When the possessor is in nominative case the possessum can be modified by numerals and/or adjectives, but it cannot take an article. It means that the possessor and the possessum form an NP, their order is fixed and the verb can not intervene. In possessive contructions the possessum agrees with its possessor in person and number.

(2)   Peti   kutyája
      Peter+N+Nom dog+N+s3
      Peter's dog

When the possessor is in dative case there are two individual NPs for it and its possessum. This means that their order is not fixed[11] and the verb can intervene.

(3)   Petinek   elveszett   a   kutyája
      Peter+N+Dat lose+V+Past the+Article dog+N+s3
      Peter's dog is lost.

The most neutral realization of the iterated possessive construction is when the first possessor is in nominative case, and the second one is in dative case.

(4)   Peti   kutyájának a   nyakörve
      Peter+N+Nom dog+N+s3 the+Article collar+N+s3
      Peter's dog's collar

We measured the distance between the possessor and the possessum in nominative case using the Pázmány Corpus. We were looking for structures that start with a word in nominative case and end with the closest word having a possessive affix. The possessor's position was marked with 0 and the position of the possessed was determined automatically, compared to the possessor. With this method more than 7.700.000 phrases were matched. Figure 5 shows the positions of possessed, given in percent.

The +1 position of the possessum covers 52.46 % of the cases. It means that the possessor is followed immediately by the possessum (e.g. *Chopin művei* '[the] works of Chopin'). The +2 position has 27.45 %. The intervening word is usually an adjective (e.g. *Bozsik legfontosabb tulajdonsága* 'Bozsik's most important property') or a numeral (e.g. *ingatlanok 10 százaléka* '10 % of [the] real estates'). 10.66 % goes to the +3 position. The two intervening words are mostly an adverb and an adjective/numeral (e.g. *népesség csaknem 60 százaléka* 'almost 60 % of the population'), sometimes a complex substantive derived from a verb (e.g. *döntések hatályon ívül helyezése* 'repeal of decisions').

---

[11] The most neutral is the possessor-possessum order, the reverse is still grammatical but somehow marked.

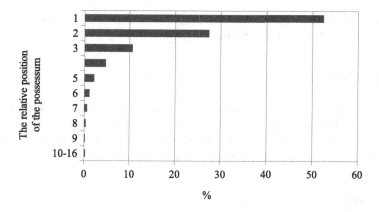

Fig. 5. The distance of the nominative possessor and its possessum (in nominative)

The summarized frequency of the latter positions is less than 10 %. These phrases usually include enumerations or a participle where the derived verb keeps its arguments and adjuncts to its left (see Example 5 found in Pázmány Corpus (+16 position of the possessum[12]).

(5) Krisztina   különleges, Swarovski kristályokból és   minőségi
     Kristina+N special,   Swarovski crystal   and high-quality
     japán   gyöngyökből készült, egyedi tervezésű romantikus, nőies
     Japanese pearl   made,   unique designed romantic,   feminine
     nyaklánca
     necklace+Ps+s3

     'Kristina's special, romantic, feminine necklace with unique design, made of Swarovski crystals and high quality Japanese pearls'

As we can see, a trigram-window is sufficient in 80 % of the possible cases. Even if the possessor stands without a suffix that could indicate the grammatical case (so it is analysed as nominative), the parser is able to make a decision whether the word is a possessor or not. If a word having a possessive affix can be found in the window of the word originally marked as nominative, it is highly possible that the word without grammatical case is actually the possessor.

In 20 % of the measured cases, there is more than one intervening word within the possessive structure. More than half of these cases include co-ordinations (enumeration of the possessum's attributes), and the presence of embedded participles is frequent as well. In case of these complex NPs, a decision about the possessor's role can not be made with the help of a trigram-window but in a latter phase of processing. Even so, we have to emphasize that this problem does not occur in four fifths of the possessive structures. The large distance between the possessor and the possessum occurs rather in – mostly formal – written texts.

---

[12] Punctuation marks are counted as separate tokens.

We assume that there is an other parsing strategy for handling these long-term dependencies which is a topic of an other research.

5 Conclusion

The data extracted from the corpus are consistent with the results of our entropy experiment. The human processor tries to close the different phrases as soon as possible, so they will appear in a trigram-window. Therefore the first phase of the Sausage Machine can be observed both in production and perception.

References

1. Indig, B., Prószéky, G.: Magyar szövegek pszicholingvisztikai indíttatású elemzése számítógéppel. Alkalmazott nyelvtudomány **15**(1–2), 29–44 (2015)
2. Pléh, C., Németh, K., Varga, D., Fazekas, J., Várhelyi, K.: Entropy measures and predictive recognition as mirrored in gating and lexical decision over multimorphemic hungarian noun forms. Psihologija **46**(4), 397–420 (2013)
3. Elman, J.L.: An alternative view of the mental lexicon. Trends Cogn. Sci. **8**(7), 301–306 (2004)
4. Frazier, L., Fodor, J.D.: The sausage machine: a new two-stage parsing model. Cognition **6**(4), 291–325 (1978)
5. Prószéky, P., Indig, B., Vadász, N.: Performanciaalapú elemző magyar szövegek számítógépes megértéséhez. In: Bence, K. (ed.) "Szavad ne feledd!": Tanulmányok Bánréti Zoltán tiszteletére, pp. 223–232. MTA Nyelvtudományi Intézet, Budapest (2016)
6. Endrédy, I.: Nyelvtechnológiai algoritmusok korpuszok automatikus építéséhez és pontosabb feldolgozásukhoz (Language Tehcnology Algorithms for Automatic Corpus Building and More Precise Data Processing). PhD thesis, Pázmány Péter Catholic University Faculty of Information Technology, Budapest, 6 2016. (in Hungarian)
7. Kimball, J.: Seven principles of surface structure parsing in natural language. Cognition **2**(1), 15–47 (1973)
8. Kutas, M., Hillyard, S.A.: Brain potentials during reading reflect word expectancy and semantic association. Nature **307**, 161–163 (1984)
9. Lerdahl, F., Jackendoff, R.: A Generative Theory of Tonal Music. The MIT Press, Cambridge (1983)
10. Antal, L.: A megnyilatkozások tagolása morfémák szerint. Magyar nyelvőr **86**(2), 189–202 (1962)
11. Antal, L.: A formális nyelvi elemzés. Gondolat, Budapest (1964)
12. Miller, G.A.: Language and Communication. McGraw Hill, New York (1951)
13. Shannon, C.E.: A mathematical theory of communication. SIGMOBILE Mob. Comput. Commun. Rev. **5**(1), 3–55 (2001)
14. Shannon, C.E., Weaver, W.: A Mathematical Theory of Communication. University of Illinois Press, Champaign (1963)

Simulating Stochastic Dynamic Interactions with Spatial Information and Flux

Ozan Kahramanoğulları[1,2]

[1] Department of Mathematics, University of Trento, Trento, Italy
[2] Centre for Computational and Systems Biology,
The Micrososft Research - University of Trento, Rovereto, Italy

Abstract. We present a conservative extension to rule based modeling languages with constructs for component attributes and functions that modify these attributes; the language has a stochastic semantics, and it is equipped with flux analysis. We show that the constructs of this language, called M, bring an ease especially in modeling biological systems, where spatial information is of essence. We discuss the language on models from molecular biology such as membrane diffusion systems, and actin polymerization networks, as well as models from ecology, where spatial behavior of animals as in bird flocks and fish schools are studied.

1 Introduction

The recent advances in systems and synthetic biology are now giving rise to an increased integration of modeling languages. The capabilities that these technologies offer make it possible to model, simulate and analyze biological phenomena with the aim of complementing and accelerating the investigations in life sciences. The compact constructs of such languages for expressing various phenomena, as they are considered in different areas of biology, speed up the modeling process. As a result, specialized domain-specific languages contribute to investigations on a great variety of phenomena from molecular biology [1,5,10,15,16], pharmacology [12], ecology [4,8,9], and others, e.g., [11].

Among many mathematical and computational formalisms used to model biological systems, probably the most common representation schemes are those that are based on chemical reaction networks (CRN). The formalism of CRN is quite convenient as it finds deterministic and stochastic interpretations in terms of simulations. While the deterministic simulations are easily performed as numeric solutions of ordinary differential equation systems, the discrete stochastic simulations, which we consider here, are commonly performed by resorting to the Gillespie algorithm [6]. This algorithm and its many variations provide the semantics for the rule based languages, commonly used in many systems biology applications with results that provide insights to biological questions. In a nut shell, the rule based languages such as BNG and Kappa [1,5,15] provide compact representations for CRNs. This, in return, makes it possible for these languages to express biological system models with only few rules, in contrast to many, sometimes even infinite number of reactions of simple CRN representations.

© Springer International Publishing AG 2016
C. Martín-Vide et al. (Eds.): TPNC 2016, LNCS 10071, pp. 149–160, 2016.
DOI: 10.1007/978-3-319-49001-4_12

Here, we introduce a modeling language, called M, that extends some of the more common notations that are in use in rule based languages with the gain of an increased expressive power. M extends the constructs of the rule based languages with those for encoding attributes of model components and functions that modify these attributes. These encodings become instrumental, for example, for implementing spatial information and arbitrary constraints on model dynamics that account for the encoded information. Our implementation of the simulation engine conservatively extends the Gillespie algorithm to accommodate these features for the models that employ them. Moreover, the simulation algorithm makes use of the analysis methods, introduced in [13], for quantifying the stochastic fluxes due to the continuous time Markov chain semantics. The constructs that we introduce bring an ease to the modeling and analysis of certain phenomena that are more challenging in standard rule based languages. However, some of these constructs can be implemented by not-so-straight-forward encodings in stochastic Pi-calculus, that is, SPiM [2,10,14,16].

In the following, we introduce the syntax and semantics of M, and discuss its properties as a modeling language. We illustrate its features on a number of example models with varying detail and structure of model components. In particular, we present how simple CRN models and rule based models are accommodated, and how flux analysis can be easily applied to these models. We illustrate how geometric information can be encoded to capture classes of models from biology and ecology such as those for protein diffusions on membranes, and movements of animals as in bird flocks or fish schools. We show how the geometric information can be used to render movies that reflect the emerging geometric structures in molecular biology as in actin dynamics.[1]

2   Syntax

Each M model consists of a set of rules, a description of the initial state, and a number of directives that specify the kind of data to be output at the end of a simulation. These directives determine the data to be recorded besides the time series resulting from the simulation. This is because simulations with these models can generate different kinds of information such as the evolution of the species in space with respect to their coordinates, stochastic fluxes at arbitrary time intervals, or the evolution of other species parameters defined below.

The rules for the interactions are defined with the grammar in Fig. 1, where the curly brackets denote the optional components. Here, Name, Species, x, y, z, v_1, ..., v_k, Site, and Bond are strings. f_x, f_y, and f_z as well as Rate and Exp are functions with type float on any subset of all the variables in the rule. f_1, ..., f_k are also functions on any subset of the variables in the rule, however with types $Type_1$, ..., $Type_k$, respectively. If the Rate value is not given for a rule, it is assigned a default value of 1.0. Sites is associative and commutative, so the order of the Site expressions does not matter.

---

[1] Prototype modules that implement the language components are available for download at our website. http://sites.google.com/site/ozankahramanogullari/M.

{Name :} Reactants -> Products {with Rate} {if Condition} ;

Reactants ::= o | Reactant + ⋯ + Reactant

Reactant ::= Species{ReactantArguments} | Reactant.Reactant

ReactantArguments ::= ({CoordinateVariables} ; {Variables} ; {Sites})

CoordinateVariables ::= $c(x)$ | $c(x,y)$ | $c(x,y,z)$

Variables ::= v_1 : Type$_1$, ... , v_k : Type$_k$

Type ::= int | float | bool | string

Sites ::=   Site{! Bond} , ... , Site{! Bond}

Products ::= o | Product + ⋯ + Product

Product ::= Species{ProductArguments} | Product.Product

ProductArguments ::= ({CoordinateFunctions} ; {Functions} ; {Sites})

CoordinateFunctions ::= : cf(f_x) | cf(f_x,f_y) | cf(f_x,f_y,f_z)

Functions ::= : $f_1, ..., f_k$

Condition ::= Atom |

       not Condition | Condition && Condition | Condition or Condition

Atom ::= Exp > Exp | Exp >= Exp | Exp = Exp | Exp =< Exp | Exp < Exp

Fig. 1. The grammar that defines the rules of language M.

The definition of the rules above extends the standard definition of the chemical reaction networks (CRN), and also rule based languages such as BNG [1], Kappa [5], or others [15]. It is immediate that any chemical reaction of a CRN can be written as a rule of the above form that does not involve any CoordinateVariables, Variables, Sites or Condition expressions. Similarly, any BNG rule can be mapped to a rule with Sites and Variables as defined above, and modifications on *complexes* can be modeled by using the associative and commutative '.' construct in Reactant and Product primitives. These permit a number of common modeling expressions, including BNG style rules; in particular, the following are valid in language M:

1. Reactions (that create or destroy molecules), e.g., A + B -> C;
2. Rules for forming a bond, e.g., A(b) + B(a) -> A(b!0).B(a!0);
3. Rules for breaking a bond, e.g., A(b!0).B(a!0) -> A(b) + B(a);
4. Rules for changing a component state, e.g., X(x) -> X(x+1);

Besides these expressions that are common to other modeling languages, the definition above permits other constructs, in particular:

5. Variables and functions on species coordinates, and conditions on their interactions, e.g., to model two species that exchange their locations if they are
   less than 2 units apart from each other:

$$\texttt{A(c(x,y))} + \texttt{B(c(p,q))} \ \texttt{->} \ \texttt{A(c(p,q))} + \texttt{B(c(x,y))} \ \texttt{if} \ (x-p)^2 + (y-q)^2 < 4;$$

6. Other variables and functions on species, and conditions on their interactions
   to model various attributes of species, e.g., to model state changes given as
   modifications of arguments under specific conditions:

$$\texttt{A(p,r)} \ \texttt{->} \ \texttt{A(p*2,"very-high")} \ \texttt{if} \ p > 10 \ \&\& \ r = \texttt{"high"};$$

In any model, these constructs can be combined and used together to express
arbitrarily complex phenomena including conditional complexation and decom-
plexation, and positioning in space with respect to species interactions.

The initial state at the beginning of a simulation is defined by the grammar
below, which is used to describe the species that are present at time zero.

Quantity InitialSpecies ;

InitialSpecies $::=$ Species{SpeciesArguments} | InitialSpecies.InitialSpecies

SpeciesArguments $::=$ ({Coordinates} ; {Constants} ; {Sites})

Coordinates $::=$ c(c_x) | c(c_x,c_y) | c(c_x,c_y,c_z)

Constants $::=$ $c_1, \ldots, c_k$

Here, Quantity is an integer. c_x, c_y, and c_z are real numbers. $c_1, \ldots, c_k$ are constants with types that agree with those in reactant and product definitions in
the rules. These constructs are used to specify the *state* of the system at time
zero, which is then modified by the rules at each simulation step.

The modifications performed by the rules are recorded in a number of log
files as state updates according to the directives of the model. Each of these log
files contain various aspects of the simulation trace, including the time series of
the model species. These directives are given by the following grammar:

{directive time-series OutputSpecies , . . . , OutputSpecies; }

OutputSpecies $::=$ Species{OutputArguments} | OutputSpecies · OutputSpecies

OutputArguments $::=$ ({OutputCoordinates} ; {OutputParameters} ; {Sites})

OutputCoordinates $::=$ c(t_x) | c(t_x,t_y) | c(t_x,t_y,t_z)

OutputParameters $::=$ $t_1, \ldots, t_k$

{directive coordinates; }

{directive parameters; }

{directive flux; }

Here, t_x, t_y, and t_z vary over real numbers and variables. $t_1, \ldots, t_k$ vary over
constants and variables with types that agree with those in reactant and product

definitions in the rules. These constructs are used to specify the species and complexes, the time-series of which are recorded. If a coordinate or parameter is specified with a variable instead of a constant, then all the species that match that expression are counted. The instructions 'directive coordinates' and 'directive parameters', respectively, write to separate files the modifications on species coordinates and species parameters by individual rule instances. This way, for example, the movement of species in space as a result of the stochastic simulation dynamics can be plotted as a movie. If 'directive flux' is included in the model, then the initial state and the rules will be annotated off-line by the preprocessing engine with respect to the algorithm described in [13]. In this respect, the monitoring of the stochastic fluxes during simulation does not require any syntactic notation in the modeling language. The flux information is then written to a separate file.

Given a model with the syntax above, the pre-processing engine performs a number of syntactic checks on the input model. These are as follows.

1. All the occurrences of the same species in different rules and initial conditions agree with each other in terms of their arguments, their arity and their types. For example, for a species A, the language does not permit two occurrences with A(1.0,"free") and A("free",1.0), as one of them has a parameter with type float as the first argument and the other with type string.

2. All the occurrences of all the species in different rules and initial conditions agree with each other in terms of the arity of their coordinates. For example, given two species A and B, the language does not permit two occurrences with A(c(1.0)) and B(c(3.0,1.0)), as one of them has a coordinate with one dimension whereas the other has two dimensions. However, species without any coordinate parameter are permitted in the presence of others with coordinates. These coordinate-free species are then to be interpreted as "freely diffusing". (However, as it is explained below, the coordinate parameters do not have any effect on the simulation dynamics, unless they are specified to affect it by means of conditions or rate functions.)

3. Any Bond expression is permitted to occur at maximum two Site expressions in any Reactants, Products, or Species expression.

4. The variable occurrences in any Reactant expression is a superset of those in the Product, Rate and Condition expression of the same rule.

5. The Species expressions in the initial conditions are subset of those that occur in the Reactants and Products expressions.

3   Semantics and Implementation

The models of language M that do not include any species parameters are CRN models. Thus, it is immediate that the continuous time Markov chain (CTMC) interpretation of CRNs, given by the Gillespie algorithm [6], provides a semantics for simulations with these models. Similarly, rule-based models are implemented by resorting to the CTMC semantics; this is done by generating the chemical reactions from the rules at every state when they become applicable. This way, a rule based model can be used to simulate a system that would potentially require an infinite number of reactions as a simple CRN. Examples to such models include polymerization models [2,3].

The semantics of language M extends the CTMC semantics of the rule based languages to those models that include species coordinates and other parameters and functions that operate on these parameters under given conditions. This is done by considering any two species or any two complexes distinct if they differ in terms of any of their parameters. As a result of this, species and complexes at any state of the simulation that are modified by the rules are grouped with respect to their bonds as in rule based models, and also with respect to their parameters. For identifying and comparing the individual species and complexes, we employ a canonical form for the complexes given by the '.' construct. Because any syntactic expression $A.B$ or $B.A$ refer to the same complex, imposing a pre-defined lexicographic order on these entities provides a canonical form.

Following the standard CTMC semantics of the CRN with respect to the Gillespie algorithm, the propensity of each rule is computed in the usual way, whereby the rate of the rule is multiplied by the number n of possible combinations in the current state that match the Reactants. If a rule has a Condition, only those matches that satisfy the Condition are considered; as the number of such combinations is $m \leq n$, the propensity is computed by using m instead of n. Then, as the rule to be applied is selected by the standard procedure of the Gillespie algorithm, an instance of Reactants is randomly picked from m combinations, and the rule is applied to this instance. Although this procedure is linear-time, considering the individual differences of the species with respect to their parameters introduces an overhead to the simulation, which can be avoided for the models that do not involve parameters such as pure CRN models. This is done by inspecting the model automatically with respect to the constructs that it employs, and by automatically simplifying the data structures and procedures according to the level of complexity introduced by these constructs.

According to the algorithm in [13], the fluxes are computed by labeling each species with a unique id, which is a natural number assigned to each species during the creation of that species. If the flux directive is set in the model description, the simulation engine performs this labeling to produce the *simulation trajectory* with respect to the definitions in [13]. Fluxes are collected during the simulation in terms of the flow of species between rules. The flux algorithm conservatively extends the Gillespie algorithm, and thereby constructs several data structures, which reveal a variety of statistics about resource creation and consumption during the simulation. This information is logged into a file to be used to quantify the causal interdependence and relative importance of the reactions at arbitrary time intervals. As it is the case for complexes and parameters of species, computation of fluxes introduces a computational overhead due to the tracking of individuals. However, this overhead becomes relevant only if the fluxes are being monitored during simulation.

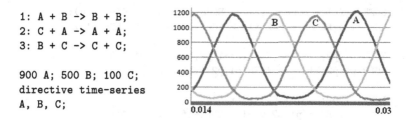

```
1: A + B -> B + B;
2: C + A -> A + A;
3: B + C -> C + C;

900 A; 500 B; 100 C;
directive time-series
A, B, C;
```

Fig. 2. M implementation of a CRN that models an oscillator, and a time-series of it.

4 Example Models

In the following, we present a number of models with varying expressivity to illustrate the constructs above in use. While the individual models are valid in isolation, the concepts they use can be combined for incrementally richer models.

Simple CRNs and Rule Based (BNG-Style) Models

CRN models as in [12] are implemented with the common notation. For a simple example, consider the oscillator model in M, depicted in Fig. 2 together with a time-series plot. Here, the rates are set to 1.0 by default.

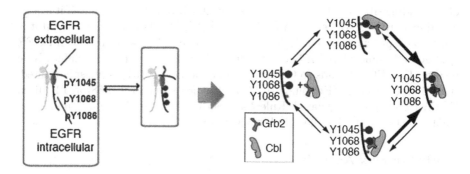

Fig. 3. Schematic EGFR model. EGFR forms a dimer with another EGFR, and thereby facilitates the binding of its ligand EGF. The ligand bound EGFR has a higher phosphorylation affinity of its tyrosin residues. The phosphorylated residues then become binding sites for other proteins. The phosphorylated sites Y1068 or Y1086 become available for the binding of the protein Grb2, whereas phosphorylated Y1045 is a binding site for Cbl. Cbl and Grb2 bind each other, independent from their binding to EGFR.

Let us now consider a more complex model that would require hundreds of reactions as a CRN model, however can be modeled with few rules in M as in other rule based languages. We consider the Epidermal Growth Factor Receptor

```
1: EGFR(egfr) + EGFR(egfr) -> EGFR(egfr!a).EGFR(egfr!a);
2: EGFR(1,egfr!b) + EGF(r) -> EGFR(1!a,egfr!b).EGF(r!a);

3: EGFR(p1,p2;1!a) -> EGFR(p1+1,p2;1!a) if p1 = 0;
4: EGFR(p1,p2;1!a) -> EGFR(p1,p2+1;1!a) if p2 < 2;

5: EGFR(p1,p2;y45) + Cbl(egfr) ->
            EGFR(p1,p2;y45!a).Cbl(egfr!a) if p1 = 1;
6: EGFR(p1,p2;y68or86) + Grb2(egfr) ->
            EGFR(p1,p2;y68or86!a).Grb2(egfr!a) if p2 > 0;
7: Grb2(c) + Cbl(g) -> Grb2(c!a).Cbl(g!a);

100 EGFR(0,0;egfr,1,y45,y68or86);   100 EGF(r);
60 Cbl(egfr,g); 10 Grb2(egfr,c);

directive time-series EGFR(p1,p2;egfr!a,1!b,y45!c,y68or86!d).
                      EGFR(p1,p2;egfr!a,1!f,y45!g,y68or86!h);
```

Fig. 4. A model that implements the dynamics depicted in Fig. 3.

(EGFR), as depicted in Fig. 3. In the model in Fig. 4, for simplicity we use default rates, which can be easily replaced with the actual kinetic rates by using the 'with Rate' construct. We also omit the reverse rules for simplicity. Here, Rule 1 states that two EGFR form a dimer, no matter what the state of their other binding sites are. Rule 2 states that an EGFR binds to its ligand if it is part of a dimer. Rule 3 states that Y1045 on EGFR (p1) gets phosphorylated if it is not already phosphorylated. Rule 4 states that one of Y1068 or Y1086 on EGFR (p2) gets phosphorylated if both of them are not already phosphorylated. Rule 5 states that EGFR binds to Cbl if the Y1045 on EGFR (p1) is phosphorylated. Rule 6 states that EGFR binds to Grb2 if at least one of Y1068 or Y1086 on EGFR (p2) is phosphorylated. Rule 7 states that Cbl and Grb2 bind, no matter what the state of their other binding sites are.

Stochastic Flux Analysis

Thanks to the automatic annotation of the model species, if 'directive flux' is included in the model, flux information is automatically generated and written in a separate file with respect to the algorithm in [13]. For example, the oscillator model in Fig. 2 produces the fluxes depicted in Fig. 5 at three distinct non-steady-state intervals, denoted within the square brackets, where respectively A, B and C increase. Here the fluxes quantify the amount of resources that flow between the reactions within these intervals.

Models with Space and Geometric Information

The constructs of language M permit the definition of the dynamic behavior of the species to depend on the geometric state or the spatial constraints. In

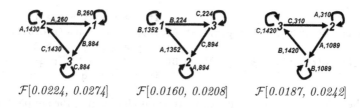

$\mathcal{F}[0.0224,\ 0.0274]$ $\mathcal{F}[0.0160,\ 0.0208]$ $\mathcal{F}[0.0187,\ 0.0242]$

Fig. 5. Flux configurations of the simulation with the oscillator network depicted in Fig. 2, for different time intervals, where the species A, B and C increase.

this setting, species can alter their position in space with respect to arbitrary functions defined on their parameters or the parameters of the species they interact with. For a simple example, we consider a class of models that are commonly used, for example, to study the behavior of diffusing proteins on membranes [7]. A diffusion model on a two dimensional grid, where a particle moves either north or east, is given by the two rules below.

```
move_x: A(c(x,y)) -> A(c(x+1,y)); move_y: A(c(x,y)) -> A(c(x,y+1));
1 A(c(0,0)); directive coordinates;
```

Another class of models that we consider here as an example is individual based models in ecology [4] that are used for simulating the spatial behavior of animals in groups as in fish schools or bird flocks. The birds in a migrating flock of birds, for instance, adjust their distances with their neighbors by synchronizing on few simple rules [8,9,17]. This gives rise to the emergent behavior known as *flocking*. Although there are much more refined characterizations, the most basic form of flocking behavior is modeled by three simple principles:

1. Separation, that is, avoid crowding neighbors.
2. Alignment, that is, steer towards average heading of neighbors.
3. Cohesion, steer towards average position of neighbors.

The constructs of M permit describing these principles as model rules with arbitrary level of detail or precision. To illustrate this, let us take a simpler setting on the two-dimensional plane, whereby all the birds move in the same direction along the x-axis, and each bird synchronizes with its neighbors. Among other rules that describe the movement of the birds, the rules below provide a simple implementation of these three principles. However, models with arbitrary detail can be similarly accommodated as well as rules with greater control.

```
separation_1: B(c(x,y)) + B(c(p,q)) -> B(c(x,y+0.1)) + B(c(p,q-0.1))
                         if y > q && y - q < 1;
separation_2: B(c(x,y)) + B(c(p,q)) -> B(c(x,y-0.1)) + B(c(p,q+0.1))
                         if y < q && q - y < 1;
alignment_1: B(c(x,y))  + B(c(p,q)) -> B(c(x+0.1,y)) + B(c(p,q))
                         if x < p && p - x > 1;
alignment_2: B(c(x,y))  + B(c(p,q)) -> B(c(x,y)) + B(c(p+0.1,q))
```

```
                           if x > p && x - p > 1;
cohesion_1:  B(c(x,y)) + B(c(p,q)) -> B(c(x,y-0.1)) + B(c(p,q+0.1))
                           if y > q && y - q > 2;
cohesion_2:  B(c(x,y)) + B(c(p,q)) -> B(c(x,y+0.1)) + B(c(p,q-0.1))
                           if y < q && q - y > 2;
```

Another class of models that are more than challenging for simple CRNs is polymerization models as these models would require an infinite number of CRN reactions to capture unbounded polymerization [3]. The situation gets even more complicated when the polymers have rich structures as it is the case for actin [2], where each monomer in a polymer can have a number of states depending on being bound to ADP, ADP-P_i or ATP or other actin binding proteins. The following M model illustrates how polymerization can be modeled by two rules.

```
1: A(l,r) + A(l,r) -> A(c(0);l,r!a).A(c(1);l!a,r);
2: A(c(x);l!a,r) + A(l,r) -> A(c(x);l!a,r!b).A(c(x+1);l!b,r);
```

```
1000 A(l,r); directive time-series A(l!a,r!b);  directive coordinates;
```

Here, Rule 1 states that two free monomers bind to form a dimer, and Rule 2 states that a free monomer binds to the right-end of a filament, and thereby becomes the new end-most monomer of the filament. The important point to observe in this model is how the coordinate information is updated, that is, each free monomer gets a coordinate information when it binds to an existing filament. This concept, which is here illustrated for one dimensional space, can be easily generalized for models in two or three dimensions. In particular, the images depicted in Fig. 7 are obtained from the screen shots of movies generated by stochastic simulation on actin polymerization models by applying theses ideas [2].[2] These models are constructed by encoding the geometric information as coordinate parameters and the dynamics as functions that alter this information.

The actin filaments in Fig. 6 are polymers of monomers that grow along an axis [2,14]. As in the polymer model implementation above, the free actin do not have coordinate parameters, because they are assumed to be free in the cytosol. However, all the bound actin monomers are equipped with a coordinate

Fig. 6. Graphical representation of the formation of a polymer, consisting of three monomers, that is, a trimer. Af denotes the monomer that is freely diffusing, whereas Al and Ar, respectively, denote the monomers that are bound on the left and bound on the right to other monomers. Ab denotes a monomer that is bound to other monomers on both sides. The trimer then consists of the chain of Ar, Ab, and Al.

---

[2] https://www.youtube.com/watch?v=38KCf8nHQz0.

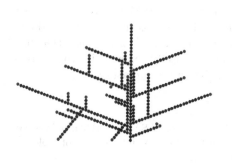 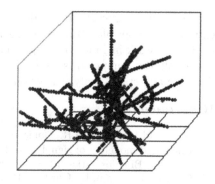

Fig. 7. Example screen shots captured from the movies generated by stochastic simulations with actin models that contain encodings of geometric information. The image on the left is from a 2D simulation where the filaments branch, however they do not rotate along the growth axis. The image on the right is obtained from a model that contains the 3D encoding of the branching as well as the helical rotations.

parameter. When a free monomer binds to a filament, the free monomer evolves to a bound state, while receiving the coordinate information from the filament that it binds to. When branching filaments are considered, we adopt this idea to include the rotation of the filaments with respect to the axis of growth. This is because the angle between a mother actin filament and a daughter filament is measured as 70 degrees. Moreover, actin filaments have a helical shape with a rotating structure, repeating every 13 subunits. In order to model these rotations, we equip each rule with a function that implements a rotation matrix on the coordinates with respect to the growth vector of its filament axis. In this setting, due to the inclusion of 'directive coordinates', as the simulation evolves simulation steps are recorded in a separate file with respect to the emerging coordinate dynamics. This information is then used, for example, to render movies that reflect the dynamics emerging from the species interactions.

5   Discussion

We have introduced a modeling language that extends common rule based languages with constructs for encoding species attributes, and functions that modify them, as well as features for stochastic flux analysis. The example models above should provide a flavor of the possible applications that make use of spatial information as well as flux analysis.

For the models that makes use of all the constructs of language M, the simulation algorithm results in reduction in efficiency in comparison to, for example, pure CRN models. This overhead is due to the increase in the information monitored and modified within the data structures during simulation. However, our design of the simulation algorithm inspects the constructs that are used in the model, and enables certain data structures only if they are required for the model in use. In this respect, 'pure' models that do not exploit M features can be easily exported to other platforms that provide the fastest algorithm for the task.

Future work includes the implementation of a modeling platform that integrates all the components of M, and incrementally extends it with various dynamic and static analysis methods available in the literature.

References

1. Blinov, M.L., Faeder, J.R., Goldstein, B., Hlavacek, W.S.: BioNetGen: software for rule-based modeling of signal transduction based on the interactions of molecular domains. Bioinformatics **20**, 3289–3292 (2004)
2. Cardelli, L., Caron, E., Gardner, P., Kahramanoğulları, O., Phillips, A.: A process model of actin polymerisation. In: FBTC 2008, vol. 229. ENTCS, pp. 127–144. Elsevier (2008)
3. Cardelli, L., Zavattaro, G.: On the computational power of biochemistry. In: Horimoto, K., Regensburger, G., Rosenkranz, M., Yoshida, H. (eds.) AB 2008. LNCS, vol. 5147, pp. 65–80. Springer, Heidelberg (2008). doi:10.1007/978-3-540-85101-1_6
4. DeAngelis, D.L., Gross, L.J.: Individual-based Models and Approaches in Ecology. Chapman and Hall, New York (1992)
5. Feret, J., Danos, V., Krivine, J., Harmer, R., Fontana, W.: Internal coarse-graining of molecular systems. PNAS **106**(16), 6453–6458 (2008)
6. Gillespie, D.T.: Exact stochastic simulation of coupled chemical reactions. J. Phy. Chem. **81**, 2340–2361 (1977)
7. Gurry, T., Kahramanoğulları, O., Endres, R.: Biophysical mechanism for ras-nanocluster formation and signaling in plasma membrane. PLoS One. **4**(7), e6148 (2009)
8. Hemelrijk, C.K., Hildenbrandt, H.: Some causes of the variable shape of flocks of birds. PLoS One. **6**(8), e22479 (2011)
9. Hildenbrandt, H., Carere, C., Hemelrijk, C.K.: Self-organized aerial displays of thousands of starlings: a model. Behav. Ecol. **21**(6), 1349–1359 (2010)
10. Kahramanoğulları, O., Cardelli, L.: An intuitive modelling interface for systems biology. Int. J. Softw. Inf. **7**(4), 655–674 (2013)
11. Kahramanoğulları, O., Cardelli, L.: Gener: a minimal programming module for chemical controllers based on DNA strand displacement. Bioinformatics (2015)
12. Kahramanoğulları, O., Morpurgo, D., Fantaccini, G., Lecca, P., Priami, C.: Algorithmic modeling quantifies the complementary contribution of metabolic inhibitions to gemcitabine efficacy. PLoS One. **7**(12), e50176 (2012)
13. Kahramanoğulları, O., Lynch, J.: Stochastic flux analysis of chemical reaction networks. BMC Systems Biol. **7**(133) (2013)
14. Kahramanoğulları, O., Phillips, A., Vaggi, F., Process modeling, rendering of biochemical structures: actin. In: Lecca, P. (ed.) Biomechanics of Cells and Tissues: Experiments, Models and Simulations, vol. 9. LNCVB, pp. 45–63. Springer, Netherlands (2013)
15. Ollivier, J.F., Shahrezaei, V., Swain, P.S.: Scalable rule-based modelling of allosteric proteins and biochemical networks. PLoS Comput. Biol. **6**(11), e1000975 (2010)
16. Phillips, A., Cardelli, L.: Efficient, Correct Simulation of Biological Processes in the Stochastic Pi-calculus. In: Calder, M., Gilmore, S. (eds.) CMSB 2007. LNCS, vol. 4695, pp. 184–199. Springer, Heidelberg (2007). doi:10.1007/978-3-540-75140-3_13
17. Reynolds, C.W.: Flocks, herds and schools: a distributed behavioral model. ACM SIGGRAPH Comput. Graph., pp. 25–34 (1987)

Implementation of Turing Machine Using DNA Strand Displacement

Wataru Yahiro[✉] and Masami Hagiya

Department of Computer Science,
Graduate School of Information Science and Technology, University of Tokyo, 7-3-1,
Bunkyo-ku, Hongo, Tokyo 113-8656, Japan
{yahiro.wataru,hagiya}@is.s.u-tokyo.ac.jp

Abstract. The computational capability of biochemical systems is one of the major interest in the area of nanotechnology. Since Bennett proposed his thought experiment of chemical Turing machine using DNA-like molecules, many attempts for DNA Turing machine have been made. However, they are based on some hypothetical assumptions or require laboratory manipulations for each step. Here we propose an implementation of Turing machine by using DNA strand displacement cascades.

1 Introduction

The development of molecular biology revealed that activities in biological cells are carried out in a highly mechanical way. The research area of molecular computing was born inspired by the insight into such biochemical processes. Researchers of molecular computing have been studying for long years the way to perform computation by biomolecules.

The attempts to implement Turing machine by biomolecules have a long history. The first theoretical proposal was done by Bennett [2]. However, because it required hypothetical enzymes and polymers, it was only a theoretical consideration. Many other theoretical proposals used existing enzymes, but they required laboratory manipulations for each step of Turing machine [1,6].

Recently, DNA strand displacement (DSD) is widely known as a powerful framework for molecular computation. It was shown that multi-stack machines, which are Turing-universal model of computation, can be constructed within this framework [3,4]. In these works, a polymer of DNA molecules was used to resemble a stack and stack operations were implemented as polymer modification reactions which push and pop end monomers.

We take a step further and show a way to directly construct Turing machine using DSD. In our model, computation is driven by two types of formal chemical reactions implemented by DSD. The first type is for state transitions. They push forward the computation by consuming a character and a machine state, then generating a new character and a next machine state. The second type is for tape modification. A tape is implemented as a long DNA molecule, and it is designed to be modified easily, so tape modification reactions can be realized

© Springer International Publishing AG 2016
C. Martín-Vide et al. (Eds.): TPNC 2016, LNCS 10071, pp. 161–172, 2016.
DOI: 10.1007/978-3-319-49001-4_13

by simple strand displacement reactions. In addition, tapes are autonomously extended by adding domains to which extension tapes can be attached, and it enables Turing-universal computation.

Our construction is different from works on DNA Turing machines such as those using restriction enzymes in that it does not require laboratory manipulations during the computation. Compared to the construction of multi-stack machines, our tapes can grow toward both sides if needed and it can be modified not only at the end but also at any part.

This paper mainly consists of two parts. First, in Sect. 2, we consider the case where the tape length is fixed, and show that an arbitrary space-bounded Turing machine can be simulated by DSD. Second, in Sect. 3, we introduce reactions for signal-driven tape extending, which enable Turing-universal computation.

In this paper, we assume that readers are familiar with the basic rules of DNA strand displacement [8].

2   Space-Bounded DSD Turing Machine

2.1   Definitions

We have to modify the definition of well-known Turing machine so that it is suitable to the framework of DSD. Our basic idea is roughly the same as that of stack machines [3,4]. The configuration of a machine is represented by a chemical solution that contains three types of special chemical species, which stand for states, characters and tapes, respectively, and the computation is driven by two types of chemical reactions, which are in charge of state transitions and tape operations respectively.

We clarify the basic notions of formal language theory used in this paper. Let Σ be a finite alphabet. The set of all finite-length strings over Σ is denoted by Σ^*. Let U, V be languages. The concatenation of languages is denoted by UV. For a character $a \in \Sigma$, a single-word language $\{a\}$ is often denoted by a itself. Next we define a labeled alphabet. Let D be a set of symbols called labels. A labeled alphabet is an alphabet $\Sigma^D = \{a^d \mid a \in \Sigma, d \in D\}$. We denote a subset of Σ^D that have a fixed label by $\Sigma^d = \{a^d \mid a \in \Sigma\}$ where $d \in D$.

Let us give the formal definition of a variant of Turing machine, which we call DSD Turing machine or DSDTM for its short hand.

Definition 1. *let $D = \{L, R\}$ be a set of labels. A DSD Turing machine M is defined as a 6-tuple $M = (Q, \Sigma, \delta, q_0, F, a_0^d)$ where*

- *Q is a finite set of states,*
- *Σ is a finite set of symbols called alphabet,*
- *$\delta \subseteq (Q \backslash F) \times \Sigma^D \times Q \times \Sigma^D$ is a set of 4-tuples called state transition reactions,*
- *$q_0 \in Q$ is the initial state,*
- *$F \subseteq Q$ is a set of final states,*
- *$a_0^d \in \Sigma^D$ is an initial character.*

We call elements of Σ^L and Σ^R, respectively, L-type characters and R-type characters.

Definition 2. *A tape of a DSD Turing machine M is defined as a string $T \in (\Sigma^L)^*(\Sigma^R)^*$. A head is defined as a partition (boundary line) between L-type characters and R-Type characters.*

In the following text, a tape is denoted as $T = [a_1a_2...a_n|a_{n+1}...a_{n+m}]$, where the vertical bar | represents the position of the head. Note that the "head" is defined as a partition while that of ordinary Turing machines is defined as a pointer to a character.

Definition 3. *A configuration of a DSD Turing machine M is defined as a 3-tuple $C = (q, a^d, T)$ where $q \in Q$ is a state, $a^d \in \Sigma^D$ is an extra character and $T \in (\Sigma^L)^*(\Sigma^R)^*$ is a tape.*

A configuration (q_0, a_0^d, T_0) is especially called an initial configuration, where T_0 is an initial tape that is given as an input. Likewise, when a configuration contains a state $q_f \in F$, it is called a terminal configuration. This definition is a formalization of a chemical solution in which q, x^d and T represent formal chemical species. Chemical solutions are often formalized as a multiset [3,4,7], but we use a tuple in order to clarify that the solution contains exactly one molecule of each species. This situation is exactly the same as in the previous works on stack machines [3,4].

A state transition rule of a DSDTM is represented as a formal reaction $(q, a^d, p, x^{d'}) \in \delta$. It is called a state transition reaction. A state transition reaction is a formal chemical reaction, as its name indicates, so we denote it by $q + a^d \rightarrow p + x^{d'}$ in the following text. According to the combination of labels, there are four types of state transition reactions as written below.

$$q + a^L \rightarrow p + x^L \tag{1}$$
$$q + a^L \rightarrow p + x^R \tag{2}$$
$$q + a^R \rightarrow p + x^L \tag{3}$$
$$q + a^R \rightarrow p + x^R \tag{4}$$

These are called an LL-type reaction (1), an LR-type reaction (2), an RL-type reaction (3) and an RR-type reaction (4), respectively. We often write a LD-type reaction or a DR-type reaction to partially fix labels.

The operations for a tape are also defined as formal chemical reactions. They are called tape modification reactions and written as follows.

$$a^L + [...c|bd...] \rightleftharpoons [...ca|d...] + b^R \tag{5}$$

Tape modification reactions edit the content of the tape and move the head simultaneously. The forward reaction pushes an L-type character into left of the head and pops an R-type character which was at right of the head. The backward reaction is a mere inverse of the forward reaction. The only requirement for tape modification reactions is that the content of the opposite side of the pushed character is not empty. For example, tape modification reaction is not defined between an extra character a^L and a tape $[bc|]$ because there is no character to pop. Conversely, except for this corner case, tape modification reactions occur whenever an extra character and a tape exist. Note that this limitation implies that tape modification reactions cannot change the length of the tape.

Now we describe how the computational process of DSDTM proceeds. A DSDTM performs computation as rewriting its configuration by state transition reactions and tape modification reactions. The transition rules between configurations are defined as follows.

Definition 4. *Let C and C' be configurations of a DSD Turing machine M. The transition from C to C' is denoted by $C \Rightarrow C'$. A transition from $C = (q, a^d, [a_1...a_n | a_{n+1}...a_{n+m}])$ is enabled when the destination fulfills one of the following conditions.*

- $C \Rightarrow (p, x^{d'}, [a_1...a_n | a_{n+1}...a_{n+m}])$ *when* $q + a^d \to p + x^{d'} \in \delta$.
- $C \Rightarrow (q, a^R_{n+1}, [a_1...a_n a | a_{n+2}...a_{n+m}])$ *when* $a^d \in \Sigma^L$ *and* $m > 0$.
- $C \Rightarrow (q, a^L_n, [a_1...a_{n-1} | a a_{n+1}...a_{n+m}])$ *when* $a^d \in \Sigma^R$ *and* $n > 0$.

The first one is a transition by a state transition reaction and others are by tape modification reactions.

Transitions of a DSDTM are essentially nondeterministic, but we can make it "practically" deterministic by imposing two conditions on δ. First, δ must be (partially) functional. That is to say, for any q and a^d, there exists at most one state transition reaction $q + a^d \to p + x^{d'} \in \delta$. Second, any state q can react with characters of only one type. When both a state transition reaction and a tape modification reaction is simultaneously possible, q can react with different characters and it might make the computation nondeterministic. For example, let a configuration be $(q, x^R, [a|b])$ and δ include two state transition reactions $q + a^L \to p + c^R$ and $q + x^R \to p' + d^L$. If a tape modification reaction occurs first, the transition path will be $([a|b], q, x^R) \Leftrightarrow ([|xb], q, a^L) \Rightarrow ([|xb], p, c^R)$. On the other hand, if a state transition reaction occurs first, it will be $([a|b], q, x^R) \Rightarrow ([a|b], p', d^L) \Leftrightarrow ([ad|], p', b^R)$, so the path will be forked. However, any transition by tape modification reactions is reversible and a tape modification reaction always emits a character whose label is opposite to its reactant, so we can avoid undesired nondeterminism by limiting the type of characters to react with each state. Accordingly, we can guarantee that a computational path of DSDTM can be uniquely determined except for going back by tape modifications. This is why we said that "practically" deterministic at the beginning of this paragraph.

2.2   DSD Turing Machine vs. Turing Machine

Since DSDTMs have rules for state transition and tape modification, they seem equivalent to Turing machine in its computational power. So, we prove the theorem that DSDTM can simulate an arbitrary space-bounded Turing machine.

Theorem 5. *Let a space-bounded Turing machine be $M_{TM} = (Q, \Sigma, \delta, q_0, F)$, where Q is a set of state, Σ is a finite alphabet, $\delta : (Q \backslash F) \times \Sigma \rightarrow Q \times \Sigma \times \{L, R\}$ is a transition function, $q_0 \in Q$ is the initial state and $F \subseteq Q$ is the set of final states. There exists a space-bounded DSD Turing machine M that can simulate M_{TM}.*

Proof. Here we describe the main ideas of the proof. First, we regard a character at right of the head of a DSDTM as the head of a Turing machine. For example, in a tape of a DSDTM $[ab|cd]$, the character c is assumed to be pointed by Turing machine's head. In this proof, we refer to the head of a Turing machine simply by the head, and that of a DSDTM by the partition in order to avoid overlapping of the word "head". Second, we introduce additional character used for tape manipulation. Finally, we translate each transition rule into state transition reactions by subdividing each step of M_{TM} into some substeps.

Specifically, we can construct a desired DSDTM as follows. Let the DSDTM be $M = (Q', \Sigma \cup \{H\}, \delta', q_0, F, H^L)$ where $H \notin \Sigma$ is an additional character and $Q' \supseteq Q$ has some additional states, while q_0 and F are directly inherited from M_{TM}. So, all that is left is to translate transition rules.

Let $\delta(q, a) = (p, x, d)$ be a transition rule. Because our assumption about the head is asymmetric, the implementation varies according to direction d. They can be implemented as follows, respectively.
$\delta(q, a) = (p, x, L)$:

$$q + a^R \rightarrow q_a + x^R \tag{6}$$
$$q_a + H^L \rightarrow q_a' + H^R \tag{7}$$
$$q_a' + b^L \rightarrow q_{ab} + H^L \tag{8}$$
$$q_{ab} + H^R \rightarrow p + b^R \tag{9}$$

where (8) is defined for every $b^L \in \Sigma^L$.
$\delta(q, a) = (p, x, R)$:

$$q + a^R \rightarrow q_a + H^R \tag{10}$$
$$q_a + H^L \rightarrow q_a' + x^L \tag{11}$$
$$q_a' + H^R \rightarrow p + H^L \tag{12}$$

Figure 1 shows how each substep works. First, no matter what the direction is, each cycle starts with a configuration $C = (q, H^L, [...b|a...])$ where a tape $[...b|a...] \in (\Sigma^L)^*(\Sigma^R)^*$ does not include either H^L or H^R. The only possible transition from C is $C \Leftrightarrow (q, a^R, [...bH|...])$. This step corresponds to reading a character on the head of Turing machine.

From this point, the computational path branches according to the direction indicated by the original transition function. In the case of $\delta(q, a) = (p, x, L)$, the reaction (6) and succeeding tape modification reaction rewrite the character on the head. The reaction (7) is to read the character on left of the partition, because we have to switch its direction label in order to move the head toward left.

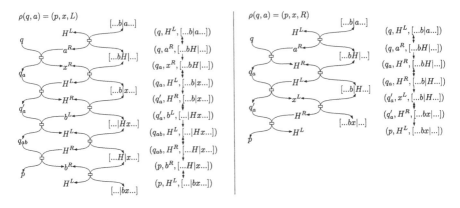

Fig. 1. A simulation of a Turing machine by a DSDTM

Fig. 2. The structure of formal species q, a^L, a^R and $[a...b|c...d]$

The reaction (8) recognizes the character and the next reaction (9) produces a switched character and the new state p. After the final substep, the configuration will be $(p, b^R, [...H|x...])$, and it can change to $(p, H^L, [...|bx...])$, which is the entry point of the next cycle.

The translation of $\delta(q, a) = (p, x, R)$ is slightly easier, because we only have to care about the character on the head. The first reaction (10) is to recognize the character on the tape. The second reaction (11) produces a new character x^L to be written. The final reaction (12) produces new basic state p, then the configuration reaches the entry point of next cycle.

Accordingly, it is proved that for any Turing machine M_{TM}, there exists an DSDTM M that can simulate M_{TM}. Moreover, M needs only a constant number of substeps to simulate each step of M_{TM}, so DSDTM can perform computation as fast as Turing machine.

2.3   Formal Species

Figure 2 illustrates the structure of formal species q, a^L, a^R and $[a...b|c...d]$. A state q and characters a^L and a^R are represented by short upper strands, which we call state strands and character strands. The structure of state strands is inherited from [4]. The two long domains ^-q and ^+q are unique to q, but all state strands have a toehold domain U in common. The structure of character strands a^L and a^R are like mirror images. The domains S and T are shared among all character strands, so each character strand has only one unique domain.

A tape $[a...b|c...d]$ is a long complex of DNA molecules. The bottom strand of it, which we name a substrate strand, is a single long strand. The substrate strand

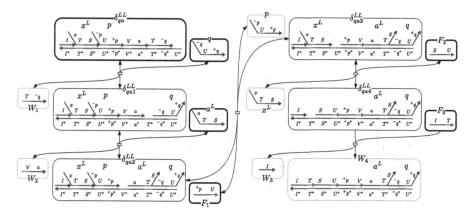

Fig. 3. The implementation of a state transition reaction $q + a^L \rightarrow p + x^L$. The bold frames indicate species required to be present initially. The blue frames indicate end products.

has a long domain S^* and a toehold domain T^* alternatively and repeatedly, and has T^* at the both ends. The content of the tape is represented by character strands attached to the substrate strand. Though almost all domains of the substrate strands are covered with character strands, only one toehold T^* is exposed and it works as a head. On the side of $3'$ end (left in Fig. 2) from the head, only L-type character strands are allowed. Conversely, on the side of $5'$ end (right in Fig. 2) from the head, only R-type character strands are allowed. Definition 2 reflects this structure. Needless to say, the structure of a substrate strand itself is independent of any character, so it is capable of representing arbitrary sequence of characters.

2.4   State Transition Reaction

Our implementation of state transition reactions is similar to that of irreversible formal chemical reactions in [4]. Figure 3 shows an LL-type state transition reaction $q + a^L \rightarrow p + x^L$ (1) in detail. We assume that δ_{qa}^{LL}, F_1, F_2 and F_3 exist in sufficiently large amount at any time so that the reaction can occur whenever reactants of the state transition reaction are present. In contrast, there are exactly one copy of q and x^L as we mentioned in the definition of a configuration. W_1, W_2, W_3 and W_4 are waste strands produced during the reaction.

The reaction is implemented by a chain of strand displacement proceeding from the $5'$ end to the $3'$ end. The existence of both q and a^L is confirmed by the first two steps. The next two steps is driven by fuel species and produce a new state and a character. The final step makes the entire process irreversible.

Other types of state transition reactions (2), (3) and (4) can be implemented similarly. Figure 4 shows the implementation of other types of state transition reactions. For the LR-type reaction (2), δ_{qa}^{LR} has almost the same structure as that of δ_{qa}^{LL}. On the other hand, those of RD-type reactions are quite different.

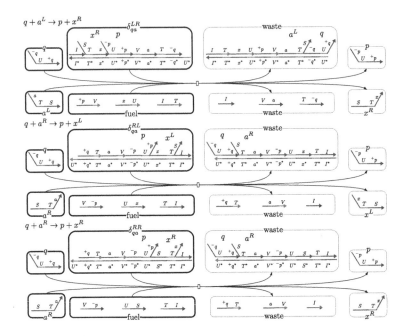

Fig. 4. The implementations of other types of state transition reactions

For example, δ_{qa}^{RL} for the RL-type reaction (3) has the first toehold U^* on the $3'$ end in order to recognize the unique domain of an R-type character. In other words, branch migration proceed to opposite directions between LD-type reactions and RD-type reactions. The difference between δ_{qa}^{RL} and δ_{qa}^{RR} is just as that of LD-type reactions.

2.5 Tape Modification Reaction

The implementation of tape modification reactions is simpler than that of state transition reactions. Figure 5 illustrates the tape modification reaction $a^L + [...c|bd...] \rightleftharpoons [...ca|d...] + b^R$ (5). As Fig. 5 shows, both forward and backward reaction are simple strand displacement reaction. By the forward reaction, a^L is pushed into the tape and b^R is popped, and the only exposed toehold T^*, which we decided as the head, moves right. The backward reaction is mere inverse of the forward reaction.

3 Space-Unbounded DSD Turing Machine

3.1 Definitions

The implementation we described above is not Turing-universal because of its limitation in the size of tape. Generally speaking, Turing-universality requires a model of computation to be able to use unbounded space. So, we implement in our architecture a function to extend the tape whenever more space is needed.

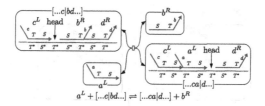

$$a^L + [...c|bd...] \rightleftharpoons [...ca|d...] + b^R$$

Fig. 5. The implementation of tape modification reaction

Definition 6. *Let* $D = \{L, R\}$ *and* $I = \{1, 2\}$ *be sets of labels. A space-unbounded DSD Turing machine is defined as a 9-tuple* $M = (Q, \Gamma, \oslash, \{[,]\}^I, \Sigma, \delta, q_0, F, a_0^d)$ *where*

- Q *is a finite set of states,*
- Γ *is a finite set of symbols called alphabet,*
- $\oslash \in \Gamma$ *is the blank character,*
- $\{[,]\}^I$ *is a set of the terminal characters,*
- $\Sigma = \Gamma \backslash \{\oslash\}$ *is a set of symbols called input alphabet,*
- $\delta \subseteq Q \times \Gamma^D \times Q \times \Gamma^D$ *is a set of 4-tuple called state transition reactions,*
- $q_0 \in Q$ *is the initial state,*
- $F \subseteq Q$ *is the set of final states,*
- $a_0^d \in \Sigma^D$ *is a initial character.*

Some definitions need to be modified in order to enable space-unbounded computation. A tape of a space-unbounded DSDTM is defined as a string $T \in [^I(\Gamma^L)^*(\Gamma^R)^*]^I$, and denoted by $[^i a_1 a_2 ... a_n | a_{n+1} ... a_{n+m}]^j$. It looks similar to that of space-bounded DSDTM, but $[^i$ and $]^j$ represent actual characters. Tape modification reactions are not changed essentially, but we clarify the following two special cases when the head reaches the end of the tape.

$$a^L + [^i...b|]^j \rightleftharpoons [^i...ba| +]^j \tag{13}$$

$$[^i|b...]^j + a^R \rightleftharpoons [^i+ |ab...]^j \tag{14}$$

Strictly speaking, $[^i...ba|$ and $|ab...]^j$ do not match the definition of tapes, but we do not distinguish them to avoid unnecessary redundancy.

Next, we introduce two kinds of reactions to extend tapes. The first type of reactions are tape generating reactions. They are written as follows.

$$[^i \rightarrow [^j\oslash... \oslash + \oslash^L \tag{15}$$

$$]^i \rightarrow \oslash...\oslash]^j + \oslash^R \tag{16}$$

where $[^j\oslash...\oslash$ and $\oslash...\oslash]^j$ are additional tapes of L-type and R-type, respectively, We have to impose the condition on the labels that $i \neq j$. This requirement seems unnatural but we will explain the reason later. There are four tape generating reactions according to the label of terminal characters. The second

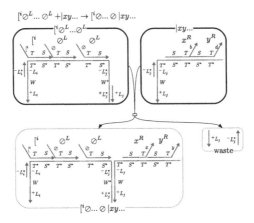

Fig. 6. The implementation of tape extending reaction

type of reactions are tape extending reactions. They attach an additional tape
to an existing tape as follows.

$$\left[{}^i \oslash ... \oslash + |a_1...a_n\right]^j \rightarrow \left[{}^i \oslash ... \oslash |a_1...a_n\right]^j \tag{17}$$

$$\left[{}^i a_1...a_n| + \oslash...\oslash\right]^j \rightarrow \left[{}^i a_1...a_n| \oslash ...\oslash\right]^j \tag{18}$$

Let us describe how a tape is extended by these reactions. Let the configuration
be $C = (q, a^R, [{}^i|b...]^j)$. The transition $C \Rightarrow (q, [{}^i, |ab...]^j)$ is enabled by the tape
modification reaction (14). Next, a new additional tape $[{}^k\oslash^L... \oslash^L$ $(k \neq i)$ and a
blank character $\oslash^L$ are generated by the reaction (15). Then the tape extending
reaction (17) attaches the additional tape to the existing tape, and the tape is
extended into $[{}^k\oslash... \oslash |ab...]^j$. Finally, the configuration become $(q, \oslash^L, [{}^k\oslash... \oslash$
$|ab...]^j)$. Compared to C, it looks as if the blank character is popped out by
moving the head to left. A tape can be extended to right similarly.

Needless to say, space-unbounded DSDTMs can simulate an arbitrary space-
unbounded Turing machines, so they can perform Turing-universal computation.

3.2   Tape Extending Reaction

We have to change the structure of tapes in order to realize tape extending
reactions. Figure 6 shows the implementation of an extendable tape and the
reaction to extend the tape to left. Compared to Fig. 2, extendable tapes have
additional domains to bind each other on both ends of substrate strands. We call
them joint sections. The process of tape extending reaction itself is quite simple.
As in Fig. 6, the existing tape $|xy..$ has a toehold domain W exposed and the
additional tape has the complement toehold W^*, so they can bind each other,
and two joint sections are bound irreversibly by branch migration.

Note that the joint sections of both ends of an additional tape have different
labels (that is, $i \neq j$) because of the condition of labels in tape generation

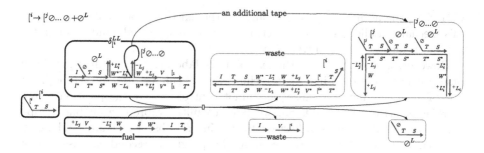

Fig. 7. The implementation of new tape generating reaction

reactions (15) and (16). This is necessary because if they have the same label, they can be bound by each other and the additional tape make a loop by itself. So, we have to use at least two different types of joint sections.

3.3 Tape Generating Reaction

Tape generating reactions can be realized in a way similar to the state transition reactions. Figure 7 illustrates the tape generating reactions (15). The complex $\delta_{[^i}^{LL}$ corresponds to δ_{qa}^{LL} in Fig. 3. The additional tape $[^j \oslash ... \oslash +\oslash^L$, which is drawn as a black curved line on $\delta_{[^i}^{LL}$ in Fig. 7, is attached to $\delta_{[^i}^{LL}$ turned upside down. It is bound by joint sections of both ends and the content part of the tape is rounded. Other types of tape generating reactions is are similar.

4 Conclusions

In this paper, we proposed a way to implement (a variant of) Turing machine with DNA molecule using DNA strand displacement cascades. In the first half, we implemented the space-bounded version of Turing machine. It can be constructed by two types of reactions, state transition reactions and tape modification reactions. State transition reactions change the state of Turing machine and produce a new character. Basic approach to implementing them is to use mediating complexes as in the stack machine [4]. However, in our construction, since characters have directionality in order to designate the movement of the head in tape operations, we must design the mediating complex taking the directionality into consideration. On the other hand, tape modification reactions are for the tape operations. Our design of tapes made it possible to modify their content easily, so tape modification reactions themselves can be realized by simple toehold-mediated strand displacement reactions.

In the second half, we constructed the space-unbounded version of Turing machine by improving the structure of tapes. We introduced joint parts at which an additional tape can be attached and terminal characters behave as the signals for generating additional tapes. Once the head has reached the end of the tape, the terminal character is emitted and it triggers the tape generating reaction.

After that, the additional tape is bound to the existing tape by the joint part. This mechanism allows our construction to perform space-unbounded computation and achieves Turing-universality.

However, when it comes to the feasibility of laboratory experiment, we have some points to notice. First, it is technically difficult to directly synthesize a tape of arbitrary input because we cannot control exactly the position where a character strand is bound. So, we have to initially prepare an blank tape $[\oslash ... \oslash \,|]$, which can be synthesized by mixing a substrate strand and many blank characters $\oslash^L$, then give an input by program. Second, we use a long DNA molecule as a storage, but actual DNA molecules are easily breakable. So, although our framework theoretically enables space-unbounded computation, the size of memory is practically bounded by the durability of DNA molecules. Finally, since the basic idea of performing computation by interaction between free-floating molecules is inherited from the implementation of the stack machine [4], our constructions could not overcome problems deriving from it. Especially, our system will not run correctly if there are two or more copies of state strands in the solution, but it is difficult to prepare an exact number of molecules in laboratory. On the third problem, it is not altogether impossible to overcome by making a femtoliter droplets that contains single molecule using a special laboratory technique [5]. Another possible solution is to change the frameworks so that an arbitrary copy of machines in the same solution. For example, if we can link the state with the tape somehow and construct each machine by an independent single molecule as in Bennett's scheme. This can also improve the first problem because parallelism enhance the probability that tapes survive.

References

1. Beaver, D.: A universal molecular computer. DNA Based Comput. **27**, 29–36 (1996)
2. Bennett, C.H.: The thermodynamics of computationa review. Int. J. Theor. Phys. **21**(12), 905–940 (1982)
3. Lakin, M.R., Phillips, A.: Modelling, simulating and verifying turing-powerful strand displacement systems. In: Cardelli, L., Shih, W. (eds.) DNA 2011. LNCS, vol. 6937, pp. 130–144. Springer, Heidelberg (2011). doi:10.1007/978-3-642-23638-9_12
4. Qian, L., Soloveichik, D., Winfree, E.: Efficient turing-universal computation with DNA polymers. In: Sakakibara, Y., Mi, Y. (eds.) DNA 2010. LNCS, vol. 6518, pp. 123–140. Springer, Heidelberg (2011). doi:10.1007/978-3-642-18305-8_12
5. Rondelez, Y., Tresset, G., Tabata, K.V., Arata, H., Fujita, H., Takeuchi, S., Noji, H.: Microfabricated arrays of femtoliter chambers allow single molecule enzymology. Nature Biotechnol. **23**(3), 361–365 (2005)
6. Rothemund, P.W.: A DNA and restriction enzyme implementation of Turing machines. DNA Based Comput. **27**, 75–119 (1996)
7. Soloveichik, D., Cook, M., Winfree, E., Bruck, J.: Computation with finite stochastic chemical reaction networks. Natural Comput. **7**(4), 615–633 (2008)
8. Soloveichik, D., Seelig, G., Winfree, E.: DNA as a universal substrate for chemical kinetics. Proc. Nat. Academy Sci. **107**(12), 5393–5398 (2010)

Machine Learning

A Quantum Annealing Approach to Biclustering

Lorenzo Bottarelli, Manuele Bicego, Matteo Denitto, Alessandra Di Pierro[(✉)],
and Alessandro Farinelli

University of Verona, Strada le Grazie 15, 37134 Verona, Italy
alessandra.dipierro@univr.it

Abstract. Several problem in Artificial Intelligence and Pattern Recognition are computationally intractable due to their inherent complexity and the exponential size of the solution space. One example of such problems is biclustering, a specific clustering problem where rows and columns of a data-matrix must be clustered simultaneously. Quantum information processing could provide a viable alternative to combat such a complexity. A notable work in this direction is the recent development of the D-Wave^{TM} computer, whose processor is able to exploit quantum mechanical effects in order to perform quantum annealing. The question motivating this work is whether the use of this special hardware is a viable approach to efficiently solve the biclustering problem. As a first step towards the solution of this problem, we show a feasible encoding of biclustering into the D-Wave^{TM} quantum annealing hardware, and provide a theoretical analysis of its correctness.

1 Introduction

Biclustering, also known in other scenarios as co-clustering, is a term used to encompass a large set of data mining techniques generally aimed at "performing simultaneous row-column clustering" of a data matrix [19]. It is used in several different scenarios, such as document analysis [11], market segmentation [12], recommender systems [20] and, most importantly, expression microarray data analysis [2,15,19,22,24]. In this last scenario, the starting point is a matrix whose rows and columns represent genes and experiments, respectively. Each entry of the matrix measures the expression level of a gene in a specific experiment. Biclustering aims to find clusters of genes which show a coherent behavior in subsets of experiments. This permits the discovery of co-regulation mechanisms. Addressing this issue can provide invaluable information to biologists, given the ever increasing amount of data that they have to analyse.

Different biclustering techniques have been proposed in the past [1,5,7,10, 27], each one characterized by different features, such as computational complexity, effectiveness, interpretability and optimization criterion – cf [15,19,24]) for a general review. A significant part of these approaches aim at adapting a given clustering technique to the biclustering problem, for example by repeatedly performing rows and columns clustering. However, an interesting recent chunk of works aim at proposing novel models for biclustering, where rows and columns

© Springer International Publishing AG 2016
C. Martín-Vide et al. (Eds.): TPNC 2016, LNCS 10071, pp. 175–187, 2016.
DOI: 10.1007/978-3-319-49001-4_14

are analysed simultaneously (as opposed to clustering rows and columns separately) [27]. This has several advantages for what concerns the performance of the biclustering process that is significantly more accurate. However, such accuracy comes at a price as such models typically involve a large amount of variables and relationships. Specifically, the typical biclustering instance is represented by a matrix with thousands of column/rows [19]. Moreover, the underlying optimization task required by the model is inherently intractable leading to severe restrictions on the practical applicability of those approaches. In order to combat such complexity, recent works typically relax the model or use heuristic, greedy approaches, hence giving up optimality of the solution.

In this paper we investigate the applicability of a metaheuristic, called Quantum Annealing (QA) [14,16,26], to the global optimization problems underlying biclustering, by following some recent developments in the construction of quantum devices that physically realise quantum annealing. Similarly to the classical Simulated Annealing, QA is an optimization metaheuristic that seeks the global optimum of an objective function by following a process inspired by the thermodynamic process of annealing. In this search, QA is more effective than the classical method as it employs quantum fluctuations in order to escape local minima, i.e. it uses some quantum effects that allows the tunneling through narrow barriers separating local minima, rather than climbing over them as done classically by using thermal fluctuations. Apart from the recent theoretical demonstrations, this has also been demonstrated experimentally [9]. A fundamental contribution in this direction is due to D-Wave Systems Inc., which has commercialized some analog quantum devices designed to use quantum annealing to solve quadratic optimization problems.

Various works investigated the possibility of addressing typical Artificial Intelligence (AI) and Pattern Recognition (PR) problems by using QA. Examples include image recognition [21], Bayesian network structure learning [23] and hard operational planning problems [25]. As done in [25] or in [21] for image recognition, we show here an encoding of biclustering as a Quadratic Unconstrained Binary Optimization (QUBO) problem [17], i.e. as a problem where the aim is to find an assignment for binary variables so as to minimize a quadratic objective function. The QUBO format corresponds to the input format required for the D-Wave^{TM} superconducting adiabatic quantum computing processors. To the best of our knowledge this is the first study in this direction. A sampling algorithm for clustering was proposed in [18] which is inspired by quantum annealing. However, this algorithm is designed for classical computers, while here we investigate the possible exploitation of a radically different computing machine, i.e. the D-Wave^{TM} quantum computer, for biclustering.

The contributions of this paper can be summarized as follows: (1) We introduce the first QUBO model for the biclustering problem; more specifically, we formulate the biclustering problem as a repeated search for the largest biclusters following well known approaches such as [4,7], where biclusters are extracted one at a time from the data-matrix. (2) We analyse the model proving that it is correct, i.e. that the optimal solution of the QUBO model is the optimal solution for the one-bicluster problem. (3) We discuss the practical applicability of our model considering the current architecture of the D-Wave^{TM} machine.

2 Background and Related Work

In this section we first detail the biclustering problem, then provide some necessary notions on quantum annealing and on the D-wave^{TM} architecture. Finally, we present the QUBO formalization for generic optimization problems.

2.1 Biclustering

As already mentioned, biclustering has been used in various application domains with different techniques. However, in its most general form, biclustering can be defined as the simultaneous clustering of rows and columns of a given data-matrix [19]. The goal is then retrieving the subsets of rows and columns that have a coherent behavior, where "coherence"is defined according to the specific application domain (e.g. Euclidean distance, Pearson correlation, etc.).

In this paper we follow a standard technique [4,7], where biclusters are extracted one by one from the data-matrix. In particular, we focus on the problem of finding the largest bicluster in a data matrix, which in the rest of the paper we will refer to as the *one-bicluster* problem. The other biclusters can then be retrieved by masking the bicluster(s) already found (i.e. setting to a predefined value the relevant entries of the data-matrix) and by iterating the process.

Hence our problem takes as input a real-valued data matrix A with N rows and M columns, and returns a subset of rows and columns that identifies the largest, most coherent bicluster. Each real value of the data-matrix $a_{i,j}$ encodes an "activation" level for a specific configuration. For example, for expression microarray data rows typically represent genes and columns experimental conditions, hence each entry $a_{i,j}$ represents the activation level of gene i under the experimental condition j. Our goal is to return the set of genes that exhibits a coherent behavior under the same subset of experimental conditions.

2.2 Quantum Annealing and D-Wave^{TM}

Among the various approaches to quantum information processing, a particularly interesting one is *adiabatic quantum optimization* and the closely related phenomenon of quantum annealing (QA), which allows us to replace exhaustive searches in global optimization problems with heuristic algorithms approximating the global optimum to the aim of finding a satisfactory solution. QA is a meta-heuristic based on the quantum adiabatic theorem[1], whose basic strategy can be described as follows: first, the system is initialized to a simple state

---

[1] According to the quantum adiabatic theorem, a quantum system that begins in the non-degenerate ground state of a time-dependent Hamiltonian will remain in the instantaneous ground state provided the Hamiltonian changes sufficiently slowly.

and then the conditions are slowly (adiabatically) changed to reach a complex final state that describes the solution to a computational problem of interest. It is in some way similar to the classical simulated annealing (SA) [13], which instead borrows a metaphor from the physical process used in metallurgy to create a defect-free crystalline solid. Rather then thermal fluctuations used in SA to control the search, in the quantum case the computation is driven by *quantum fluctuations* and the tunneling field strength replaces temperature to control acceptance probabilities [14]. The QA optimization scheme has been implemented directly on quantum hardware by the Canadian company D-Wave Systems Inc. The D-Wave^TM devices are able to minimize an objective function expressed in accordance to the Ising Model of statistical mechanics. The Ising energy minimization problem is NP-hard [3] and it is equivalent to the QUBO model presented in the next section.

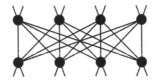

Fig. 1. D-Wave^TM unit cell as shown in [8]

In order to solve an instance of a QUBO problem with a D-Wave^TM machine we will need to adapt the logical formulation of a given problem to the physical fixed architecture of the quantum processor. This architecture is composed by a matrix of unit cells (Fig. 1) that is a set of 8 qubits disposed in a bipartite graph. These unit cells are connected in a structure called *chimera graph*.

The current version of the machine (D-Wave 2X^TM) has 12×12 unit cells for a total of 1152 qubits (cf [9] for more details on its hardware and performance).

2.3   Quadratic Unconstrained Binary Optimization Problems

The goal of a Quadratic Unconstrained Binary Optimization problem (QUBO) is to find the assignment to a set of binary variables $x_1...x_n$ so as to minimize an objective function that has the following form:

$$O(x_1, ..., x_n) = \sum_{i=1}^{n} a_i x_i + \sum_{1 \leq i < j \leq n} b_{i,j} x_i x_j \qquad (1)$$

We can also represent an instance of a QUBO problem with a weighted graph where each node represents a binary variable x_i, a linear coefficient a_i encodes the value associated to the node x_i and a quadratic coefficient $b_{i,j}$ represents the value associated to the edge between nodes x_i and x_j. With this representation, setting $x_i = 1$ corresponds to selecting the node x_i, while $x_i = 0$ corresponds to eliminating the node x_i from the graph. Hence, the objective function corresponds to the sum of all values in the graph and its minimization is equivalent to decide which nodes to remove (where removing a node implies the removal of all edges that are incident to that node), in such a way that the summation of the values remaining in the graph is the lowest possible.

3   The QUBO Model for Biclustering

In this section, we detail our QUBO model for the one-bicluster problem. We first describe a binary model for the one-bicluster problem, then we show how such a model can be encoded as a QUBO.

3.1   A Binary Model for One-Bicluster

We now present the objective function for the binary one-bicluster problem and in what follows we explain how it is derived. Given a real-valued data matrix A with N rows and M columns the objective function for the binary one-bicluster problem is the following:

$$\arg \max_{(c_{1,1},\cdots,c_{N,M})} \left(\sum_{i,j} a_{i,j} c_{i,j} - \sum_{i,j,t,k} O_{i,j,t,k} c_{i,j} c_{t,k} + \sum_{i<t} B_{i,t} \right) \qquad (2)$$

where $1 \leq i, t \leq N$; $1 \leq j, k \leq M$.

In the first two terms we have $N \times M$ binary variables $c_{i,j}$ that encode whether a given entry $a_{i,j}$ of the data matrix A belongs to the bicluster or not (where $c_{i,j} = 1$ indicates that the entry $a_{i,j}$ does belong to the bicluster).

Also, in this function we can identify two forces: one that encourages points to group together, namely the first term in (2), and one that avoids points that are not coherent to be in the same group (i.e., the second term in (2)). Such term is based on a value $O_{i,j,t,k}$ which measures the coherence between two points $a_{i,j}$ and $a_{t,k}$. The function $O_{i,j,t,k}$ depends on which kind of biclusters we wish to analyse. In particular, following the relevant literature (e.g., [27]) we consider two types of coherence:

Constant: which aims at penalizing points that have a different activation level and hence identifies biclusters that have a single coherent value.

$$O_{i,j,t,k} = w|a_{i,j} - a_{t,k}| \qquad (3)$$

Additive: which identifies biclusters that encode an evolution of the activation values over columns.

$$O_{i,j,t,k} = w(a_{i,j} - a_{t,j} + a_{t,k} - a_{i,k})^2 \qquad (4)$$

$$C = \begin{pmatrix} 1\,0\,1\,1\,0 \\ 0\,0\,0\,0\,0 \\ 1\,0\,1\,1\,0 \\ 1\,0\,1\,1\,0 \end{pmatrix} \longrightarrow \begin{pmatrix} 1\,1\,1\,0\,0 \\ 1\,1\,1\,0\,0 \\ 1\,1\,1\,0\,0 \\ 0\,0\,0\,0\,0 \end{pmatrix} \qquad\qquad C = \begin{pmatrix} 1\,0\,1\,1\,0 \\ 0\,0\,0\,0\,0 \\ 1\,0\,0\,1\,0 \\ 0\,1\,1\,1\,0 \end{pmatrix}$$

(a)   (b)

Fig. 2. Example of: a valid assignment and its permutation that results in a full rectangle of ones (2a); an invalid assignment, no permutation can result in a full rectangle of ones (2b)

In both (3) and (4) the weight w can be adjusted to balance such two forces: setting w to high values favours the coherence of the points inside the biclusters while setting w to low values favours the creation of large biclusters. Such weight must be determined experimentally and it is domain dependent.

In order to solve our problem, we need to restrict the feasible variable assignments so that only valid assignments correspond to a bicluster. In other words, we need to rule out assignments that do not correspond to a subset of rows and columns that have all entries selected (see Fig. 2b for an example of a non-valid assignment). To do so we add one constraint stating that, given two rows of the output matrix C, they have to share the same configurations or one of them must be zero. The constraint between rows i and t is expressed in Eq. (2) by the term:

$$B_{i,t} = \begin{cases} 0, & \text{if } (\sum_k c_{i,k} = 0) \vee (\sum_k c_{t,k} = 0) \vee (\sum_k (c_{i,k} - c_{t,k}) = 0) \\ -\infty, & \text{otherwise} \end{cases} \quad (5)$$

Such constraint ensures that there is a permutation of rows and columns that forms a submatrix with all entries selected (i.e., visually a full rectangle of ones).

Another interesting way to look at an admissible configuration is that it can be described by fixing the same value for all the elements of a column with an exception for the elements that belong to a disabled row. For example, considering Fig. 2a (before permutations) the configuration can be expressed as: Columns $\{1,3,4\}$ take value 1, columns $\{2,5\}$ take value 0 and row 2 is disabled (all the element are 0). Hence any admissible configuration can be uniquely identified by this type of description. This description is useful to better understand the QUBO model we describe next.

3.2   The QUBO Model for the One-Bicluster Problem

We now provide a QUBO formulation for the binary model described above. For ease of explanation let us start with a QUBO representation that does not consider the bicluster constraint (i.e., the $B_{i,t}$ elements in Eq. (2)). To build such model by using the graph-based representation of QUBOs, we create a node $x_{i,j}$ for each variable $c_{i,j}$. Considering that the QUBO formulation has to be minimized, we then assign a value $-a_{i,j}$ to each node. For each pair of nodes

$(x_{i,j}, x_{t,k})$ we assign to the edge between them a positive value $O_{i,j,t,k}$ calculated according to the Eqs. (3) or (4). Note that the latter has value 0 for points on the same row or the same column, hence for such measure the horizontal and vertical edges are absent from the graph. The corresponding objective function for the QUBO problem will then be:

$$\arg \min_{(x_{1,1}, \cdots, x_{N,M})} \left(\sum_{i,j} -a_{i,j} x_{i,j} + \sum_{i,j,t,k} O_{i,j,t,k} x_{i,j} x_{t,k} \right) \qquad (6)$$

where $1 \leq i, t \leq N$; $1 \leq j, k \leq M$. It is easy to see that the assignment that maximizes function (2) without the bicluster constraint is the same that minimizes the QUBO objective function (6). Figure 3 shows a graphical representation of such a simplified QUBO model for a 2×2 input data matrix.

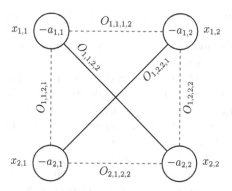

Fig. 3. A graphical representation of our QUBO model for a 2×2 data-matrix, the (red) dotted edges are absent in case of additive coherence measure (4).(Color figure online)

Now, in order to consider the bicluster constraint we must add some extra nodes to the QUBO model so as to ensure that the assignments generated are valid (i.e., they represent a subset of rows and columns). As mentioned in Sect. 3.1 an admissible configuration should set all variables in the same column to the same value except for the variables that belong to disabled rows. To express this, we create two types of constraints: column constraints and row constraints. A column constraint ensures that all variables in a column have the same value. To do so we add to each node a positive value V and we add a new node to the graph with a value equal to $N(B - V)$ where $B > V$. We call this new node the *column switch* and we indicate with s_j the variable that corresponds to the node switch for column j. Finally, we set the value of the edges between the column switch and the N nodes to $-B$ (see Fig. 4a for a graphical representation). Intuitively, if k of the N nodes are selected and the switch is not active (i.e., $s_j = 0$), we add to the objective function a value kV. If we select the switch and the k nodes we add $k(V - B) + N(B - V)$. Since we are minimising

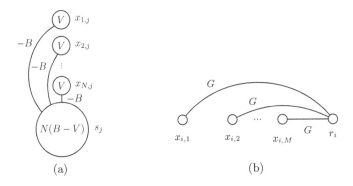

Fig. 4. Graphical representation of: a column constraint (4a); a row constraint (4b)

the objective function the best configuration will be either selecting all nodes (with a contribution of $N(V - B) + N(B - V) = 0$) or not selecting any node (again with a contribution of zero). All other configurations will add a positive value to the objective function.

A row constraint should force all variables in a row to be zero when a specific condition holds (i.e., we decide to not consider that row). To enforce this we add a new node to the graph with a value 0 and we call this new node the *row switch*. We indicate with r_i the variable that corresponds to the node switch for row i (see Fig. 4a for a graphical representation). Then, we set the edges between the row switch and the M nodes to a positive value G. Intuitively, when the $r_i = 0$ any configuration for the M nodes contributes with a null value to the objective function, hence they are equally desirable. However, if $r_j = 1$ then selecting any of the M nodes will increase the objective function of a value G. Hence, in this case the best configuration is the one that does not select any of the M nodes.

Finally we combine the first graph (Fig. 3) without the bicluster constraint (from now on called the *inner graph*) with the row and column constraints and by adding from each row switch to every column switch an edge with value $V - B$. The objective function has now the following form:

$$
\arg \min_{(x_{1,1}, \cdots, x_{N,M})} \sum_{i,j} \Big(V x_{i,j} - B x_{i,j} s_j + G x_{i,j} r_i + (V - B) r_i s_j
$$

$$
+ (B - V) s_j - a_{i,j} x_{i,j} + \sum_{t,k} O_{i,j,t,k} x_{i,j} x_{t,k} \Big) \tag{7}
$$

In order to ensure that our QUBO formulation is a proper model for the one-bicluster problem we must show that for all valid solutions the extra constraints (i.e., row and column constraints) contribute with a zero value, while for all non-valid solutions they contribute with a strictly positive value. In particular, we prove the following theorem:

Theorem 1 (Model validity). *Given a model of a data-matrix with N rows and M columns and values $B > V > 0$ and $G > B - V$, for all assignments*

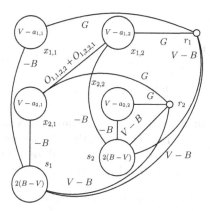

Fig. 5. Graph of the complete model for $N = 2$ and $M = 2$ with the additive coherence similarity metric (4) and the simplification proposed at the end of this section.

that do not violate a row or a column constraint such extra constraints provide a null contribution to the objective function. For all other configurations the contribution is greater than 0.

Proof (Proof sketch). From Eq. (7) we can observe that in each addend of the summation, the terms that depend on the constraint structure are $Vx_{i,j} - Bx_{i,j}s_j + Gx_{i,j}r_i + (V - B)r_is_j + (B - V)s_j$. Hence, each addend depends exclusively on three binary variables, namely a node from the inner graph $x_{i,j}$ and the two switches r_i and s_j. By analyzing exhaustively the eight cases we can reach the desired conclusion.

In order to complete the model we have to identify the appropriate values for V, B and G. To do so, we observe that a configuration that does not comply with all the switches constraints should increase more than the decrease in value that can derive from taking such a configuration in the inner graph, namely the values assigned to the structure should be high enough to ensure that the objective function does not minimize for the non-valid configurations. Although intuitively we can simply choose high values, to maintain the range of possible values as small as possible, we investigate what the lowest admissible ones are. Let us indicate with R a configuration for the row switches, S a configuration for the column switches, X a configuration for the inner graph nodes in compliance with the switches and $\overline{X}$ a configuration where any subset of X does not comply with the corresponding switches. We can then show the following theorem:

Theorem 2 (Determining V, B, G). *Given the specific switches configurations R and S and the valid solution (X, R, S), we have that:*

$$O(\overline{X}, R, S) - O(X, R, S) > 0 \iff (V > V_m \wedge B > B_m \wedge G > G_m) \quad (8)$$

for all invalid solutions $(\overline{X}, R, S)$, *where*

$$V_m = \max_{i,j}\{a_{i,j}\} \quad B_m = V + \max_{i,j}\{-a_{i,j} + \sum_{t,k} O_{i,j,t,k}\}$$

$$G_m = B - V + \max_{i,j}\{a_{i,j}\} \tag{9}$$

Proof (Proof sketch). In a similar way to what we explained in Theorem 1, we can analyze the cases of Eq. (7) considering the configurations of the three binary variables $x_{i,j}$, r_i and s_j. We can then calculate the values V_m,B_m,G_m by imposing $O(\overline{X}, R, S) - O(X, R, S) > 0$ between the eight cases.

Theorems 1 and 2 ensure that by building the model as described above, for any valid configuration (i.e. a configuration that describes a bicluster) the contribution of the column and row constraints to the objective function is null. For all valid assignments the objective function reported in Eq. (7) reduces to Eq. (6), hence the configuration that minimizes Eq. (7) is the same that maximizes Eq. (2) (i.e., the most coherent, largest bicluster). Moreover, for any non valid assignment (i.e. an assignment that does not encode a bicluster) the contribution of the row and column constraints will be strictly positive hence such configuration will always be discarded in favor of a valid assignment.

The proposed model can be further simplified. In particular, we can reduce the number of edges (quadratic terms) by observing that if a couple of nodes (in the inner graph) on different rows and columns are active (i.e., two nodes on the opposite corners of a rectangle) also the other two nodes on the other diagonal of the rectangle must be active to comply with the switches. The terms $O_{i,j,t,k}x_{i,j}x_{t,k}$ and $O_{t,j,i,k}x_{t,j}x_{i,k}$ either contribute both or none to the objective function. Hence, we can add both values $O_{i,j,t,k} + O_{t,j,i,k}$ to a single edge and remove the other one. Hence, regardless of the coherence measure used, we can remove half of the diagonal edges. An example of the complete simplified model is shown in Fig. 5.

3.3   Minor Embedding the QUBO Model on the D-Wave[TM] Architecture

In order to solve a QUBO model on a D-Wave[TM] machine, an arbitrary logical graph has to be embedded into the physical structure of the processor. This requires a mapping of the physical qubits into the problem's variables, i.e. to determine which physical qubits should represent which variable of the QUBO problem. In order to perform this operation we adopt the approach developed in [6] for finding graph minors. More specifically, we use a minor embedding technique. Note that, even if the number of nodes of the model is smaller than the number of qubits of the processor, it is not always possible to find a valid embedding. In particular, the embedding into the hardware architecture usually requires more variables, since some nodes are represented by several physical qubits due to the sparse connectivity of the hardware graph.

We applied this minor embedding technique to our model using the code provided by authors of [6] with the aim to determine the dimension of the matrices and the sparsification required to always find a valid embedding. Results show that the dimensions of the matrices that can be analysed on D-Wave^{TM} are significantly smaller than typical data for biclustering. Specifically, we can embed matrices up to 7×7 on the processor of the current version of the D-Wave^{TM} machine (1152 qubits). Nonetheless, it is possible to decompose large matrices into smaller ones, achieving good results in terms of accuracy for the retrieved biclusters.

4   Conclusions

In this paper we have introduced a QUBO model for the one-bicluster problem. The results suggest that nowadays the use of such an approach would be possible only for small matrices on the current processor of the D-Wave^{TM} machine as explained in Sect. 3.3. Nonetheless, this paper takes a first important step towards an effective use of quantum annealing for biclustering.

Several challenges will need to be addressed for the development of future improved quantum annealers. Critical issues such as longer coherence times, calibration accuracy, etc. are objects of intense study by researchers in both academy and industry as well as by the quantum enhanced optimization (QEO) group of the Intelligence Advanced Research Projects Agency (IARPA) of the US government. Solving these issues will hopefully lead in a near future to the implementation of quantum annealing that will be more flexible both in terms of connectivity and choice of cost function, thus adding value to studies like the one proposed in this paper.

References

1. Ayadi, W., Elloumi, M., Hao, J.: Bimine+: An efficient algorithm for discovering relevant biclusters of DNA microarray data. Knowl. Based Syst. **35**, 224–234 (2012)
2. Badea, L.: Generalized clustergrams for overlapping biclusters. In: IJCAI, pp. 1383–1388 (2009)
3. Barahona, F.: On the computational complexity of Ising spin glass models. J. Phys. A: Math. Gen. **15**(10), 3241–3253 (1982)
4. Ben-Dor, A., Chor, B., Karp, R., Yakhini, Z.: Discovering local structure in gene expression data: The order-preserving submatrix problem. J. Comput. Biol. **10**(3–4), 373–384 (2003)
5. Bicego, M., Lovato, P., Ferrarini, A., Delledonne, M.: Biclustering of expression microarray data with topic models. In: International Conference on Pattern Recognition (ICPR2010), pp. 2728–2731 (2010)
6. Cai, J., Macready, W.G., Roy, A.: A practical heuristic for finding graph minors. ArXiv e-prints, June 2014
7. Cheng, Y., Church, G.: Biclustering of expression data. In: Proceedings of the Eighth International Conference on Intelligent Systems for Molecular Biology (ISMB00), pp. 93–103 (2000)

8. Dahl, E.D.: Programming with D-Wave: Map Coloring Problem (2013). http://www.dwavesys.com/sites/default/files/Map%20Coloring%20WP2.pdf

9. Denchev, V.S., Boixo, S., Isakov, S.V., Ding, N., Babbush, R., Smelyanskiy, V., Martinis, J., Neven, H.: What is the computational value of finite-range tunneling? Phys. Rev. X **6**(3), 031015 (2016)

10. Denitto, M., Farinelli, A., Franco, G., Bicego, M.: A binary factor graph model for biclustering. In: Fränti, P., Brown, G., Loog, M., Escolano, F., Pelillo, M. (eds.) S+SSPR 2014. LNCS, vol. 8621, pp. 394–403. Springer, Heidelberg (2014). doi:10.1007/978-3-662-44415-3_40

11. Dhillon, I.: Coclustering documents and words using bipartite spectral graph partitioning. In: Proceedings of the International Conference on Knowledge Discovery and Data Mining, pp. 269–274 (2001)

12. Dolnicar, S., Kaiser, S., Lazarevski, K., Leisch, F.: Biclustering : overcoming data dimensionality problems in market segmentation. J. Travel Res. Q. Publ. Travel Tourism Res. Assoc. **51**(1), 41–49 (2012)

13. Farhi, E., Goldstone, J., Gutmann, S.: Quantum Adiabatic Evolution Algorithms versus Simulated Annealing. eprint, January 2002. arXiv:quant-ph/0201031

14. Finnila, A.B., Gomez, M.A., Sebenik, C., Stenson, C., Doll, J.D.: Quantum annealing: A new method for minimizing multidimensional functions. Chem. Phys. Lett. **219**, 343–348 (1994)

15. Flores, J.L., Inza, I., Larranaga, P., Calvo, B.: A new measure for gene expression biclustering based on non-parametric correlation. Comput. Methods Programs Biomed. **112**(3), 367–397 (2013)

16. Kadowaki, T., Nishimori, H.: Quantum annealing in the transverse Ising model. Phys. Rev. E **58**(5), 5355–5363 (1998)

17. Kochenberger, G., Hao, J., Glover, F., Lewis, M., Lü, Z., Wang, H., Wang, Y.: The unconstrained binary quadratic programming problem: a survey. J. Comb. Optim. **28**(1), 58–81 (2014)

18. Kurihara, K., Tanaka, S., Miyashita, S.: Quantum annealing for clustering. In: Proceedings of the Twenty-Fifth Conference on Uncertainty in Artificial Intelligence, pp. 321–328. UAI 2009, AUAI Press, Arlington, Virginia, United States (2009)

19. Madeira, S., Oliveira, A.: Biclustering algorithms for biological data analysis: a survey. IEEE Trans. Comput. Biol. Bioinform. **1**, 24–44 (2004)

20. Mukhopadhyay, A., Maulik, U., Bandyopadhyay, S., Coello, C.: Survey of multi-objective evolutionary algorithms for data mining: Part ii. Evol. Comput. IEEE Trans. **18**(1), 20–35 (2014)

21. Neven, H., Rose, G., Macready, W.G.: Image recognition with an adiabatic quantum computer I. Mapping to quadratic unconstrained binary optimization, ArXiv e-prints, April 2008

22. Oghabian, A., Kilpinen, S., Hautaniemi, S., Czeizler, E.: Biclustering methods: Biological relevance and application in gene expression analysis. PLoS ONE **9**(3), e90801 (2014). http://dx.doi.org/10.1371%2Fjournal.pone.0090801

23. O'Gorman, B., Babbush, R., Perdomo-Ortiz, A., Aspuru-Guzik, A., Smelyanskiy, V.: Bayesian network structure learning using quantum annealing. Eur. Phys. J. Spec. Top. **224**(1), 163–188 (2015). http://dx.doi.org/10.1140/epjst/e2015-02349-9

24. Prelić, A., Bleuler, S., Zimmermann, P., Wille, A., Bühlmann, P., Gruissem, W., Hennig, L., Thiele, L., Zitzler, E.: A systematic comparison and evaluation of biclustering methods for gene expression data. Bioinformatics **22**(9), 1122–1129 (2006)

25. Rieffel, E.G., Venturelli, D., O'Gorman, B., Do, M.B., Prystay, E.M., Smelyan-skiy, V.N.: A case study in programming a quantum annealer for hard operational planning problems. Quantum Inform. Process. **14**, 1–36 (2015)
26. Santoro, G.E., Tosatti, E.: Optimization using quantum mechanics: quantum annealing through adiabatic evolution. J. Phys. A Math. Gen. **39**(36), R393–R431 (2006)
27. Tu, K., Ouyang, X., Han, D., Honavar, V.: Exemplar-based robust coherent biclustering. In: SDM, pp. 884–895. SIAM (2011)

Determining Player Skill in the Game of Go with Deep Neural Networks

Josef Moudřík[1]([✉]) and Roman Neruda[2]

[1] Department of Theoretical Computer Science and Mathematical Logic,
Faculty of Mathematics and Physics, Charles University,
Malostranské náměstí 25, Prague, Czech Republic
j.moudrik@gmail.com
[2] Institute of Computer Science, The Czech Academy of Sciences,
Pod Vodárenskou věží 2, Prague, Czech Republic
roman@cs.cas.cz

Abstract. The game of Go has recently been an exuberant topic for AI research, mainly due to advances in Go playing software. Here, we present an application of deep neural networks aiming to improve the experience of humans playing the game of Go online. We have trained a deep convolutional network on 188,700 Go game records to classify players into three categories based on their skill. The method has a very good accuracy of 71.5 % when classifying the skill from a single position, and 77.9 % when aggregating predictions from one game. The performance and low amount of information needed allow for a much faster convergence to true rank on online Go servers, improving user experience for new-coming players. The method will be experimentally deployed on the Online Go Server (OGS).

Keywords: Computer Go · Machine learning · Board games · Skill assessment · Deep neural networks

1 Introduction

Computer Go is a field which mainly focuses on developing programs for playing the game. In this work, we focus on analyzing existing game records using deep neural networks with the aim to improve current ranking systems on online Go servers. This allows the servers to offer better suited opponents to the users, thus enabling them to have a better gaming experience.

Deep neural networks are currently a very hot topic of research, radically changing hard fields such as computer vision, or natural language processing [1,9,10,19]. The boom in deep architectures is allowed by abundance of data, graphical processing units (GPUs) with huge computational power and smart models. As there is probably much room for improvement in all three factors, we can only expect such models to proliferate.

Go is a two-player full-information board game played on a square grid (usually 19×19 lines) with black and white stones; the goal of the game is to control

C. Martín-Vide et al. (Eds.): TPNC 2016, LNCS 10071, pp. 188–195, 2016.
DOI: 10.1007/978-3-319-49001-4_15

the board by means of surrounded territory and captured enemy stones. Go has traditionally been an excellent testing ground for artificial intelligence, as the game has been considered to be extremely challenging. Only recently has the AI surpassed humans, when Google's AlphaGo beat world's top professional player Lee Se-dol [20], causing much surprise among most computer Go researchers.

In the game of Go, the strength of amateur players is measured by *kyu* (student) and *dan* (master) ranks. The kyu ranks decrease from about 25 kyu (an absolute beginner) to 1 kyu (a fairly strong player), the scale continues by dan ranks, 1 dan (somewhat stronger than 1 kyu), to 6 dan (a very strong player). Often, the ranks are modelled using an underlying continuous quantity called *rating*.

A rating system is a way to numerically express player's strength. In online Go servers, this is necessary so that users can be matched to other users with similar skill and so that users' skills can be compared. Often, mathematical models such as ELO [5] or Bayesian approaches [7] are used. After a game, these systems take information about the result (win/loss/draw) and modify the user's rating. As draws are quite rare in Go, this makes up for only a slightly more than 1 bit of information per game. As a result, the current systems take nontrivial number of games to converge to true players' rating, causing problems for new-coming players, often forcing them to play games with opponents of unfitting skill.

For instance, after the AlphaGo vs. Lee Se-dol match, Online Go Server (OGS) [17] had a large influx of beginners, who often chose incorrect rank as their baseline, causing some frustration and work for intervening administrators. A similar problem with ranking is also caused by players who are much stronger than they declare. Such players often cause dismay amongst similarly-ranked (yet weaker) players, and it is often again a task for administrator to find such players and correct their rating.

Obviously, some more information about the players' skill would be very helpful and one of possible source are the games themselves. In our previous work [2,11,14,15], we pioneered a machine-learning approach to predict the player's strength and playing style from game records. Our methods used features based on various statistics (patterns played, etc.), but these required a sample of at least 10 games to be reasonably accurate, which is still impractical to tackle the rating problem. This paper presents a new approach to this problem.

In this work, we set out to investigate the possibilities of estimating the strength of a player using as little information as possible, the natural starting point being a single position. Such small sample sizes naturally call for smarter utilization of the information; for this, we employ deep neural networks. The proposed methodology is being experimentally deployed on OGS.

The rest of the paper is organized as follows. Section 2 presents the dataset, preprocessing and augmentation used. Section 3 gives information about the architecture of the deep neural network used. Section 4 gives an overview about the experiments we have performed, and reflects on the results. The paper is concluded by Sect. 5, which sums up the work, discusses the application and proposes future work.

2 Dataset

The dataset was created from 188,700 public game records from March 2015 to February 2016. The games were downloaded from OGS. Because OGS is a relatively new server, it does not have many strong players (also not many games played by them). Therefore, we only chose games in which players are between 2 dan and 25 kyu. Of all the games, 20,000 were used as a validation set (used for tuning hyper-parameters of the model) and 20,000 reserved for testing (used for final evaluation). Each game is viewed as a sequence of positions.

The dataset consists of 3,426,489 pairs (X, y). Each sample X (an encoding of a position and 4 last moves) is classified into 3 classes y based on the skill of the player. The three classes used are: strong players (2 dan–7 kyu), intermediate players (8 kyu–16 kyu) and weak players (17 kyu–25 kyu). Three classes were chosen instead of direct regression (or a classification with more classes) because the problem is quite hard and more precise methods would not work robustly enough given the low amount of information from a single position.

In the following paragraphs, we describe the steps we took to process the game records in order to create the dataset for the deep neural network.

Planes: Every single sample X was encoded as 13 binary planes, each of size 19×19. A point on each plane gives information about the particular intersection. Out of the 13 planes, 4 encode the number of liberties (an empty intersection next to a group of stones) for player whose turn it is (the planes being 1, 2, 3 or 4 and more liberties), 4 encode liberties for opponent stones in the same fashion. One plane encodes positions of empty intersections and the last four planes show the last move, the second-last move, the third-last move and the fourth-last move. The planes used were proposed by D. Schmicker [18].

Subsampling: During training, the network tended to memorize positions from the games, causing serious overfitting and poor performance on unseen data. To fight this, we increased the number of games in a dataset and subsampled the positions: every fifth position (plus previous four moves) is taken from each game (randomly). For instance, from a game of 250 moves we get 50 pairs (X, y) on average. Together with data augmentation, this prevented overfitting very efficiently.

Data Augmentation: To prevent overfitting, we devised the following simple data-augmenting strategy. During training, each sample from each mini-batch was randomly transformed into one of its 8 symmetries; this is possible since board in the game of Go is symmetrical under reflection and rotation. This helps the network to build representations that are invariant to symmetry and reflection, thus improving generalization.

Equalization and Shuffling: In the training data, we made sure that all the classes have precisely the same number of examples. This makes comparison of different models easy, as it makes sure that the network is not exploiting uneven distribution of the targets.

Finally, all the training examples were shuffled well, so that all batches in the learning process have roughly the same distribution of targets, the motivation being to improve the gradient in the batches. In our experience, uneven distributions of classes among many consecutive mini-batches cause the network to exploit the irregularities, leading to poor performance.

3 Architecture and Training

The network has 4 convolutional layers followed by two fully connected layers of 128 neurons and finally a 3-way softmax layer. The first convolutional layer has filters of size 5×5, the remaining layers have filters of size 3×3. All the neurons in the network were activated using non-saturating nonlinearity $f(x) = \max(x, 0)$, the so-called *rectified linear units* (ReLUs) [16]. Compared to saturating non-linear activations, such as tanh, ReLU units speed up the convergence considerably. Every convolutional layer operated on the full 19×19 input, outputs of the network were padded by zeros again to 19×19, the convolutions were applied with a stride of 1. The number of filters in the network is 512 for the first layer and 128 for all the other layers. Batch normalization [8] was used in all the convolutional layers. Batch normalization normalizes layer inputs as a part of the model, allowing higher learning rates while acting as a regularizer.

All weights in the network were initialized with normalized initialization as described in [6]. In total, the network has 6,985,475 parameters, majority between the last convolutional and the first fully connected layer.

The best generalization and performance on the validation set was achieved when we trained the network in two phases, see Fig. 2. For two epochs, we had used stochastic gradient descent (SGD) with Nesterov momentum [3] of 0.8, learning rate of 0.01, and mini-batches of size 32. After this, the network was fine-tuned for 4 epochs using SGD without momentum, learning rate of 0.01 and mini-batches of size 128.

The loss function used was the categorical cross-entropy:

$$L(t, p) = -\sum_i t[i] log(p[i]),$$

where t is one-hot vector specifying the true label and p is the probability predicted by the softmax. The categorical cross-entropy basically penalizes confident (high $p[i]$) predictions that are wrong, and the resulting numerical outputs can thus be interpreted as class membership confidence.

Network was trained for 6 epochs and in total, the learning took 2 days on NVIDIA GeForce GTX 580 with 1.5 GB of memory. To design, test and train the model, we have used the Keras deep-learning framework [4].

4 Experiments and Results

We have performed several experiments, the baseline being the prediction from a single position. Additionally, we have investigated possibilities for aggregating

Table 1. Summary of results. All accuracies reported are measured on testing data. The last column reports percentage of examples where the correct label was within top two classes. The last three rows show accuracies of aggregated predictions from a single game. Label *Augmented* indicates that prediction was made from 8 symmetrical board positions and averaged, instead of simply predicting from the position alone. Label *Cropped* indicates that only predictions from move 30 on were taken.

Model	Accuracy	Accuracy (Top-2)
Single position	71.5 %	94.6 %
Single position (Augmented)	72.5 %	94.9 %
Aggregated per game, mode (Augmented)	76.8 %	N/A
Aggregated per game, sum (Augmented)	77.1 %	96.4 %
Aggregated per game, sum (Augmented, Cropped)	77.7 %	96.7 %
Aggregated per game, sum (Augmented, Weighted)	77.9 %	96.8 %

multiple predictions. Finally, we investigated the dependency of accuracy on move number. All the experiments are described in paragraphs below. The results are summarized in Table 1.

Predictions from Single Position: Firstly, we measured the baseline accuracy of prediction for single positions, which is 71.5 % on testing data, the confusion matrix can be seen in Fig. 1. We further improved this accuracy by a novel trick. Since we train the network on augmented positions (8 symmetries), the network should be roughly invariant under reflection and rotation. Therefore, it makes sense to present the network with all 8 symmetrical copies of a single position and average the resulting predictions. This improves the accuracy by roughly 1 %. The intuition why this works is that the symmetrical positions essentially form an ensemble, averaging out outliers.

Aggregating Predictions: Another interesting thing to study is how to improve accuracy by aggregating multiple predictions. A natural way is to sum up predictions from individual positions and then take the class with the maximal sum (accuracy of 77.1 %). Another possibility we have tried is to take the most frequent (mode) class (accuracy of 76.8 %).

Accuracy by Move: Next, we investigated the dependence of accuracy on the move number, as shown in Fig. 3. The results indicate that the accuracy is bad at the beginning of the game, but improves rapidly afterwards. This is very understandable, as the games of Go often have very similar opening sequences (e.g. players usually start by playing into the corners). The figure also shows size of data samples at each move, as different games have different lengths. This also explains why the accuracy curve jumps near the end, this is caused by the low number of samples. The figure naturally suggests a way to improve the aggregation, and that is either to crop off moves at the beginning of the game (improvement in accuracy of 0.6 %, see Table 1), or — better — to weight the

		Predicted Label	
	Strong	Intermediate	Weak
	0.79	0.18	0.02
True Label	0.21	0.63	0.15
	0.03	0.19	0.78

Fig. 1. Normalized confusion matrix of predictions on testing data.

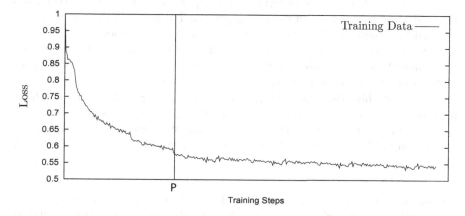

Fig. 2. Evolution of Loss function during training. The P point marks the place where the fine tuning phase of training was started, see Sect. 3.

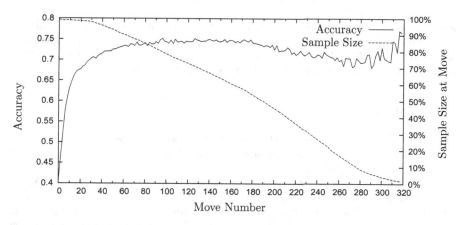

Fig. 3. Dependency of accuracy on the move number (measured on validation set). The dashed line shows sample size at given move in testing data — some games end earlier than others.

predictions proportionally to their accuracy (improvement of 0.8 % in accuracy). As this weighting can be considered hyper-parameter tuning, the weights (as well as Fig. 3) were computed using the validation set.

5 Conclusions and Future Work

In this work, we have proposed a novel methodology for information-efficient way of predicting player strength using deep neural networks. In comparison with other approaches, much less information is needed. This is naturally balanced by a relatively coarse discretization of the target domain (strength is divided into 3 classes).

The methodology will be experimentally deployed on Online Go Server, aiming to improve convergence of the rating system. The precise way to incorporate the predicted class into the rating system is yet to be determined. A general idea on how to do this is to use the predicted classes as a prior for the underlying rating model. As the number of games in the model increases, the importance of the prior would naturally decrease.

The results hint that the performance of the network is touching the limit given by the amount of information provided. A natural next step would be to extend the system to use information from one whole game. Recurrent neural networks could be the ideal tool for this; we plan to investigate this in the near future.

Resources. To promote further research and to ease reproducibility of this study, we have published the game records, datasets and the model file (including the weights of the best network we have found). All the files can be found at [13].

The dataset processing was performed using our open-source toolkit, see [12].

Acknowledgments. Authors would like to thank Martin Pilát for valuable discussions. This research has been partially supported by the Czech Science Foundation project no. P103-15-19877S. J. Moudřík has been supported by the Charles University Grant Agency project no. 364015 and by SVV project no. 260 333.

References

1. Andor, D., Alberti, C., Weiss, D., Severyn, A., Presta, A., Ganchev, K., Petrov, S., Collins, M.: Globally normalized transition-based neural networks. arXiv preprint (2016). arXiv:1603.06042
2. Baudiš, P., Moudřík, J.: On move pattern trends in a large go games corpus. Arxiv, CoRR. http://arXiv.org/abs/1209.5251
3. Bengio, Y., Boulanger-Lewandowski, N., Pascanu, R.: Advances in optimizing recurrent networks. In: 2013 IEEE International Conference on Acoustics, Speech and Signal Processing, pp. 8624–8628. IEEE (2013)
4. Chollet, F.: Keras (2015). https://github.com/fchollet/keras
5. Elo, A.E.: The Rating of Chessplayers, Past and Present. Arco, New York (1978)
6. Glorot, X., Bengio, Y.: Understanding the difficulty of training deep feedforward neural networks. Aistats **9**, 249–256 (2010)
7. Herbrich, R., Minka, T., Graepel, T.: Trueskill (tm): A bayesian skill rating system. In: Advances in Neural Information Processing Systems, pp. 569–576 (2006)
8. Ioffe, S., Szegedy, C.: Batch normalization: Accelerating deep network training by reducing internal covariate shift. arXiv preprint (2015). arXiv:1502.03167

9. Krizhevsky, A., Sutskever, I., Hinton, G.E.: Imagenet classification with deep convolutional neural networks. In: Advances in Neural Information Processing Systems, pp. 1097–1105 (2012)

10. Mikolov, T., Dean, J.: Distributed representations of words and phrases and their compositionality. Adv. Neural Inform. Process. Syst. **26**, 3111–3119 (2013)

11. Moudřík, J.: Meta-learning methods for analyzing Go playing trends. Master's thesis, Charles University, Faculty of Mathematics and Physics, Prague, Czech Republic (2013). http://www.j2m.cz/jm/master_thesis.pdf

12. Moudřík, J.: deep-go-wrap: Toolkit designed to ease development of your deep neural network models for the game of Go. (2016). https://github.com/jmoudrik/deep-go-wrap

13. Moudřík, J.: Source code and resources (2016). http://j2m.cz/~jm/archive/2016-08-02/

14. Moudřík, J., Baudiš, P., Neruda, R.: Evaluating go game records for prediction of player attributes. In: 2015 IEEE Conference on Computational Intelligence and Games (CIG), pp. 162–168. IEEE (2015)

15. Moudřík, J., Neruda, R.: Evolving non-linear stacking ensembles for prediction of go player attributes. In: 2015 IEEE Symposium Series on Computational Intelligence, pp. 1673–1680. IEEE (2015)

16. Nair, V., Hinton, G.E.: Rectified linear units improve restricted Boltzmann machines. In: Proceedings of the 27th International Conference on Machine Learning (ICML-10), pp. 807–814 (2010)

17. OGS: Online Go Server (OGS) (2016). http://online-go.com

18. Schmicker, D.: Planes for move prediction, maillist entry. http://computer-go.org/pipermail/computer-go/2015-December/008324.html

19. Szegedy, C., Liu, W., Jia, Y., Sermanet, P., Reed, S., Anguelov, D., Erhan, D., Vanhoucke, V., Rabinovich, A.: Going deeper with convolutions. In: Proceedings of the IEEE Conference on Computer Vision and Pattern Recognition, pp. 1–9 (2015)

20. Wikipedia: Alphago versus lee sedol – wikipedia, the free encyclopedia (2016). https://en.wikipedia.org/w/index.php?title=AlphaGo_versus_Lee_Sedol&oldid=732449782, Accessed 12 Sep 2016

Flexible Generalized Fuzzy Petri Nets
for Rule-Based Systems

Zbigniew Suraj[1(✉)], Piotr Grochowalski[1], and Sibasis Bandyopadhyay[2]

[1] Chair of Computer Science, University of Rzeszów, Rzeszów, Poland
zbigniew.suraj@ur.edu.pl
[2] Department of Mathematics, Visva Bharati, Santiniketan, India

Abstract. In 2015, the modified generalised fuzzy Petri nets ($mGFP$-nets) were proposed. This paper describes an extended class of $mGFP$-nets called flexible generalised fuzzy Petri nets ($FGFP$-nets). The main difference between the latter net model and the $mGFP$-net concerns transition operator Out_1 appearing in a triple of operators (In, Out_1, Out_2) in a $mGFP$-net. The operator Out_1 for each transition is determined automatically by the $GTVC$ algorithm, using the value of In and the value of truth degree function β in the net. This modification has significant influence on optimization of the modelled system by the $FGFP$-nets. The choice of suitable operators for the modelled system is very important, especially in systems described by incomplete, imprecise and/or vague information. The proposed approach can be used both for control design as well as knowledge representation and modelling of reasoning in decision support systems.

Keywords: Fuzzy petri net · Fuzzy logic · Knowledge representation · Approximate reasoning · Control · Decision support system

1 Introduction

Petri nets have become an important computational paradigm to represent and analyse a broad class of systems. As a computational paradigm for intelligent systems, they provide a graphical language to visualize, communicate and interpret engineering problems [5,12]. The concept of a Petri net has its origin in C.A. Petri's dissertation [13]. In the last four decades, several extensions of Petri nets have been proposed improving such aspects as hierarchical nets, high level nets or temporal nets [6]. For some time Petri nets have been gaining a growing interest among people in Artificial Intelligence and Systems Biology due to its adequacy to represent the reasoning process as a dynamic discrete event system [4,7,10,11]. In 1988, C.G. Looney proposed in [9] so called *fuzzy Petri nets* (*FP*-nets). In his model logical propositions can be associated with Petri nets allowing for logical reasoning about the modelled system. In this class of Petri net models not only crisp but also imprecise, vague and uncertain information is admissible and taken into account. Several authors proposed different classes of fuzzy Petri

© Springer International Publishing AG 2016
C. Martín-Vide et al. (Eds.): TPNC 2016, LNCS 10071, pp. 196–207, 2016.
DOI: 10.1007/978-3-319-49001-4_16

nets [4]. These models are based on different approaches combining Petri nets and fuzzy sets introduced by L.A. Zadeh in 1965 [19]. Recently, a new class of *FP*-nets (*mGFP*-nets [16]) has been introduced. The main difference between this net model and the existing *FP*-nets [4] concerns the definition of the operator binding function δ. This function, similarly to generalised fuzzy Petri nets (*GFP*-nets) [18], connects transitions with triples of operators (In, Out_1, Out_2). The meaning of the first and third operator in the *mGFP*-nets is the same as in the case of *GFP*-nets. However, in the *mGFP*-net model, the meaning of the second operator in the triple (called transition operator) is significantly different. In the *GFP*-net model the operator Out_1 belongs to the class of *t*-norms, whereas in the *mGFP*-net model it is assumed that it belongs to the class of inverted fuzzy implications [15]. Due to this change the latter net model modifies existing interpretation of transition firing rule in *GFP*-nets. Since there exist infinitely numerous fuzzy implications in the field of fuzzy logic, and the nature of the marking changes variously in given *mGFP*-nets depending on used implication function, it is very difficult to select suitable implication functions for particular applications. However, taking into account the *GTVC* algorithm for determining the optimal inverted fuzzy implication [15] for the transition operator Out_1 depended on the current marking of the net, the net model presented in the paper is more flexible than the *mGFP*-net one. The choice of suitable operators for the modelled system is very important, especially in control systems described by incomplete, imprecise and/or vague information.

The aim of this paper is to describe an extended class of *mGFP*-nets called *flexible generalised fuzzy Petri nets*. The main difference between the latter net model and the *mGFP*-net concerns the transition operator Out_1 appearing in a triple of operators (In, Out_1, Out_2) in a *mGFP*-net. The operator Out_1 for each transition is determined automatically by the *GTVC* algorithm, using the value of In and the value of truth degree function β in the net. This modification has significant influence on optimization of the modelled system by the *FGFP*-nets. The proposed approach can be used both for control design as well as knowledge representation and modelling of approximate reasoning in decision support systems.

The text is organized as follows. In Sect. 2, basic notions and notation concerning triangular norms and fuzzy implications are recalled. Moreover, the algorithm for determining the optimal inverted fuzzy implication from a set of basic fuzzy implications is described. Section 3 provides a brief introduction to *mGFP*-nets. In Sect. 4, *FGFP*-nets formalism is presented. A simple example coming from the control domain is given in Sect. 5. Section 6 includes concluding remarks.

2 Preliminary Notions

In this section, we remind both basic notions and notation concerning triangular norms and fuzzy implications, as well as the *GTVC* algorithm. For further details, see [2,8,15].

2.1   Triangular Norms

Let $[0, 1]$ be the interval of real numbers from 0 to 1 (0 and 1 are included).

A function $t : [0, 1] \times [0, 1] \rightarrow [0, 1]$ is said to be a t-norm if it satisfies, for all $a, b, c \in [0, 1]$, the following conditions: (1) it has 1 as the unit element, (2) it is monotone, commutative, and associative. A function $s : [0, 1] \times [0, 1] \rightarrow [0, 1]$ is said to be an s-norm if it satisfies, for all $a, b, c \in [0, 1]$, the following conditions: (1) it has 0 as the unit element, (2) it is monotone, commutative, and associative.

More relevant examples of t-norms are the minimum $t(a, b) = min(a, b)$ and the algebraic product $t(a, b) = a * b$. However, the examples of s-norms are the maximum $s(a, b) = max(a, b)$ and the probabilistic sum $s(a, b) = a + b - a * b$.

The set of all triangular norms is denoted by TN.

2.2   Fuzzy Implications

A function $I : [0, 1] \times [0, 1] \rightarrow [0, 1]$ is said to be a *fuzzy implication* if it satisfies, for all $x, x_1, x_2, y, y_1, y_2 \in [0, 1]$, the following conditions: (1) $I(., y)$ is decreasing, (2) $I(x, .)$ is increasing, (3) $I(0, 0) = 1$, $I(1, 1) = 1$, and $I(1, 0) = 0$.

The set of all fuzzy implications is denoted by FI.

Table 1 contains a sample of basic fuzzy implications. For their extended list, refer to ([2], page 4).

Table 1. A sample of basic fuzzy implications

Name	Year	Formula of basic fuzzy implication
Gödel	1932	$I_{GD}(x, y) = \begin{cases} 1 \; if \; x \leq y \\ y \; if \; x > y \end{cases}$
Goguen	1969	$I_{GG}(x, y) = \begin{cases} 1 \;\; if \; x \leq y \\ \frac{y}{x} \; if \; x > y \end{cases}$
Kleene-Dienes	1938	$I_{KD}(x, y) = max(1 - x, y)$
Yager	1980	$I_{YG}(x, y) = \begin{cases} 1 \;\; if \; x = 0 \; and \; y = 0 \\ y^x \; if \; x > 0 \; or \; y > 0 \end{cases}$

In the paper [15], a method of choosing suitable fuzzy implications has been proposed. The method assumes that there is given a basic fuzzy implication $z = I(x, y)$, where x, y belong to $[0,1]$. x is interpreted as the truth value of the antecedent and is known, whereas z is interpreted as the truth value of the implication and is also known. In order to determine the truth value of the consequent y, the inverse function $InvI(x, z)$ is needed to be computed. Moreover, this method allows to compare two fuzzy implications. If the truth value of the antecedent and the truth value of the implication are given, we can easily optimize the truth value of the implication consequent by means of inverse fuzzy implications. In other words, one can choose the fuzzy implication which

Table 2. Inverted fuzzy implications for the fuzzy implications from Table 1

Formula of inverted fuzzy implication	Domain of inverted fuzzy implication
$InvI_{GD}(x,z) = z$	$0 \le z < x, x \in (0,1]$
$InvI_{GG}(x,z) = x*z$	$0 \le z < 1, x \in (0,1]$
$InvI_{KD}(x,z) = z$	$1 - x < z \le 1, x \in (0,1]$
$InvI_{YG}(x,z) = z^{\frac{1}{x}}$	$0 \le z \le 1, x \in (0,1]$

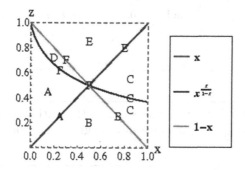

Fig. 1. The unit square $[0,1] \times [0,1]$ divided into 6 separable areas

has the greatest truth value of the implication consequent or greater truth value than other implication. Using this method we formulate a new model of fuzzy Petri nets proposed in this paper (see Sect. 4).

Table 2 lists inverse fuzzy implications and their domains for the fuzzy implications from Table 1. The resulting inverse functions can be compared with each other so that it is possible to order them. However, in general case, some of those functions are incomparable in the whole domain. Therefore, the domain is divided into separable areas within which this property is fulfilled.

The division of the unit square into 15 areas allows to compare the fuzzy implications with one another [15]. However, if we are only interested in finding the optimal implication which has the greatest truth value of the implication consequent, it is enough to divide the unit square into 6 areas A–F (see Fig. 1 and Table 3).

2.3   Algorithm

The algorithm presented below determines a basic fuzzy implication which has the greatest truth value of the consequent, and the truth value of the antecedent as well as the truth value of the implication are given. This algorithm uses the inverse fuzzy implications and their domains are presented in Table 2. The **if-then** clauses corresponding to specific cases are shown in Table 3.

Table 3. Table of optimal functions

No	Area	The optimal function
A	$z \geq x$ and $z < x^{\frac{x}{1-x}}$	I_{GG}
B	$z < x$ and $z \leq 1 - x$	I_{GD}
C	$z > 1 - x$ and $z < x$	$I_{GD} = I_{KD}$
D	$z > 1 - x$ and $z \geq x$	I_{KD}
E	$z > x^{\frac{x}{1-x}}$ and $z \leq 1 - x$	I_{YG}
F	$z = x^{\frac{x}{1-x}}$ and $x \in (0, \frac{1}{2}]$	$I_{GG} = I_{YG}$

Algorithm *GTVC*

Input: x - the truth value of the antecedent, z - the truth value of the implication
Output: I - fuzzy implication which has the greatest truth value of the consequent

---

if $(z \geq x$ and $z < x^{\frac{x}{1-x}})$ or $(z = x^{\frac{x}{1-x}}$ and $x \in (0, \frac{1}{2}])$ **then** $I \leftarrow I_{GG}$;
/* **case** A or F */
if $(z < x$ and $z \leq 1 - x)$ or $(z > 1 - x$ and $z < x)$ **then** $I \leftarrow I_{GD}$;
/* **case** B or C */
if $(z > 1 - x$ and $z \geq x)$ **then** $I \leftarrow I_{KD}$;
/* **case** D */
if $(z > x^{\frac{x}{1-x}}$ and $z \leq 1 - x)$ **then** $I \leftarrow I_{YG}$;
/* **case** E */
return I;
   This algorithm is a compact version of the algorithm presented in [15].

3   Modified Generalised Fuzzy Petri Nets

In the paper, we assume that the reader is familiar with the basic notions of Petri nets [12].

Definition 1. *[16] A modified generalised fuzzy Petri net is said to be a tuple $N = (P, T, S, I, O, \alpha, \beta, \gamma, Op, \delta, M_0)$, where: (1) $P = \{p_1, p_2, \ldots, p_n\}$ is a finite set of places; (2) $T = \{t_1, t_2, \ldots, t_m\}$ is a finite set of transitions; (3) $S = \{s_1, s_2, \ldots, s_n\}$ is a finite set of statements; (4) the sets P, T, S are pairwise disjoint; (5) $I: T \to 2^P$ is the input function; (6) $O: T \to 2^P$ is the output function; (7) $\alpha: P \to S$ is the statement binding function; (8) $\beta: T \to [0,1]$ is the truth degree function; (9) $\gamma: T \to [0,1]$ is the threshold function; (10) $Op = TN \cup FI$ is a union of triangular norms and inverted fuzzy implications called the set of operators; (11) $\delta: T \to Op \times Op \times Op$ is the operator binding function; (12) $M_0: P \to [0,1]$ is the initial marking, and 2^P denotes a family of all subsets of the set P.*

As for the graphical interpretation, places are denoted by circles and transitions by rectangles. The function I describes the oriented arcs connecting places with transitions, and the function O describes the oriented arcs connecting transitions with places. If $I(t) = \{p\}$ then a place p is called an *input place* of a transition t, and if $O(t) = \{p'\}$, then a place p' is called an *output place* of t. The initial marking M_0 is an initial distribution of numbers in the places. It can be represented by a vector of dimension n of real numbers from $[0,1]$. For $p \in P$, $M_0(p)$ can be interpreted as a truth value of the statement s bound with a given place p by means of the statement binding function α. Pictorially, the tokens are represented by means of grey "dots" together with suitable real numbers placed inside the circles corresponding to appropriate places.

We assume that if $M_0(p) = 0$ then the token does not exist in the place p. The numbers $\beta(t)$ and $\gamma(t)$ are placed in a net picture under the transition t. The first number is usually interpreted as the truth degree of an implication corresponding to a given transition t. The role of the second one is to limit the possibility of transition firings, i.e., if the input operator In value for all values corresponding to input places of the transition t is less than a threshold value $\gamma(t)$ then this transition cannot be fired (activated). The operator binding function δ connects similarly to *GFP*-nets [18] transitions with triples of operators (In, Out_1, Out_2). The meaning of the first and third operator is the same as in the case of *GFP*-nets. The first operator in the triple is called the input operator, and the third one is the output operator. The input operator In concerns the way in which all input places are connected with a given transition t. In the case of the input operator we assume that it can belong to one of two classes, i.e., t- or s-norms. However, the second operator in the triple (i.e., Out_1) is now called the transition operator and its meaning is significantly different. In the *GFP*-net model the operator Out_1 belongs to the class of t-norms, whereas in the *mGFP*-net we assume that it belongs to the class of inverted fuzzy implications. The transition operator Out_1 and the output operator Out_2 concern the way in which the next marking is computed after firing the transition t. In the case of the output operator we assume similarly to *GFP*-nets that it can belong to the class of s-norms.

Let N be a *mGFP*-net. A marking of N is a function $M: P \to [0,1]$.

The *mGFP*-net dynamics defines how new markings are computed from the current marking when transitions are fired.

Let $N = (P, T, S, I, O, \alpha, \beta, \gamma, Op, \delta, M_0)$ be a *mGFP*-net, M be a marking of N, $t \in T$, $I(t) = \{p_{i1}, p_{i2}, \ldots, p_{ik}\}$ be a set of input places for a transition t and $\beta(t) \in (0,1]$. Moreover, let $\delta(t) = (In, Out_1, Out_2)$ and D be the domain of a transition operator Out_1, i.e., the domain of an inverted fuzzy implication corresponding to the transition t.

A transition $t \in T$ is *enabled* for marking M, if the value of input operator In for all input places of the transition t by M is positive and greater than, or equal to, the value of threshold function γ corresponding to the transition t, and the value belongs to the domain of a transition operator Out_1 of t, i.e., the following two conditions must be satisfied:

1. $In(M(p_{i1}), M(p_{i2}), \dots, M(p_{ik})) \geq \gamma(t) > 0$,
2. $In(M(p_{i1}), M(p_{i2}), \dots, M(p_{ik})) \in D$.

Only enabled transitions can be fired. If M is a marking of N enabling transition t and M' is the marking derived from M by firing transition t, then for each $p \in P$ a procedure for computing the next marking M' is as follows:

1. Numbers in all output places of t are modified in the following way: at first, the value of input operator In for all input places of t is computed, next, the value of output operator Out_1 for the value of In and for the value of truth degree function $\beta(t)$ is determined, and finally, a value corresponding to $M'(p)$ for each $p \in O(p)$ is obtained as a result of output operator Out_2 for the value of Out_1 and the current marking $M(p)$.
2. Numbers in the remaining places of net N are not changed.

Formally, for each $p \in P$

$$M'(p) = \begin{cases} Out_2(Out_1(In(M(p_{i1}), M(p_{i2}), \dots, M(p_{ik})), \beta(t)), M(p)) \\ \text{if } p \in O(t), \\ M(p) \text{ otherwise.} \end{cases}$$

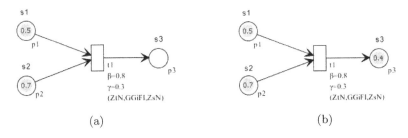

(a)   (b)

Fig. 2. A $mGFP$-net with: (a) the initial marking, (b) the marking after firing t_1

Example 2. Consider a $mGFP$-net in Fig. 2(a). For the net we have: the set of places $P = \{p_1, p_2, p_3\}$, the set of transitions $T = \{t_1\}$, the input function I and the output function O in the form: $I(t_1) = \{p_1, p_2\}$, $O(t_1) = \{p_3\}$, the set of statements $S = \{s_1, s_2, s_3\}$, the statement binding function α: $\alpha(p_1) = s_1$, $\alpha(p_2) = s_2$, $\alpha(p_3) = s_3$, the truth degree function β: $\beta(t_1) = 0.8$, the threshold function γ: $\gamma(t_1) = 0.3$, and the initial marking $M_0 = (0.5, 0.7, 0)$. Moreover, there are: the set of operators $Op = \{ZtN, ZsN\} \cup \{GGiFI\}$, where $ZtN(a, b) = min(a, b)$ (Zadeh t-Norm), $ZsN(a, b) = max(a, b)$ (Zadeh s-Norm), $GGiFI(x, z) = x * z$ (Goguen inverted Fuzzy Implication) (see Table 2) and the operator binding function δ defined as follows: $\delta(t_1) = (ZtN, GGiFI, ZsN)$. The transition t_1 is enabled by the initial marking M_0. Firing transition t_1 by the marking M_0 transforms M_0 to the marking $M' = (0.5, 0.7, 0.4)$ (Fig. 2(b)).

For further details, see [16].

4   Flexible Generalised Fuzzy Petri Nets

This section presents the main contribution to the paper. Using the $GTVC$ algorithm from Subsect. 2.3 we reformulate the definition of $mGFP$-net as follows:

Definition 3. *A flexible generalised fuzzy Petri net is said to be a tuple $N' = (P, T, S, I, O, \alpha, \beta, \gamma, Op, \delta, M_0)$, where: (1) $P, T, S, I, O, \alpha, \beta, \gamma, M_0$ have the same meaning as in Definition 1; (2) $Op = TN \cup OPTInvFI$ is a union of triangular norms and optimal inverted fuzzy implications determined by the GTVC algorithm (Subsect. 2.3) called the set of operators; (3) $\delta: T \rightarrow Op \times Op \times Op$ is the operator binding function.*

The operator binding function δ connects similarly to $mGFP$-nets transitions with triples of operators (In, Out_1, Out_2). The meaning of the first and third operator is the same as in the case of $mGFP$-nets. However, in this net model, the value of the second operator in the triple (i.e., Out_1) for each transition t in the $FGFP$-net is determined automatically by the $GTVC$ algorithm using the value of In and the value of truth degree function β.

It is easy to see that the role of a given transition t in the $FGFP$-net changes dependently on the current marking of the net. In the $mGFP$-net model we also assume that the operator belongs to the class of inverted fuzzy implications, but this operator is defined in advance by the users depending on their knowledge and experience.

In many cases, taking into account various combinations of the values of In and the value of truth degree function β for a given transition t, the choice of the suitable inverted fuzzy implication by the user is very difficult or sometimes impossible. However, considering the $GTVC$ algorithm (see Subsect. 2.3) the user can indicate the operator Out_1 as being chosen by the algorithm during the execution of the $FGFP$-net.

The dynamics of $FGFP$-nets is defined in an analogous way to the case of $mGFP$-nets.

Example 4. Consider an $FGFP$-net in Fig. 3(a). We assume that in the net: the sets P, T, S, and the functions I, O, α, β, γ, M_0 are described analogously to Example 1. However, the set of operators $Op = \{ZtN, ZsN\} \cup \{KDiFI\}$,

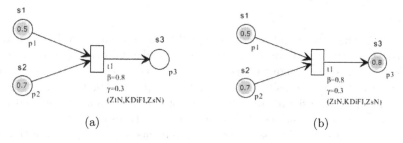

(a)   (b)

Fig. 3. A $FGFP$-net with: (a) the initial marking, (b) the marking after firing t_1

where $KDiFI(x, z) = z$ (Kleene-Dienes inverted Fuzzy Implication, see Table 2) denotes the optimal inverted fuzzy implication determined automatically by the $GTVC$ algorithm. The operator binding function δ is defined as follows: $\delta(t_1) = (ZtN, KDiFI, ZsN)$. The transition t_1 is enabled by the initial marking M_0. Firing transition t_1 by the marking M_0 transforms M_0 to the marking $M' = (0.5, 0.7, 0.8)$ (Fig. 3(b)).

5   Example

In order to illustrate our methodology, let us describe a simple example coming from the domain of control. For this goal, we propose to consider the following production rules describing the rule controller for a technical plant: (1) IF s_2 THEN s_4, (2) IF s_1 AND s_4 THEN s_5, (3) IF s_3 AND s_4 THEN s_6, (4) IF s_5 AND s_6 THEN s_7, where: s_1 ='Plant work is non-stable', s_2 ='Temperature sensor of plant indicates the temperature over 150 C degrees', s_3 ='Plant cooling does not work', s_4 ='Plant temperature is high', s_5 ='Plant is in failure state', s_6 ='Plant makes a huge hazard for environment', s_7 ='Turn off plant supply'.

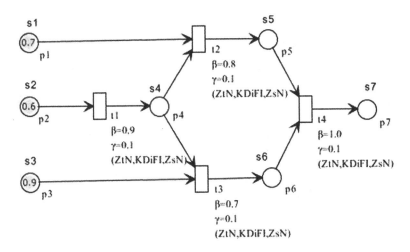

Fig. 4. An example of $FGFP$-net model of technical plant rule controller

In the further considerations we accept the assumptions as in Fig. 4, i.e., (1) the logical operator AND we interpret as min (Zadeh t-Norm); (2) to the statements $s_1, s_2,..., s_7$ we assign the fuzzy values 0.7, 0.6, 0.9, 0, 0, 0, 0, respectively; (3) the truth-values of transitions t_1, t_2, t_3, t_4 are equal to 0.9, 0.8, 0.7, 1.0, respectively; (4) all the threshold values for these four transitions are equal to 0.1; (5) the $GTVC$ algorithm (Subsect. 2.3) determines the transition operator Out_1 for all net transitions. Firstly, assessing the statements s_1, s_2, s_3, we see that the transition t_1 can be fired by the initial marking $M_0 = (0.7, 0.6, 0.9, 0, 0, 0, 0)$.

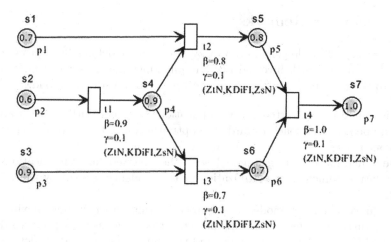

Fig. 5. *FGFP*-net model from Fig. 4 after simulation with *KDiFI* interpretation for the transition operator Out_1

The *GTVC* algorithm determines the transition operator $Out_1 = KDiFI$ (the Kleene-Dienes inverted fuzzy implication, see Table 2) for the transition t_1 by M_0. If t_1 is fired then we obtain the new marking $M' = (0.7, 0.6, 0.9, 0.9, 0, 0, 0)$. Two new transitions t_2 and t_3 are enabled by M'. If one chooses a sequence of transitions $t_2 t_3$ then they obtain the marking $M'' = (0.7, 0.6, 0.9, 0.9, 0.8, 0.7, 0)$. After firing the enabled transition t_4 the final value, corresponding to the statement s_7, equal to 1.0 is obtained (see Fig. 5). It is worth to observe that the same inverted fuzzy implication as for the transition t_1 is assigned by the *GTVC* algorithm to the remaining transitions for all markings reachable from the initial marking M_0. Secondly, if we interpret these four transitions as the Goguen fuzzy implications, and if we choose the same sequences of transitions as above, we obtain the final value for the statement s_7 equal to 0.38. We omit the detailed computations performed in this case. Thirdly, if we execute the similar simulation of approximate reasoning for four transitions considered above and, if we interpret the transitions as the Yager fuzzy implications, we obtain the final value for s_7 equal to 1.0. It is easy to observe that the final value 1 for the statement s_7 is the greatest (optimal).

This example shows clearly that different interpretations of the transitions may lead to quite different decision results. It is also possible to see that using the *GTVC* algorithm we automatically obtain the best interpretation for fuzzy implications. Certainly, it is limited to a set of considered fuzzy implications. In the paper this set consists of only four fuzzy implications presented in Table 1.

6   Concluding Remarks

In this paper, a flexible generalized fuzzy Petri net model has been proposed in fuzzy environment with inverted fuzzy implications having some benefits compared to those proposed in the literature which can be stated as follow:

1. This paper uses inverted fuzzy implications together with t-norms and as such opens an approach towards the optimization of the truth degree at the output places.
2. The generalized Petri net model with the inverted fuzzy implications has significant influence on optimization of the modelled system by the *FGFP*-nets.
3. The fuzzy Petri net model as proposed in this paper is more flexible and hence distinct to usual ones in the sense that it gives the option to define In and Out_2 operators manually, and the third operator Out_1 is determined automatically by the algorithm presented in Subsect. 2.3. The choice of suitable operators In, Out_1, and Out_2 for the modelled system is very important, especially in real systems described by incomplete, imprecise and/or vague information.

The flexibility of choosing the operators inspires for an extension with the weighted intuitionistic fuzzy sets [1] as proposed in [14]. When an weight is associated with an input or output values then it is concerned with the reliability of the information provided, leading to more generalization in approximate reasoning process in decision support system but also it often leads to computational complexity. The flexibility of choosing operators can minimize such computational complexity. It makes the model simple and thus speeds up the approximate reasoning process. Moreover, inverted fuzzy implication helps in optimization but the method discussed here also opens the choice of using other operators, e.g. t-norm operators, if the input values does not belong to the domain of inverted fuzzy implication functions. This is the novelty of this research work.

Using a simple real-life example suitability and usefulness of the proposed approach have been proved for the control design. The elaborated approach looks promising with regard to alike application problems that could be solved in a similar manner. It is worth to mention that an experimental application has been implemented in *Java*, consisting of an editor and a simulator. The editor allows inputting and editing the *FGFP*-nets, while the simulator starts with a given initial marking and executes enabled transitions visualising reached markings and simulation parameters. All figures and simulation results presented in the paper were produced by this application.

The following research problems of our concern are both the adaptation of the *FGFP*-nets in modelling the reasoning in decision support systems using intuitionistic fuzzy sets [1] as well as the use of this approach in Systems Biology [7].

Acknowledgments. This work was partially supported by the Center for Innovation and Transfer of Natural Sciences and Engineering Knowledge at the University of Rzeszów. The authors are grateful to the anonymous referees for their helpful comments.

References

1. Atanassov, K.: Intuitionistic fuzzy sets. Fuzzy Sets Syst. **20**, 87–96 (1986)
2. Baczyński, M., Jayaram, B.: Fuzzy Implications. Springer, Heidelberg (2008)
3. Bandyopadhyay, S., Suraj, Z., Grochowalski, P.: Modified generalized weighted fuzzy petri net in intuitionistic fuzzy environment. In: Flores, V. (ed.) IJCRS 2016. LNCS (LNAI), vol. 9920, pp. 342–351. Springer, Heidelberg (2016). doi:10.1007/978-3-319-47160-0_31
4. Cardoso, J., Camargo, H. (eds.): Fuzziness in Petri Nets. Springer, Heidelberg (1999)
5. Desel, J., Reisig, W., Rozenberg, G. (eds.): ACPN 2003. LNCS, vol. 3098. Springer, Heidelberg (2004)
6. Jensen, K., Rozenberg, G.: High-level Petri Nets. Springer, Heidelberg (1991)
7. Koch, I., Reisig, W., Schreiber, F. (eds.): Modeling in Systems Biology. The Petri Net Approach. Springer, Heidelberg (2011)
8. Klement, E.P., Mesiar, R., Pap, E.: Triangular Norms. Kluwer, Boston (2000)
9. Looney, C.G.: Fuzzy petri nets for rule-based decision-making. IEEE Trans. Syst., Man, Cybern. **18**(1), 178–183 (1988)
10. Pedrycz, W., Gomide, F.: A generalized fuzzy Petri net model. IEEE Trans. Fuzzy Syst. **2–4**, 295–301 (1994)
11. Pedrycz, W.: Generalized fuzzy Petri nets as pattern classifiers. Pattern Recog. Lett. **20–14**, 1489–1498 (1999)
12. Peterson, J.L.: Petri net theory and the modeling of systems. Prentice-Hall Inc., Englewood Cliffs (1981)
13. Petri, C.A.: Kommunikation mit Automaten. Schriften des IIM Nr. 2, Institut für Instrumentelle Mathematik, Bonn (1962)
14. Suraj, Z, Bandyopadhyay, S.: Generalized weighted fuzzy petri net in intuitionistic fuzzy environment. In: Proceedings the IEEE World Congress on Computational Intelligence, IEEE WCCI 2016, 25-29 July, 2016, Vancouver, Canada, pp. 2385–2392, IEEE (2016)
15. Suraj, Z., Lasek, A., Lasek, P.: Inverted fuzzy implications in approximate reasoning. Fundam. Informat. **143**, 151–171 (2015)
16. Suraj, Z.: Modified generalised fuzzy petri nets for rule-based systems. In: Yao, Y., Hu, Q., Yu, H., Grzymala-Busse, J.W. (eds.) RSFDGrC 2015. LNCS (LNAI), vol. 9437, pp. 196–206. Springer, Heidelberg (2015). doi:10.1007/978-3-319-25783-9_18
17. Suraj, Z., Lasek, A.: Toward optimization of approximate reasoning based on rule knowledge. In: Proceedings 2nd International Conference on Systems and Informatics, ICSAI 2014, November 15-17, 2014, Shanghai, China, IEEE Systems, Man and Cybernetics Society, IEEE Catalog Numbers: CFP1473R-CDR ISBN: 978-1-4799-5457-5, pp. 281–285 (2014)
18. Suraj, Z.: A new class of fuzzy Petri nets for knowledge representation and reasoning. Fundam. Inform. **128**(1–2), 193–207 (2013)
19. Zadeh, L.A.: Fuzzy sets. Inform. Control **8**, 338–353 (1965)

Learning Grammar Rules in Probabilistic Grammar-Based Genetic Programming

Pak-Kan Wong[1(✉)], Man-Leung Wong[2], and Kwong-Sak Leung[3]

[1] The Chinese University of Hong Kong, Sha Tin, Hong Kong
pkwong@cse.cuhk.edu.hk
[2] Lingnan University, Tuen Mun, Hong Kong
mlwong@ln.edu.hk
[3] The Chinese University of Hong Kong, Sha Tin, Hong Kong
ksleung@cse.cuhk.edu.hk

Abstract. Grammar-based Genetic Programming (GBGP) searches for a computer program in order to solve a given problem. Grammar constrains the set of possible programs in the search space. It is not obvious to write an appropriate grammar for a complex problem. Our proposed Bayesian Grammar-Based Genetic Programming with Hierarchical Learning (BGBGP-HL) aims at automatically designing new rules from existing relatively simple grammar rules during evolution to improve the grammar structure. The new grammar rules also reflects the new understanding of the existing grammar under the given fitness evaluation function. Based on our case study in asymmetric royal tree problem, our evaluation shows that BGBGP-HL achieves the best performance among the competitors. Compared to other algorithms, search performance of BGBGP-HL is demonstrated to be more robust against dependencies and the changes in complexity of programs.

Keywords: Genetic programming · Estimation of distribution programming · Adaptive grammar · Bayesian network

1 Introduction

Automatic programming is a computational task to compose a set of instructions in order to form a program which accomplishes a (computational) task. Evolutionary Computation (EC) has been applied to this problem. EC include Genetic algorithm (GA) and Genetic Programming (GP) [12] which adopt Darwinian principles by stochastically modifying the population of candidate solutions (i.e. individuals). GP automatically generates and evolves parse trees (i.e. programs) composed of elements given in a terminal set and a function set through evolution processes, such as mutation and crossover. Each evolved parse tree is evaluated by a fitness function.

Programming language plays an important role in the problem of automatic programming. An executable program must be written in a programming language which formally specifies in a grammar and confines the solution space.

© Springer International Publishing AG 2016
C. Martín-Vide et al. (Eds.): TPNC 2016, LNCS 10071, pp. 208–220, 2016.
DOI: 10.1007/978-3-319-49001-4_17

A branch of EC called Grammar-Based Genetic Programming (GBGP) [24, 25] utilizes the grammar and carefully evolves the individuals. A comprehensive survey of GBGP can be found in [13].

Probabilistic Model-Building Genetic Programming (PMBGP) [22] replaces the evolutionary operators with sampling and model update. To guide the search, probabilistic models [11] are estimated from (fitter) parse trees in the past generations so when we sample from the current estimate of distribution encoded in the models, we have a higher chance of obtaining fitter parse trees. By repeating the model building and sampling procedure, the fitness of the population will iteratively improve. The final estimate of distribution reflects the principles to generate good parse trees and gives insights into the problem nature.

Despite the aforementioned advances, canonical GP and generic PMBGP approaches do not perform well when a problem becomes complex. In the context of GBGP, it may be due to an increase in the size of the terminal set, the size of the function set, the number of terms in the grammar rules or the depth of the parse trees. The search algorithm fails even after raising the population size or the total number of evaluations. It is also not obvious about how to design an appropriate grammar with a suitable structure, so that the problem can be solved effectively. To improve the search capability, many works have been done to specialize the genetic operators, such as crossover and mutation, to adapt to the problem domain based on the domain-specific knowledge. The question is whether we can automate this process. Grammar explicitly formalizes parse trees and PMBGP discovers dependence information among the grammar rules, so they together represent the knowledge to solve the search problem. In this work, we propose a system which constructs knowledge-containing grammar rules which may inspire experts to understand the problem nature. This knowledge feedback mechanism resembles the idea of discovery learning [1].

In this paper, we proposed Bayesian Grammar-Based Genetic Programming with Hierarchical Learning (BGBGP-HL) for improving the design of a grammar and automating the knowledge discovery. BGBGP-HL constructs new rules after inspecting the probabilistic distributions using a statistical approach. It can facilitate knowledge discovery while maintaining the search efficiency.

This paper is organized as follows. In the next section, relevant works on PMBGP and Grammatical Evolution are summarized. Then, we introduce the asymmetric royal tree benchmark problem and the corresponding hierarchical probabilistic context-sensitive grammar in Sects. 3 and 4 respectively. After that, the details on the work flow of the whole system are discussed in Sect. 5. The results are presented in Sect. 6. The last section is the conclusion.

2   Related Works

Our framework adopts Probabilistic Model-Building Genetic Programming (PMBGP) so the related works are summarized below. Since our system evolves grammar, studies about Grammatical Evolution (GE) (which is a non-PMBGP approach) are also summarized.

Probabilistic Model-Building Genetic Programming. The approaches can be broadly classified into two categories. The probabilistic prototype tree (PPT) model-based methods operate on a fixed-length chromosome represented in a tree structure [6,7,21]. The PPT model is completely different from our approach. Another category of approaches utilizes probabilistic context-free grammar (PCFG) [3]. A complete review can be found at [10]. Here we only summarized the recent works directly related to our approach. PAGE [8] employs PCFG with Latent Annotations (PCFG-LA) to weaken the context-free assumption. Under the context-free assumption, the dependencies between the rules and terms within a grammar rule and across multiple grammar rules cannot be captured so the search system is not capable of modeling the dependencies in a program, such as data dependencies and control dependencies. For example, the sequence of reading from and writing to the same memory resource can alter the output of a program. Subsequently, some combinations are preferable and semantically sound in good parse trees which preserve the program dependencies. The estimate of annotations can be learnt using expectation-maximization (EM) algorithm [5] or variational Bayes (VB) learning [2] as reported in PAGE-EM and PAGE-VB respectively while PAGE-VB can also infer the total number of annotations needed from the learning data. Unsupervised PAGE (UPAGE) [9] utilizes PCFG-LA mixture model to deal with local dependencies and global contexts. BAP [19] applies a learnt Bayesian network on top of a constant size chromosome and reproduces new individuals using the Bayesian network. Tanev's work [23] relies on probabilistic context-sensitive grammar (PCSG), which extends PCFG by assigning the probability according to the predefined contexts.

Grammatical Evolution. Methods to evolve grammar have also been studied in non-PMBGP approaches. One of the most prominent approaches is Grammatical Evolution (GE) [15,16]. The original version of GE adopted Backus-Naur Form for expressing the grammar. Unlike Genetic Programming (GP)[12], each individual was represented in a chromosome which can then be translated to a syntax tree and tells the system how to apply the rules using the grammar. GE has been extended and improved in terms of the genotype-phenotype mapping rules, search operators and search strategies [14,17,20].

Our Contributions. Our approach is a PMBGP approach. Contrary to the aforementioned PMBGP approaches, we employ a hierarchical PCSG model to maintain the syntactical correctness and guide the derivation of individuals by assigning a Bayesian network to each grammar rule. Our approach can also learn how to create new grammar rules by combining the existing grammar rules so as to ensure the syntactical correctness of individuals. During the evolution, the rules are gradually constructed and specialized to adapt to the problem-specific fitness evaluation function. The new rules can capture the substructure frequently occurred in the good individuals. From the best of our knowledge, it is the first attempt to discover hierarchical derivation structure and capture substructure in parse trees on hierarchical PCSG in PMBGP approaches.

3   Asymmetric Royal Tree Problem

We applied our approach on the asymmetric royal tree (ART) problem [26]. The goal of ART problem is to construct a tree with maximum score. It is a modified version of the traditional royal tree problem [18] and is designed to test a grammatical GP algorithm for the ability to learn dependencies among subtrees, including the non-terminals within the same rule and across two rules. It has a set of functions labelled by symbols from A to Z and two terminals y and z. These functions are binary and symmetric, i.e. $f(x,y) = f(y,x)$. To describe the fitness function, we firstly need to define some notations. Define an ordered list of symbols $L = (y, z, A, B, C, D, ..., Z)$, and $Prec(\alpha)$ is the preceding symbol of α in L, for instance $Prec(A) = z$. Let $Prec_2(T) = \{Prec(Root(T)), Prec(Prec(Root(T)))\}$, where $Root(T)$ is the root node of tree T.

Table 1. Optimal structure from level B to F in the asymmetric royal tree Problem

Level	S-expression	Score
B	(B (A y z) z)	36
C	(C (B (A y z) z) (A y z))	176
D	(D (C (B (A y z) z) (A y z)) (B (A y z) z))	848
E	(E (D (C (B (A y z) z) (A y z)) (B (A y z) z)) (C (B (A y z) z) (A y z)))	4096
F	(F (D (C (B (A y z) z) (A y z)) (B (A y z) z)) (E (D (C (B (A y z) z) (A y z)) (B (A y z) z))))	262,144

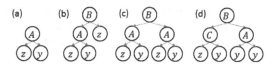

Fig. 1. Examples of asymmetric royal tree [26]. (a) A perfect tree at level A. Fitness $= 2 \times (2 \times 1 + 2 \times 1) = 8$. (b) A perfect tree at level B. Fitness $= 2 \times \{2 \times (2 \times (2 \times 1 + 2 \times 1)) + 2 \times 1\} = 36$. (c) Imperfect tree at level B. Fitness $= 2 \times 8 + 2 \times 8 = 32$. (d) Imperfect tree at level B. Fitness $= \frac{1}{3} \times (\frac{1}{3} \times 1 + \frac{1}{3} \times 1) + (2 \times 1 + 2 \times 1) \approx 4.222$

Given a tree T, where T_L and T_R are the left subtree and right subtree of tree T respectively, T is said to be perfect if T_L and T_R are both perfect subtrees and the set $\{Root(T_L), Root(T_R)\}$ is same as $Prec_2(T)$. Besides, y and z are perfect subtrees which provide the base cases. The score of T is calculated recursively using the following function $S(T)$:

$- \ S(y) = S(z) = 1$
$- \ S(T) = k_{global}(T, T_L, T_R) \times ((k_{local}(T, T_L) \times S(T_L) + k_{local}(T, T_R) \times S(T_R))),$

where $k_{global}(T, T_L, T_R)$ is 1 by default, or 2 when T_L and T_R are perfect subtrees and the set $\{Root(T_L), Root(T_R)\}$ is equal to $Prec_2(T)$. Similarly, $k_{local}(T, T_{subtree})$ is 1 by default, 2 when $Root(T_{subtree}) \in Prec_2(T)$ and $T_{subtree}$ is perfect, or $\frac{1}{3}$ when $Root(T_{subtree}) \notin Prec_2(T)$. In short, k_{global} and k_{local} give bonus or penalty to a tree. Some optimal ARTs are shown in Fig. 1. Table 1 shows the structure and score of the best ART at different depth in S-expression. The scoring system is calculated recursively from the leaf nodes to the root node.

4   Grammar Model

A program is represented in a parse tree. A parse tree is derived from the hierarchical probabilistic context-sensitive grammar (PCSG) to enforce the syntactic relations. Besides, the probabilistic dependencies among the non-terminals of a grammar rule are captured by Bayesian networks. The hierarchical PCSG used in the ART problem is shown in Fig. 2. For ease of reference, we label each rule and index each non-terminal on the right-hand side of the arrow $(- >)$ with a subscript. The grammar consists of eight rules. Consider the rule $ST.5$ in the example. ST on the left-hand side of the arrow means this rule can be chosen when we derive any non-terminal ST (e.g. ST_6). On the right-hand side of the arrow gives the content of the rule. Terminals are enclosed in square brackets. Hence, $[C]$ is a terminal. ST_6 and ST_7 are the non-terminals. In addition, a Bayesian network is attached to each rule and captures the conditional dependencies among the non-terminals of that rule. For example, the box in Fig. 2 shows the Bayesian network of rule $ST.5$. The Bayesian network captures the conditional dependencies between non-terminals ST_6 and ST_7. All terminals are constant and hence ignored. Non-terminal ST_6 (and similarly for ST_7) is associated with a random variable, which is represented using an oval. Non-terminal ST_6 has seven possible choices corresponding to the seven entries in the conditional probability table. Initially, the probabilities are uniformly distributed and the non-terminals are sampled independently of one another.

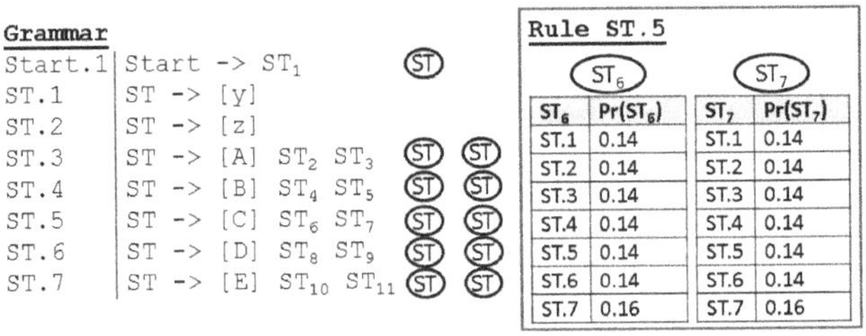

Fig. 2. Initial grammar for the asymmetric royal tree problem.

5   System Architecture

In this section, we present the details of BGBGP-HL. The entire process consists of seven steps (Fig. 3).

1. Initialize hierarchical PCSG to uniform distributions.
2. Create a new population of parse trees, some of which are derived from the hierarchical PCSG and the selected parse trees through elitism.
3. Calculate the fitness of the new parse trees in the population.
4. Select a set of diverse parse trees based on their scores.
5. Learn the Bayesian networks in each grammar rule.
6. Discover and extract new rules (structure and parameters) if the probability converges.
7. Repeat from step 2 and the selected good parse trees survive to the next generation until meeting the stopping criteria.

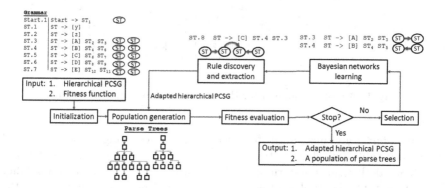

Fig. 3. System flowchart.

This paper mainly focuses on the capability of our system with the hierarchical grammar to discover new rules while the key ideas of the methods to identify and extract new rules are provided for completeness. In step 5, the Bayesian networks are learnt using K2 algorithm [4]. The samples come from the fitter parse trees being the knowledge feedback from the fitness evaluation function. After collecting the derivation choices of grammar rules in these parse trees, we obtain the statistics on how to derive *all* the non-terminals. As these records are collected from fitter parse trees, each Bayesian network actually represents dependencies of the choices of non-terminals constituted in good parse trees.

5.1   Derivation of a Parse Tree

To better understand the connection between hierarchical PCSG and parse trees, an example is present. To derive a parse tree as shown in Fig. 4, the system begins

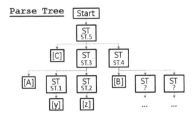

Fig. 4. A parse tree derived using the grammar in Fig. 2.

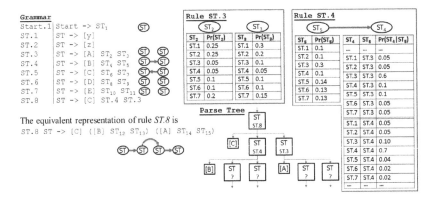

Fig. 5. Adapted grammar for the asymmetric royal tree problem.

from rule *Start.1* and picks a rule from *ST*.1 to *ST*.7 according to the conditional probability table (which is initially uniformly distribution). Suppose *ST*.5 is picked, we derive the non-terminal ST_6 following the conditional probability distribution table (i.e. table on the left in the box in Fig. 2); and similarly for the non-terminal ST_7. Let's say *ST*.3 and *ST*.4 are then picked. Again, we perform a random sampling recursively according to the probability distributions until all the leaf nodes in the parse tree are terminals.

5.2   Grammar Rules Discovery and Extraction

In this section, we introduce the general idea of our method to discover and extract new rules from the set of Bayesian networks of each rule.

Discovery of interesting assignments. In BGBGP-HL, new rules are generated by combining existing rules. However, the number of possible combinations is very large. For example, the rule *ST*.5 can be combined with different rules to generate new rules with one-level of hierarchy, such as

$$ST \rightarrow [C]\ ST.1\ ST_7$$
$$ST \rightarrow [C]\ ST.2\ ST_7$$
...
$$ST \rightarrow [C]\ ST_6\ ST.1$$

$ST \rightarrow [C]\ ST_6\ ST.2$

...

$ST \rightarrow [C]\ ST.1\ ST.1$

...

There are $9 \times 9 - 1 = 80$ possible combinations for generating new rules from the rule $ST.5$. Thus, the system needs to identify some interesting assignments. It will analyse the conditional probability tables associated with the nodes (i.e. random variables) of the Bayesian network of a rule to determine promising combinations. Using Fig. 6 as an example, we firstly identify choices that are almost certain. We compute the Shannon entropy (which is a measure of randomness of a random variable) of ST_6 for every parent configuration ST_7. As the entropy is below 0.5 bit, the randomness of random variable ST_6 is quite low. We have shaded the rows with entropy less than 0.5 bit in Fig. 6 (left).

Extraction of a rule. Interesting assignment choices for conditional probability table $Pr(ST_6|ST_7)$ are marked with a asterisk (*) as shown in Fig. 6 (right). However, some inappropriate rules can still be generated if rules are created directly based on some expansion choices. For example, $ST \rightarrow [C]\ ST.3\ ST.3$ will be created. But this rule is equivalent to $ST \rightarrow [C]\ [A]\ ST\ ST\ [A]\ ST\ ST$, which is not suitable for the ART problem.

In order to avoid this issue, it is necessary to further analyse these expansion choices to identify the general patterns of them. In this paper, C5.0 is applied to group and generalize the interesting expansion choices in *all* conditional probability tables of the same rule. Feature attributes in the training data are the choices of random variables in the conditional probability table and the class attribute is whether the corresponding entry is marked. C5.0 identifies the predictive features and produces conjunctions of features that lead to the class labels. For example, we may obtain a decision tree as depicted in Fig. 7. We select branches that predict the interesting expansion choices and with accuracy over 95 %. Then, we can collect from the branches for a set of conjunctive conditions to describe the interesting assignments. For instance, in the previous decision for non-terminal ST_6, the two conjunctive rules are $(ST_6 \in \{ST.3\})$ and $(ST_6 \in \{ST.4\} \wedge ST_7 \in \{ST.3\})$.

Pr(ST₆|ST₇)	Random variable ST₆									Random variable ST₆						
	ST.1	ST.2	ST.3	ST.4	ST.5	ST.6	ST.7	Entropy		ST.1	ST.2	ST.3	ST.4	ST.5	ST.6	ST.7
ST.1	0.05	0.01	0.06	0.70	0.11	0.05	0.02	1.57	ST.1							
ST.2	0.02	0.00	0.02	0.93	0.03	0.00	0.00	0.47	ST.2				*			
ST.3	0.01	0.01	0.98	0.00	0.00	0.00	0.00	0.16	ST.3			*				
ST.4	0.00	0.02	0.95	0.00	0.01	0.01	0.01	0.38	ST.4			*				
ST.5	0.02	0.04	0.80	0.02	0.00	0.09	0.03	1.13	ST.5							
ST.6	0.14	0.24	0.18	0.19	0.05	0.01	0.19	2.52	ST.6							
ST.7	0.19	0.14	0.07	0.13	0.19	0.17	0.07	2.71	ST.7							

Fig. 6. Conditional probability table $Pr(ST_6|ST_7)$ (left) and the table of interesting expansion choices (right).

Creation of a hierarchical derivation rule. Since each non-terminal of a grammar rule has its own set of conjunctive conditions, we need to find a consensus of these conjunctive conditions. Thus, a combined conjunctive condition

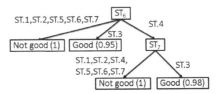

Fig. 7. An illustration showing a decision tree generalizes the decision table of the conditional probability table. The number enclosed by a pair of brackets is the accuracy of the branch.

suggests a possible assignment to all non-terminals in a grammar rule. It also ensures the consistency across all the non-terminals. For example, if a grammar rule contains only two non-terminals ST_6 and ST_7, $(ST_6 \in \{ST.4\}) \wedge (ST_6 \in \{ST.3, ST.4\} \wedge ST_7 \in \{ST.3\})$ gives $(ST_6 \in \{ST.4\} \wedge ST_7 \in \{ST.3\})$. This combined conjunctive condition produces a grammar rule: $ST \rightarrow [C] \, ST.4 \, ST.3$.

6 Comparative Experiments

To demonstrate the search effectiveness and the capability of discovery hierarchical knowledge of our algorithm, we implemented BGBGP-HL and tested it with a benchmark problem: the asymmetric royal tree (ART) problem. Apart from the classic GBGP, it was compared with two existing PMBGP methods: PAGE-EM [8], and PAGE-VB [8], which were superior to univariate model (PIPE), adjacent model (EDP model) and simple GP [8]. The key parameters and their values of configuration on different problems are shown in Table 2. Due to time constraints, we declare an approach fails if it cannot obtain an optimal solution in 200,000 fitness evaluations. We label our approach as BGBGP-HL.

Comparative results are shown in Table 3. We compared the four algorithms in terms of number of successes in 50 runs and reported the average number of fitness evaluation, which is the major bottleneck when the fitness evaluation has high computational complexity. This problem was difficult for GBGP, PAGE-EM and PAGE-VB. And the successful rate dropped significantly as the depth of an optimal ART increases. GBGP found the problem hard beyond level E but it performed better than PAGE-EM and PAGE-VB. BGBGP-HL outperformed the others. The number of fitness evaluations for BGBGP-HL was only 10 % of GBGP at level D and level E. One reason for BGBGP-HL to have a better performance than PAGE-EM and PAGE-VB is that the Bayesian networks in the hierarchical PCSG is comparative smaller when compared to that of PAGE-EM and PAGE-VB so sufficient amount of samples can be collected for learning the Bayesian networks. We also performed t-test between BGBGP-HL with the other approaches on the number of fitness evaluations using t-test. As shown in Table 3, the plus symbol (+) indicates BGBGP-HL was better than the corresponding approach at that tree level with statistical significance ($p < 0.05$).

We further tested the ability of BGBGP-HL by raising the depth of ART to level G. As shown in Table 4, the successful rate of BGBGP-HL slightly dropped

Table 2. Problem specific configuration.

Parameter	Value
Depth	ART: Level D, Level E, Level F, Level G
GBGP Configuration	
Parameter	Value
Population size	1,000
Crossover rate	0.9
Mutation rate	0.09
PAGE-EM Configuration	
Parameter	Value
Population size	1,000
Annotation size	8, 16
Selection rate	0.1
Elite rate	0.1
PAGE-VB Configuration	
Parameter	Value
Population size	1,000
Annotation set	{1,2,4,8,16}
Annotation exploration range	2
Selection rate	0.1
Elite rate	0.1
BGBGP-HL Configuration	
Parameter	Value
Population size	500
Accumulation size	100
Selection rate	0.4
Mutation	0.8

to 96 % at level G. The number of fitness evaluation was increased by around 2.3 times for each increase in level under the current configuration. An adapted grammar for this problem at level E is shown in Fig. 5.

To further study why BGBGP-HL performed well, we selected a case at level F for further analysis. In one of the cases, the grammar rules learnt are

ST.9	$ST \rightarrow [C]\ ST.4\ ST.3$
ST.10	$ST \rightarrow [A]\ ST.2\ ST.1$
ST.11	$ST \rightarrow [C]\ ([B]\ ST.10\ ST.2)\ ([A]\ ST.2\ ST.1)$

They are good substructures in this ART problem since they represent some of the optimal structures in the bottom level (see Fig. 1). It was also interesting to

Table 3. Results for Asymmetric Royal Tree Problem. It shows the statistics of the number of fitness evaluations in 50 runs. Column *Suc.*, *Mean* and *t-test* are the number of successful runs, the average and the result of t-test of the number of fitness evaluations in the successful runs respectively. The plus symbol (+) indicates BGBGP-HL is better with statistical significance ($p < 0.05$).

	Level D			Level E		
	Suc.	Mean	t-test	Suc.	Mean	t-test
BGBGP-HL	**50**	**3,371**	NA	**50**	**5,985**	NA
GBGP	48	11,249	+	22	19,960	+
PAGE-EM	21	6,048		13	20,846	+
PAGE-VB	**50**	15,060	+	5	63,000	+

Table 4. Results for Asymmetric Royal Tree Problem for BGBGP-HL. It shows the statistics of the number of fitness evaluations in the successful runs among the 50 runs.

	Suc.	Mean	Std. dev.
Level D	50	2,071	301
Level E	50	3,838	629
Level F	50	8,236	2,705
Level G	48	18,814	16,123

see that rule $ST.11$ was discovered after our system analysed the dependencies in rule $ST.9$. This mimics how new knowledge is constructed from the first principles. Our approach also performed similarly in the deceptive royal tree problem but we do not report the results due to the page limits.

7   Discussion and Conclusion

BGBGP-HL is a PMBGP approach that can tackle the problems with strong dependence. Meanwhile, it can construct hierarchical knowledge during evolution. Finding good parse trees is the first step to understand an optimization problem. Using our system, new grammar rules are learnt from the good parse trees. Besides, contextual (and stochastic) knowledge can be expressed using the grammar rules in hierarchical PCSG.

A new hierarchical grammar rule can represent a building block in the parse trees. It is produced because it commonly occurs in good parse trees and has to be simple to construct. Currently, although we demonstrated that BGBGP-HL can learn a relatively more complex program when compared to the other algorithms in our tests, we sometimes observed that some new rules do not represent any optimal structures. We suspected that random fluctuation of the derivation process causes a bias in the search, resulting in irrelevant rules (though they will be ignored in the subsequent generations). In the future, we will overcome this problem by deciding which rules to be removed. Removal rules may also benefit the development of a domain-specific language.

Importantly, BGBGP-HL shows the steps of how knowledge is evolved (or derived). As a result, we can better understand how to composite the existing knowledge. While the knowledge produced is hierarchical, it remains comprehensible as it is expressed in the same language.

Acknowledgments. This research is supported by General Research Fund LU310111 from the Research Grant Council of the Hong Kong Special Administrative Region and the Lingnan University Direct Grant DR16A7.

References

1. Anthony, W.: Learning to discover rules by discovery. J. Educ. Psychol. **64**(3), 325 (1973)
2. Attias, H.: Inferring parameters and structure of latent variable models by variational bayes. In: Proceedings of the Fifteenth Conference on Uncertainty in Artificial Intelligence, pp. 21–30. Morgan Kaufmann Publishers Inc. (1999)
3. Booth, T.L., Thompson, R.A.: Applying probability measures to abstract languages. Comput. IEEE Trans. **100**(5), 442–450 (1973)
4. Cooper, G.F., Herskovits, E.: A bayesian method for the induction of probabilistic networks from data. Mach. Learn. **9**(4), 309–347 (1992)
5. Dempster, A.P., Laird, N.M., Rubin, D.B.: Maximum likelihood from incomplete data via the EM algorithm. J. Royal Stat. Soc. Series B (Methodological) **39**, 1–38 (1977)
6. Hasegawa, Y., Iba, H.: Estimation of bayesian network for program generation. In: Proceedings 3rd Asian-Pacific Workshop on Genetic Programming, p. 35 (2006)
7. Hasegawa, Y., Iba, H.: A bayesian network approach to program generation. IEEE Trans. Evol. Comput. **12**(6), 750–764 (2008)
8. Hasegawa, Y., Iba, H.: Latent variable model for estimation of distribution algorithm based on a probabilistic context-free grammar. IEEE Trans. Evol. Comput. **13**(4), 858–878 (2009)
9. Hasegawa, Y., Ventura, S.: Programming with annotated grammar estimation. In: Genetic Programming-New Approaches and Successful, pp. 49–74 (2012)
10. Kim, K., Shan, Y., Nguyen, X.H., McKay, R.I.: Probabilistic model building in genetic programming: A critical review. Genet. Program. Evolvable Mach. **15**(2), 115–167 (2014)
11. Koller, D., Friedman, N.: Probabilistic Graphical Models: Principles and Techniques. MIT Press, Oxford (2009)
12. Koza, J.R.: Genetic Programming: vol. 1, On the Programming of Computers by Means of Natural Selection. MIT Press, Cambridge (1992)
13. Mckay, R.I., Hoai, N.X., Whigham, P.A., Shan, Y.: ONeill, M.: Grammar-based genetic programming: a survey. Genet. Program. Evol. Mach. **11**(3–4), 365–396 (2010)
14. O'Neill, M., Brabazon, A.: Grammatical differential evolution. In: IC-AI, pp. 231–236 (2006)
15. O'Neill, M., Ryan, C.: Grammatical evolution. IEEE Trans. Evol. Comput. **5**(4), 349–358 (2001)

16. O'Neill, M., Ryan, C.: Grammatical Evolution: Evolutionary Automatic Programming in an Arbitrary Language. Springer, Heidelberg (2003)
17. O'Neill, M., Ryan, C.: Grammatical evolution by grammatical evolution: the evolution of grammar and genetic code. In: Keijzer, M., O'Reilly, U.-M., Lucas, S., Costa, E., Soule, T. (eds.) EuroGP 2004. LNCS, vol. 3003, pp. 138–149. Springer, Heidelberg (2004). doi:10.1007/978-3-540-24650-3_13
18. Punch, W.F.: How effective are multiple populations in genetic programming. Genet. Program. **98**, 308–313 (1998)
19. Regolin, E.N., Pozo, A.T.R.: Bayesian automatic programming. In: Keijzer, M., Tettamanzi, A., Collet, P., Hemert, J., Tomassini, M. (eds.) EuroGP 2005. LNCS, vol. 3447, pp. 38–49. Springer, Heidelberg (2005). doi:10.1007/978-3-540-31989-4_4
20. Sabar, N.R., Ayob, M., Kendall, G., Qu, R.: Grammatical evolution hyper-heuristic for combinatorial optimization problems. Evol. Comput. IEEE Trans. **17**(6), 840–861 (2013)
21. Salustowicz, R., Schmidhuber, J.: Probabilistic incremental program evolution. Evol. Comput. **5**(2), 123–141 (1997)
22. Sastry, K., Goldberg, D.E.: Probabilistic model building and competent genetic programming. In: Riolo, R., Worzel, B. (eds.) Genetic Programming Theory and Practice. Genetic Programming Series, vol. 6, pp. 205–220. Springer, Heidelberg (2003). doi:10.1007/978-1-4419-8983-3_13
23. Tanev, I.: Incorporating learning probabilistic context-sensitive grammar in genetic programming for efficient evolution and adaptation of snakebot. In: Keijzer, M., Tettamanzi, A., Collet, P., Hemert, J., Tomassini, M. (eds.) EuroGP 2005. LNCS, vol. 3447, pp. 155–166. Springer, Heidelberg (2005). doi:10.1007/978-3-540-31989-4_14
24. Whigham, P.A.: Grammatically-based genetic programming. In: Proceedings of the Workshop on Genetic Programming: from Theory to Real-World Applications. vol. 16, pp. 33–41 (1995)
25. Wong, M.L., Leung, K.S.: Applying logic grammars to induce sub-functions in genetic programming. In: IEEE International Conference on Evolutionary Computation, 1995, vol. 2, pp. 737–740. IEEE (1995)
26. Wong, P.K., Lo, L.Y., Wong, M.L., Leung, K.S.: Grammar-based genetic programming with dependence learning and bayesian network classifier. In: Proceedings of GECCO 2014, pp. 959–966. ACM (2014)

Author Index

Printed in the United States
By Bookmasters